I0797455

Viella Historical Research

2

The Transformation of Confessional Cultures in a Central European City: Olomouc, 1400-1750

edited by
Antonín Kalous

with an afterword by Graeme Murdock

viella

First edition: september 2015
ISBN 978-88-6728-489-4

The publication of the work was supported from the OPVK project Confessional Culture between Middle Ages and Modern Times - Reinforcing International Research at the Department of History, Palacký University Olomouc (Konfesijní kultura mezi středověkem a moderní dobou – Posílení mezinárodního výzkumu na katedře historie Univerzity Palackého v Olomouci reg.no. CZ.1.07/2.3.00/20.0192.

Cover illustration: View of Olomouc, 1667. SOkA Olomouc.
Photo: Muzeum umění Olomouc, Markéta Ondrušková).

viella
libreria editrice
via delle Alpi, 32
I-00198 ROMA
tel. 06 84 17 758
fax 06 85 35 39 60
www.viella.it

Contents

Foreword

The present volume is a result of a common effort of eight historians, who deal with the city of Olomouc in their research as well as the general history of the period of confessional division in Europe. The appearance of this book was generously supported by a European Social Fund Project, *Confessional culture between the Middle Ages and modern times* (CZ.1.07/2.3.00/20.0192), which was run by the Department of history, Faculty of Arts, Palacký University, Olomouc from April 2013 to June 2015 in cooperation with Karin Friedrich from the Centre for Early Modern Studies at the University of Aberdeen. This book is one of the outcomes of this project. The research in Rome and the Vatican for chapters two and four was also enabled by the kind support of the Czech historical institute in Rome (*Istituto storico ceco di Roma*).

The concept of the book is, necessarily, a common product of all the authors. It resulted from discussions over the topic during the last few years: previous research on the city of Olomouc, in which all the present authors participated, is linked to two multi-volume works that have recently appeared and have inspired – among other stimuli – the publication of the current book. In 2009 a two-volume *Dějiny Olomouce* (History of Olomouc) was published and within two years a three-volume collection of studies and catalogue *Olomoucké baroko* (The Olomouc Baroque) appeared as well. Discussions over urban history and confessionalisation (with all its theoretical problems and adjustments), which constitute two basic approaches of the book, were not limited to the current authors. Thanks to the above-mentioned project, a workshop was organised in October 2013 in Aberdeen by Martin Elbel and Karin Friedrich with the participation of Graeme Murdock, Simon Ditchfield, Liudmyla Sharipova, and all the authors. The project also enabled visiting scholars at Palacký University, including – apart from the participants of the Aberdeen workshop – Nora Berend, David Frick, Norman Housley, Gábor Klaniczay, József Laszlovszky, Beata Możejko, and Miri Rubin.

The book appears in English, which means there was a number of decisions that needed to be made in terms of English terminology, which does not fully correspond to the terminology in Czech or other Central European languages. Compromises were sometimes necessary as in the case of some terms for local institutions (Czech, German or Latin terms have been added in brackets), or with the terminology for non-Catholic churches, where in general non-Catholic is used, as well as the more specific term Lutheran for the Olomouc context. Local sources also commonly use the label evangelical, but given the specific connotations of the word, it is not used in this context in English. I would wish to thank David Livingstone, who translated chapter three and Elizabeth Woock, who translated chapters four and five. Elizabeth Woock and Hana Ferencová have moreover, tried to improve the language of all the other authors, and Graeme Murdock, who wrote the afterword, also read the text at the very final stage and had a number of helpful comments on the usage of language. Tomáš Parma, with the help of the authors, acquired and organised the accompanying images, and Lenka Doová coordinated a number of activities within the project. Last, but not least, cordial thanks must go to the publisher. Andrea Settis Frugoni was able to participate in an editorial workshop in Olomouc and was the editor of the volume in the Viella publishing house, where the book was reviewed and copy-edited. As an editor, I have benefited from the work of all the above-mentioned people. Together with all the authors, we would like to dedicate the book to our families who suffered sometimes with less attention than they deserved from our side. We would like to thank them for all their support.

Antonín Kalous

Introduction. Olomouc – The City and Its History

Jaroslav Miller

Traditionally, urban history has been concerned with capital cities of the European West, large and populous centres of trade and politically autonomous republics like Venice, Nuremberg, Paris or London. With the aim of counterbalancing this rather one-sided view of the European urban landscape, social historians like Peter Clark and H. T. Gräf stressed instead the eminence of small towns, typically agricultural settlements with less than 2,000 inhabitants, which, however, represented the quintessence of urban life in premodern Europe. Yet there was also a category in between the two extremes, namely the medium-sized cities that accummulated political, economic and cultural functions while serving in some parts of Europe as regional power centres. To buttress their own prestige and the ancient origins and identity of autonomous urban republics these cities produced elaborate urban mythologies that, in the eyes of their burghers, equalled them to Nuremberg, Prague, Augsburg, Vienna or Gdańsk.

The urban map of still largely unexplored East-Central Europe was dotted with names like Bautzen, Görlitz, Jihlava, Brno, Olomouc, Bratislava (Pozsony, Pressburg), Lublin, Košice (Kassa, Kaschau) and Plzeň. As seats of bishoprics, monasteries, universities and aristocratic courts, these cities attracted immigrants from remote geographical areas and different cultural backgrounds. Urban life in these settlements was always marked by diverse interests of autonomous bodies and the coexistence of competing identities. During the early modern period such cities metamorphosed into genuinely multicultural, multireligious and multilingual environments. As a result, the integrity of their population was increasingly challenged as the community of burghers who "suffered with the town" was rivalled and sometimes undermined by subcommunities of students, clergymen, soldiers and other unassimilated groups. To modern students of municipal administration, law, political institutions, financial affairs, confessional issues and of arts, letters and culture in general, the middle-sized East-Central European city is indeed a fascinating phenomenon.

In a way the bustling early modern Moravian capital of Olomouc – with a wealthy and politically powerful bishopric and chapter, a Jesuit university and numerous monasteries and convents – was an ideal type of such an urban settlement. Innumerable panegyrics, mostly penned by leading humanists, testified to the city's political and economic significance by glorifying its beauty, material opulence, architecture, constitutional settlement and political pre-eminence among other Moravian cities. In 1549, Šimon Ennius Klatovský extolled Olomouc, "which cannot be compared to any other Moravian town as the city abounds in wealth and nurtures concord" (*Scilicet, Olmicii laudes, cui non habet urbem Aequalem lato terra Morava solo, Est opulenta satis ... In qua perpetuo felix concordia floret.*). Inspired by Plato's influential vision of an ideal state, many scholars recognised in Olomouc the perfect urban republic, well governed by a narrow circle of the wisest men and highly educated "philosophers". In celebrating the city the poet Stephanus Taurinus (1465-1520) claimed that Olomouc "prides itself on many learned men" and eulogised the erudition and expertise of the city's elders.

Humanist literature also carefully elaborated urban myth, which served to prove the singularity and historical fame of Olomouc. Adored as *Iulimons*, the city boasted of its ancient history, seemingly going back to Antiquity. According to Georgius Sibutus (1480-1528) "godlike Julius Caesar gave the city its name", while the Moravian historiographer Bartołomiej Paprocki (1540/1543-1614) recognised Caesar as a founder, but also remarked that the origins of Olomouc might have been significantly older, going back to times immemorial.[1] Many other early modern historians overtly ascribed the foundation of the city to the Roman military leader Julius Caesar, whose name the settlement bore for centuries before being Germanised to *Olmütz*.[2] Yet the myth, repeatedly recalled by urban intellectuals and historiographers, might not have been devoid of a rational core. Nestled in the Moravian basin upon the river Morava, Olomouc ranks among the oldest settlements in the country. Because of the strategic location of the place, in the second century AD the Romans indeed set up a large military camp just outside the territory of the future city, arguably the northernmost point of Roman power in Central Europe. Later populated and fortified by the Slavs, Olomouc was one of the power centres of Great Moravia, and subsequently, in the tenth to eleventh centuries the castle grew into the most significant stronghold of Přemyslid power in Moravia, the hub of provincial politics and the seat of the ruler. Olomouc's political significance in relation to other Moravian settlements was further strengthened by the opening of the first Přemyslid mint in Moravia. With the foundation (or renewal, stressing the ninth- and early tenth-century tradition) of the bishopric in 1063 and the Benedictine monastery of Hradisko (1078), Olomouc turned into the natural centre of Moravian church administration. And given its steadily growing political and economic strength, it soon overshadowed the rival urban centres in Moravia, namely Brno and Znojmo.

Though officially endowed with municipal rights as late as the 1240s, Olomouc was long before inhabited by Christian and Jewish town dwellers living in

1. See Eduard Petrů, *Humanisté o Olomouci*, Prague, Památník národního písemnictví, 1977.

2. Georgius Sibutus, "Ad sapientissimum ... senatum Olomucensem Georgii Sibuti, medicinae doctoris, poetae et oratoris laureati, carmen quo et Christianam et regiam illam urbem mirifice illustravit", in *Ad Potentissimum atque Invictissimum Ferdinandum Hungariae, et Bohemie ... Regem ...*, Vienna, 1528.

autonomous settlements adjacent to the castle. Aside from the mostly German-speaking population, which dominated from the thirteenth century, Czech-speaking and Jewish settlers also formed a significant part of the urban society. The arrangement of the city testifies to the existence of flourishing settlements prior to the city's official foundation, since the historical urban layout lacks any symmetry whatsoever, and the number of winding lanes furnish evidence of the spontaneous and uncontrolled development of the place. A historian exploring the medieval urban topography of Olomouc should give proper attention to place names, as they remained remarkably stable in the minds and hearts of town dwellers, and most of them survived over the centuries. As in other cities, street names remind us of the spatial distribution of crafts in the medieval town; but collective memory recalls also identities, buildings and urban entities that no longer exist. A site on St Michael's Hill, traditionally referred to as "At the Castle" (*Na Hradě*), gives testimony to the existence of a town fortress, while the Jewish street (*Židovská ulice, Judengasse;* today *Univerzitní ulice*) helps us to locate the Jewish settlement whose history abruptly ended in the middle of the fifteenth century.

The medieval history of Olomouc was marked by a gradual accumulation of key urban functions. The city served as the official residence of princes, the unrivalled centre of Moravian ecclesiastical power and the economic hub of the province, which had an advantage in long-distance trade (with staple rights) and artisanal production marketed within and outside its territory. Urban culture, nurtured by the city's political eminence and economic wealth, was represented from the twelfth to the fourteenth century, above all by the church scriptoria which produced a number of manuscripts of extraordinary aesthetic quality and literary value. At the same time, the city evolved its own efficient and increasingly ramified municipal administration, as evidenced by the oldest city book (1343-1420) and by the pioneering activities of urban scribe Wenceslas of Jihlava who systematised the urban archive and gave structure to urban historical documents and charters. Yet until the mid-fourteenth century the city remained under the supervision of a royal official, the reeve (*fojt*), who presided over both the city council and the law court. The municipal self-government eventually emancipated itself from the king in 1351, with mayors occupying the uppermost position in the power hierarchy. Though officially governed by the city council, Olomouc was in fact controlled by a few ancient and wealthy patrician families. Their authority, however, faded during the fifteenth century with the rising power of urban guilds and, later, the urban community, which represented all townspeople with citizenship rights. In this respect, the story of Olomouc differed from that of some other cities in Central Europe. While in Nuremberg, for instance, the aristocratic nature of the political system proved remarkably stable for centuries, in Olomouc power was gradually democratised and distributed among a larger number of burghers from diverse social backgrounds. Therefore, from the turn of the fifteenth and sixteenth centuries the urban constitution corresponded to a mixed aristocratic/democratic government with well-balanced rights and power mechanisms.

The assassination in Olomouc of King Wenceslas III (1306), the last male member of the ruling line of the Přemyslid dynasty, heralded a period of a long-term political instability and economic decline which substantially worsened the position of the city vis-à-vis Brno and Jihlava. Yet by 1400 Olomouc may have supported some five to seven thousand inhabitants, and the city ranked among the most politically and economically significant urban centres in the lands of the Bohemian Crown. As much as two-thirds of its population may have been Germans with Czechs forming a strong minority. Yet available sources provide no testimony about national turmoil until the Hussite reformation in the 1410s-1430s, which, among other things, accelerated the political, cultural and economic emancipation of the Czech-speaking population in Bohemia and Moravia. Jews, around 1400 still a marginal group of several dozen families, enjoyed a broad autonomy. Royal protection secured their peaceful symbiosis with the Christian population of the city and allowed them to build their own synagogue close to the city walls.

Because of the Hussite reformation and the collapse of central power, the fifteenth century may justly be considered the stormiest period in the history of Olomouc. The predominantly German-speaking city and seat of a bishop remained a bastion of fierce opposition to the Hussites. But costs for defending the "true faith" proved high. Several times under siege of Hussite troops the intrepid city found itself on the edge of havoc. Though Olomouc always narrowly escaped the miserable lot of some other Moravian towns captured by the Hussites, it suffered heavy economic and demographic losses with high military expenditures followed by unbearable debt.

Economic stress and the precariousness of life provoked social tensions and hatred toward some unassimilated groups of urban dwellers, in particular the Jews. The campaign waged by the Observant Franciscan John of Capestrano (1386-1456) during his repeated stays in 1451 and 1454 released latent anti-Jewish sentiments, resulting in the expulsion of Jews from the territory of the city and most of the royal towns of Moravia.

Economic and demographic hardship was, rather paradoxically, counterbalanced by the growth of Olomouc in political significance during the second half of the fifteenth century. The substantial weakening of royal power, the confessional split and the collateral rule of two kings (George of Poděbrady and Matthias Corvinus) in the Lands of the Bohemian Crown, forced leading Moravian royal cities to collaborate and organise politically. In doing so, they gradually formed a new and autonomous political body increasingly able to defend the crucial interests of burghers. This close political partnership resulted in the late fifteenth and sixteenth centuries in the rise of the burgher estate and the incorporation of royal cities into the chief Moravian institutions – the Moravian Law Court and the Moravian Diet – which were taking place alternately in the cities of Olomouc and Brno.

In a spectacular way, the city's unquestionable primacy among Moravian royal towns was confirmed in 1469 by the Olomouc election of Matthias Corvinus (1443-90) as the king of Bohemia. Under his rule Olomouc enjoyed a highly privileged stance since the city hosted royal summits. And it became one of the Central European hubs of politics and culture. This political eminence gave rise to a unique humanist culture formed by a circle of lay and ecclesiastical intellectuals whose fame extended beyond the Lands of the Bohemian Crown. Nurtured by

Olomouc bishop Stanislaus Thurzo (1470-1540), this humanist culture produced its finest fruits in the personality of John Dubravius (1486-1553), who occupied the episcopal see between 1541 and 1553. Dubravius, a high-spirited and well-educated man, distinguished himself both as a patron of the arts and historian. He authored the *Libellus de piscinis et piscium*, the first Czech treatise on fishpond cultivation. The shining genius of Dubravius, however, was preceded by other Olomouc scholars who befriended and exchanged correspondence with Konrad Celtis, Erasmus of Rotterdam and Willibald Pirkheimer. Most likely in 1502 the learned society *Sodalitas Marcomannica*, an informal assembly of noted Moravian humanists, emerged under the aegis of Olomouc bishops. Its leading spirits, Konrad Altheimer (1431-1509), Augustin Käsenbrot (1467-1513) and Stephanus Taurinus (c. 1485-1519) left behind many texts of significant literary and scholarly value and placed Olomouc on the map of humanist Europe.

In terms of culture, politics and the economy, the pre-White Mountain period (i.e. before the defeat of the estates revolt in 1620) may be labelled as a golden age in the city's history. During the sixteenth century Olomouc demographically expanded and had some ten thousand souls. On the eve of the Thirty Years' War it probably ranked among the top five most populous cities in the Bohemian lands. As a leader of a tiny group of six Moravian royal cities, Olomouc took an active part in shaping the contours of the constitutional settlement in the province prior to the White-Mountain catastrophe in 1620.

The sixteenth century also produced long-term and clearly-visible confessional frontiers within the urban society. Earlier the zealous opponent of Hussitism, the city ardently adopted the Lutheran Reformation. In mostly German-speaking Olomouc, Lutheranism overtly triumphed. But the Catholic minority was able to rely upon unabating support from bishops and, later, the increasingly active Habsburg rulers commited to the idea of restoring the Catholic faith within the monarchy. With the aim of renewing Catholic dominance Emperor Maximilian II founded the Jesuit academy in Olomouc (1566), which was provided with all university rights and privileges in 1573. With the bishopric, several monasteries and the Jesuit university, the mostly Lutheran city, paradoxically, became also a nest of Moravian re-Catholicising tendencies in the late sixteenth century. Two ambitious and politically influential bishops, Stanislaus Pavlovský (died 1598) and Francis cardinal of Dietrichstein (1570-1636), set out a plan for Catholic reform as proposed by the Council of Trent. For the rest of the sixteenth century Olomouc became the scene of sharp confessional disputes and controversies among the bishopric, the burghers and the city council.

The growing confessional tension between the non-Catholic (Lutherans, Unity of Brethren) majority and Catholic institutions destabilised the urban society in many ways. Religious issues featured ominously in city life until the end of the Thirty Years' War. The military defeat of the Bohemian Protestants on White Mountain (1620) changed political and confessional conditions in the country entirely. Still a mostly Lutheran city on the eve of the Thirty Years' War, Olomouc faced the merciless re-Catholicisation policy. And in the 1630s Catholics clearly dominated in the urban population. The Swedish occupation in 1642 and the eight-year presence of the Swedish garrison once again challenged the Catholic nature of the city. The Conventual Franciscan Paulinus Zaczkowicz and urban scribe Friedrich Flade penned in their memoirs vivid accounts of the miseries of life in occupied Olomouc and the hardships of forced coexistence between the mostly Catholic burghers and the Lutheran Swedes. In the middle of the seventeenth century the city rendered a dismal picture of misery and destitution with less than 2,000 souls and 170 houses in a habitable state. Despite massive immigration and bustling building activities the bitter consequences of warfare were not entirely eliminated before 1700. Nevertheless, in 1655 Olomouc was officially declared an imperial fortress, which heralded a new era in the city's history since it was inseparably tied with military life and the geopolitical plans of the quickly expanding Habsburg state.

Upon the departure of the Swedish troops in 1650 the confessional pendulum turned eventually to Catholicism. The faith's triumph in the city was lavishly solemnised in church processions and festive events typical of the forthcoming baroque culture. Catholic piety as reflected in arts, religious festivities and daily life of ordinary citizens featured in the story of the city for the rest of the seventeenth and most of the eighteenth centuries.

The present volume brings together a number of scholars who from different angles contribute to analysis of religious, social and political identity, and confessionalisation and Catholic piety in a late medieval and early modern Central European city.

In the impressive history of Olomouc, the Hussite wars may justly be viewed as a dramatic overture to the religious and political storms to come in the sixteenth and seventeenth centuries. As Jan Stejskal's chapter suggests, the mostly German-speaking city showed a remarkable resistence to the enticements of Hussitism; for the whole fifteenth century Olomouc remained a dauntless supporter of Catholicism. As the pillar of Sigismund of Luxembourg's power in Moravia, the Olomouc city council mercilessly punished any demonstration of Hussite heresy. Loyalty to the Catholic faith, however, ignited a bitter military conflict with the Moravian Hussite camp that inflicted a heavy blow to the Olomouc economy. The long-term stagnation of trade substantially deepened social problems, and enormous debts incurred by both the city and its burghers produced an (un)expected effect: the expulsion of Jews immediately after John of Capestrano's preaching in 1454.

The chapter by Antonín Kalous examines the politically delicate stance of the city in the turbulent, and in many ways formative, last decades of the fifteenth and early sixteenth centuries. Squeezed between its (so far) unshaken loyalty to the Catholic Church and King George of Poděbrady, who opted for the reformed Hussite faith, Olomouc carefully manouevred amidst the competing interests of church dignitaries (pope, papal legates, bishops, Hradisko monastery) and two rival secular rulers (George of Poděbrady and the king of Hungary, Matthias Corvinus). Considered a stronghold of Catholicism, the city played a strategic role in the plans of the Hungarian king and the Catholic Church in their crusade against the king of Bohemia. While papal diplomacy stood behind the military alliance of Moravian cities (Olomouc, Brno, Znojmo, Jihlava) against George of Poděbrady, Matthias Corvinus succeeded in being elected king of Bohemia in Olomouc. He also kept his royal court there. A wave of reformation in the early 1520s, however, brought sweeping change that unsettled the long-term power relationships within the region, discredited traditional political partnerships and, most importantly, contributed to the rise of the new confessional identity of the city itself.

The Reformation disturbed the social climate in Central European cities in more than one way. Firstly, it created a new dimension of conflict between urban governments and town dwellers. Secondly, religious matters soon became a pretext for interventions in urban affairs from outside, either from local aristocracy and the Catholic Church or from central power. This is why city councils typically found their space for manoeuvre and autonomy in decision-making substantially limited with regard to the burghers and external powers, who usually acted more independently. Exposed to simultaneous pressures from below and above, the city elders had to consider all risks in their reaction to the Reformation issue. Yet it was the urban political elite that eventually profited the most from the religious change. Secular patronage of municipal priests and school education gave urban governments a powerful tool to shape "public opinion" and attitudes of the citizenry. This model was not followed in all cities exposed to reform teaching, but much of it applied to Olomouc.

Because of the Reformation, Ondřej Jakubec writes, ties between Olomouc and its bishop remained loose throughout most of the sixteenth century. Bishop Mark Kuen (1553-65), especially, was unable to offer more than a weak opposition to the city's growing autonomy in matters of religion and church administration. Though the city fiercely opposed the Hussite Reformation in the fifteenth century, one hundred years later the mostly German-speaking Olomouc population was moved by and accepted the Lutheran teachings. In the second half of the sixteenth century an uneasy coexistence of Roman Catholic and Wittenberg teachings characterized Olomouc's social, political and religious life. Though Lutherans dominated in numbers and soon achieved majority in the city council, the Catholic minority systematically sought support from the bishops and Catholic clergy. Squeezed between the radicalism of zealous Lutherans and pressure from the emperors and bishops, the urban government cautiously manoeuvred to avoid conflict with the court and to forestall religiously motivated unrest in the city.

The long period of religious tolerance, once labelled by the historian Josef Válka as the era of "supraconfessional Christianity" (*nadkonfesijní křesťanství*), saw its twilight in the last decades of the sixteenth and first half of the seventeenth centuries. The gradual deterioration of the political and religious climate across Europe was paralleled by the increasing radicalism of both antagonistic camps in the Bohemian Lands. As Tomáš Parma suggests in his chapter, the foundation of a Jesuit college in 1566 (university since 1573) and the growing pressure of Olomouc bishop Francis of Dietrichstein shattered the long-term power balance in Moravia. And it substantially, although temporarily, weakened the position of Moravian non-Catholics. However, the conflict between Emperor Rudolf II and his brother Matthias in 1608-12, known as *Bruderzwist*, moved the pendulum of power in favour of the non-Catholic majority, which managed to restore its shaken authority. In 1618-20 Olomouc non-Catholics, encouraged by the triumph of the Bohemian non-Catholic estates, gained full control of the city and joined the anti-Habsburg revolt. Yet the catastrophic and rather unexpected defeat of the non-Catholic army in the battle of the White Mountain on 8 November 1620 had far-reaching demographic, political, religious and social consequences. Entangled in the "shameful rebellion", Olomouc was quickly re-Catholicised and disobedient town dwellers saw their property confiscated or were expelled from the city forever. The re-Catholicisation campaign, however, proved less effective than desired by secular and ecclesiastical authorities since some burghers considered conversion to be a merely formal act of submission to the ruling authority.

Radmila Prchal Pavlíčková is concerned with the forging of the new Catholic identity in the Olomouc urban environment, which until the Thirty Years' War remained dominantly loyal to the Lutheran faith. In doing so, she meticulously examines the formative impact of visual culture and art on the Catholic piety of Olomouc burghers. This renewed and modernised Catholic devotion featured an emotionally and visually attractive culture of Catholic pilgrimages, spectacular baroque landscapes, university theses and lavish urban rituals. Pavlíčková regards the exalted expression of faith and invigorated Catholic piety not only as the outcome of systematic state and church policy (as once suggested by Wolfgang Reinhard and Heinz Schilling), but also as the result of collective and individual endeavours of Olomouc burghers and the urban community.

Symbolic communication through the visual played a crucial role in early modern cities. Religious devotion and the piety of burghers, expressed visually through objects, symbols and images, were inseparable modes of representing communities to both their members and outsiders. In addition to their primary functions, public spaces, town halls, façades, gates, churches and cemeteries became stages for communicating status, religious zeal and political affiliations. The jubilee of 1700, as examined by Martin Elbel, aimed to celebrate the already well-established Catholic identity of Olomouc and the harmonious community of pious citizens. Yet under the façade of concord and confessional unity some latent frictions persisted. The short-term and rather bizarre conflict between the city council and the bishop's consistory over jurisdiction rights disclosed not only the increasingly visible superiority of the state in relation to the Catholic Church but also disagreements within the Church itself. Nevertheless, local tensions and the uneasy coexistence of various ecclesiastical institutions within and without the city walls substantially strengthened the flexibility of the Catholic Church, which proved able to adapt to new challenges in the decades to come.

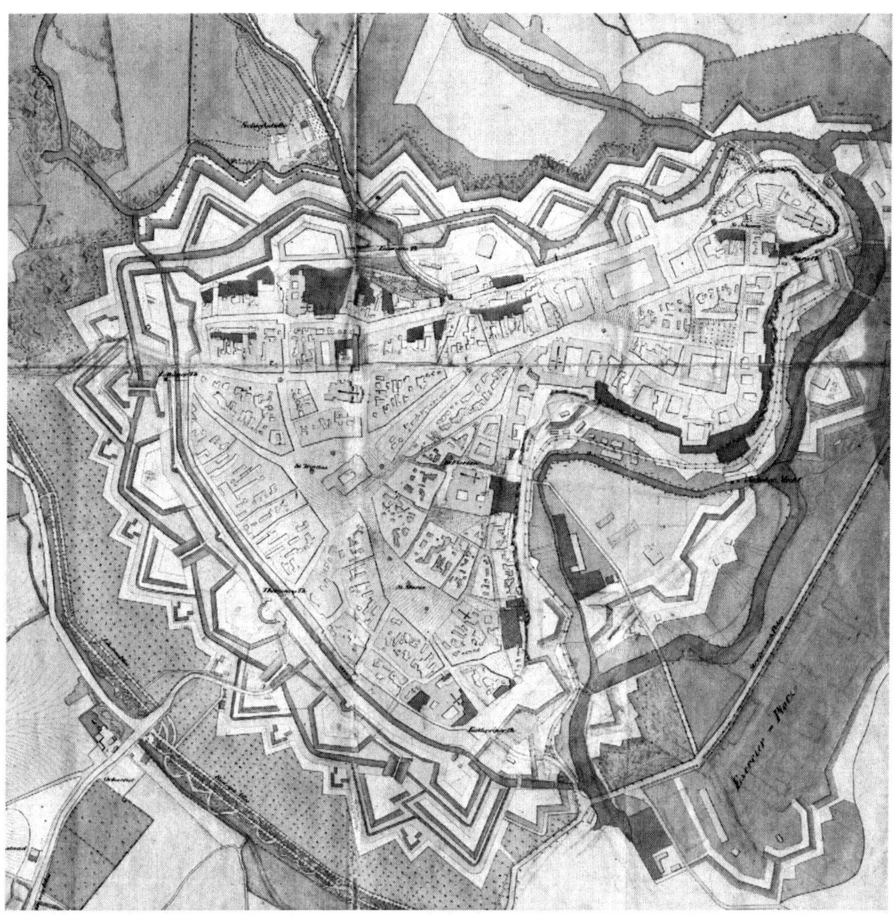

Figure 1: Map of Olomouc with the eighteenth-century fortification (mid-19th century).

19
17
15
16
8
10
7
2
3
22
20
23
22
9
12
1
13
11
18
4
14
N

Figure 2: Map of Olomouc

Legenda:
1. City hall with the chapel of St Jerome
2. Parish church of St Maurice
3. Presbytery of St Maurice
4. Parish church of St Blaise
5. Parish church of the Virgin Mary in Předhradí
6. Parish church of St Peter (former cathedral)
7. Chapel of Sts Cyril and Methodius
8. Lutheran prayer house (17th century)
9. City prison (later All Saints' chapel, now the chapel of St Jan Sarkander)
10. Hospital with the church of the Holy Ghost
11. Plague column of the Virgin Mary
12. Holy Trinity column
13. Dominican friary with St Michael's church
14. Dominican nunnery with the church of St Catherine
15. Observant Franciscan friary with the church of the Virgin Mary
16. Garden of the Observant Franciscan friary (the non-Catholic cemetery)
17. Scala santa chapel
18. Capuchin friary with the church of the Annunciation
19. Ursuline nunnery with the church of St Ursula
20. Jesuit church of the Virgin Mary of Snow (former church of Conventual Franciscans with a friary)
21. Jesuit residence
22. Jesuit University
23. Corpus Christi chapel
24. Carthusian monastery with the church of the Virgin Mary
25. Augustinian canonry with All Saints' church
26. Poor Clares nunnery with the church of St John the Baptist
27. Augustinian nunnery (later Conventual Franciscan friary) with the church of St James
28. Cathedral
29. Bishop's residence
30. Church of St Anne
31. Residence of the dean of cathedral chapter with the chapel of St Barbara
32. Residences of the members of the cathedral chapter
33. Cathedral school
34. Presbytery of the Cathedral

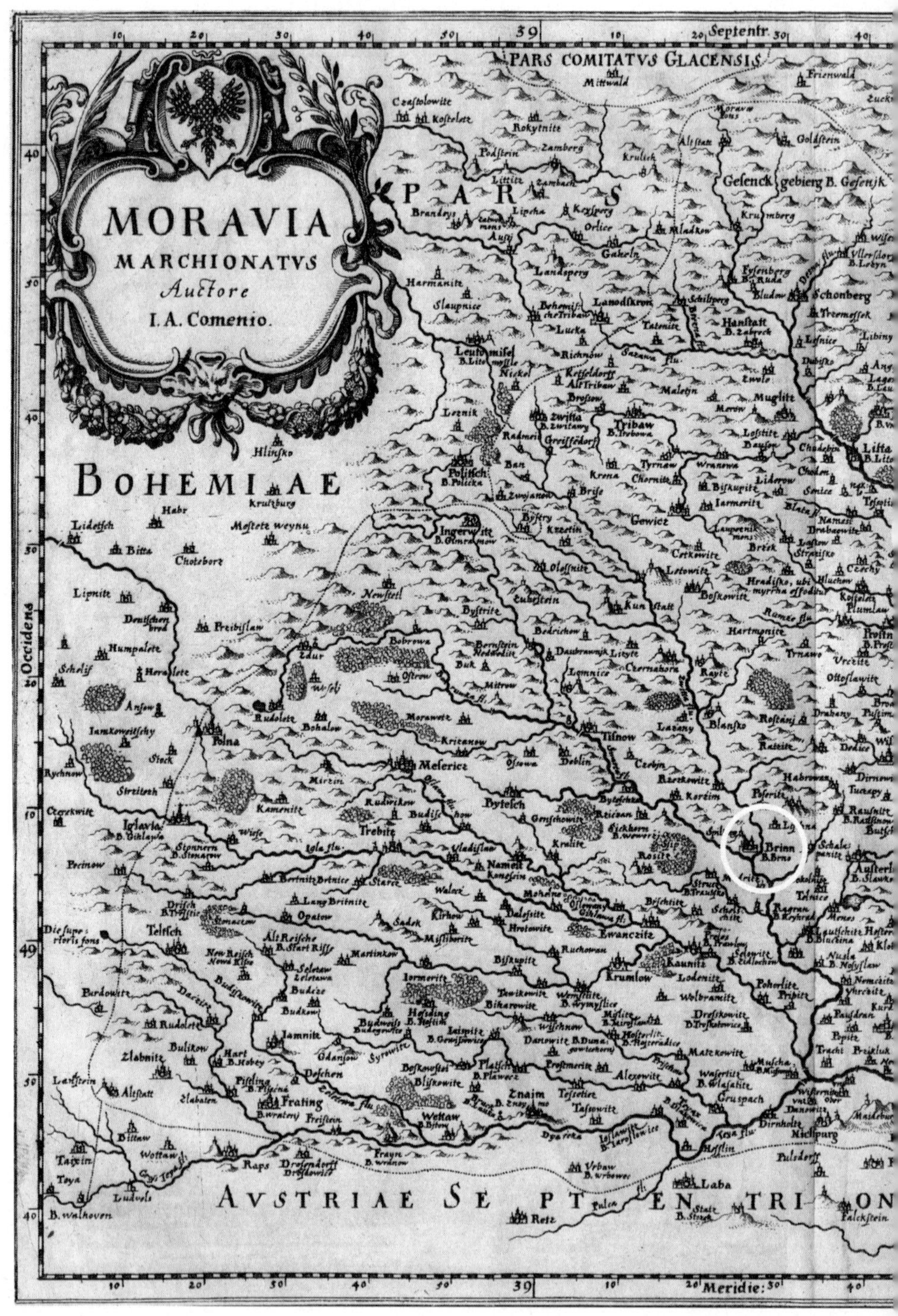
MORAVIA
MARCHIONATVS
Auctore
I.A. Comenio.
PARS COMITATVS GLACENSIS
PARS
BOHEMIAE
AVSTRIAE SEPTENTRIONALIS
Septentr.
Occidens
Meridie:
Brinn
B.Brno
Iglavia
Trebitz
Meseric
Znaim
Krumlow
Kaunitz
Tribaw
Muglitz
Schonberg
Nicolspurg
Laba
Teltsch
Frating
Polna
Bytesch
Tisnow
Blansko
Boskowitz
Lotowitz
Gewicz
Zwitta
Policzka
Auterlitz
Hanstatt

Figure 3: Johannes Amos Comenius, Map of Moravia, 1650.

1. A Catholic City in the Hussite Era, 1400-1450s

JAN STEJSKAL

Death of Margrave Jobst

Jobst (Jošt, Jodocus), the last Margrave of Moravia, died on 18 January 1411. Of the house of Luxembourg, Jobst (born c. 1354), was the eldest son of the late Margrave John Henry of Moravia († 1375), the younger brother of Emperor Charles IV. Jobst's rule was not a period of quiet development without disturbances, due to his conflicts with his brothers and his grand ambitions.[1] From 1388 Jobst held the Margravate of Brandenburg and intervened in the politics of the Holy Roman Empire. He was elected King of the Romans in 1410 after the death of King Rupert, opposing his cousin Sigismund of Luxembourg, king of Hungary. His success did not last long however. Jobst soon died, clearing the way to the throne for Sigismund who later became Holy Roman Emperor. After Jobst's death the king of Bohemia and Sigismund's brother Wenceslas IV became the new Margrave of Moravia, entrusting executive power in the province to the land captain of Moravia (*capitaneus terrae, Landhauptmann*), Laczko of Kravaře (Krawarn).[2] Laczko, as the king's deputy, became the most powerful official in Moravia and owner and supreme lord of the city of Olomouc.

The political situation in Bohemia and Moravia after the death of Margrave Jobst, and under the weak rule of King Wenceslas IV, became increasingly complex. The dispute, which was led by the teachings of the English reformer John Wycliffe, culminated in 1412. In that year Wycliffe's texts were burned in Prague by church authorities, and Jan Hus, a promoter of Wycliffe's teaching at Prague University, was expelled from the city. Land captain Laczko was the leading figure among the noble supporters of Hus. On the other hand, Laczko represented the king in Moravia and in the city of Olomouc. Therefore a conflict between Laczko and the Catholic city was imminent. The attitude of the Olomouc city council and especially the episcopal curia towards supporters of Hus (and Wycliffe) manifested in 1413. Hus himself mentioned in one of his sermons that two men – both

1. For details on the rule of the Luxembourg family in Moravia, see Jaroslav Mezník, *Lucemburská Morava 1310-1423*, Prague, Nakladatelství Lidové Noviny, 1999.

2. On Laczko and the lords of Kravaře, see Tomáš Baletka, *Páni z Kravař: Z Moravy až na konec světa*, Prague, Nakladatelství Lidové noviny, 2003.

Figure 4: Protest letter of Czech and Moravian nobility against the burgning of Jan Hus to Council of Constance, 2 September 1415, facsimile.

supporters of his cause (one of them "priest Martin") – were tortured by the Olomouc church authorities.[3]

Conflict erupted during the summer of 1415. The Council of Constance summoned Hus and later tried him for heresy (for promoting Wycliffe's teachings) and finally put him to death at the stake on 6 July 1415. Opinions on Hus's teaching and tragic death quickly divided society in the Bohemian lands. A new movement formed – the Hussites – that followed the teachings of the reformer. This predominantly religious movement also embraced social issues and in some respects strengthened Czech national awareness based on language. These factors played an important role also in the predominantly German city of Olomouc.

Disturbances broke out when news of Hus's death at the Council of Constance arrived in the Bohemian lands. Most of the protests were directed against church representatives, and especially the religious orders and their properties. Hus's supporters felt his execution was an insult to the whole country. Soon after the act the Council received protest letters from the Czech and Moravian nobility with (in Moravia) the highest dignitaries of the Margravate, including land captain Laczko of Kravaře. The execution of the popular preacher and former

3. *Dějiny Olomouce*, vol. I, ed. by Jindřich Schulz, Olomouc, Univerzita Palackého, 2009, p. 188 (Bohdan Kaňák).

rector of Prague University was perceived as an offence to the estates as well. The protest letters were sealed by 452 noblemen, an extraordinary number. Hus was not just an ordinary heretic for these people, who represented a substantial part of Bohemian and Moravian elites. The Council, however, apparently did not recognise the seriousness of the situation. They accepted the challenge and declared all those who appended their seals suspect of heresy, and summoned them personally to Constance.[4]

The lists of protesting noblemen, compiled either by their Hussite admirers or their Catholic opponents, soon circulated around the Bohemian lands. One such list written by the Carthusians from Dolany near Olomouc was surely prepared for the possible prosecution of Hus's supporters in the future.[5] Their Carthusian monastery was later seized by the Hussites and bought and destroyed by Olomouc's citizens.

Catholic City versus Hussite Nobility

The Olomouc city council was without doubt strongly against Hus's followers, as they fervently supported the Roman Catholics. The situation became clear during the summer of 1415. The city council created a surprising opposition to the country's government and to the sovereign's representative, Laczko of Kravaře. The traditional legal practice had been violated.

In summer 1415, soon after Hus's execution, a quick and unexpected trial took place in front of the municipal court. The trial is mentioned in the *Liber civitatis*, known as the Olomouc codex of Wenceslas of Jihlava.[6] Wenceslas was the city office clerk and the codex written by him contains official records. There are the annual reports regarding the city's economy and references to the poor, widows and orphans. The codex also includes a description of the duties of the mayor, councillors, clerk and other city employees and their incomes. Besides this information there are memorable reports giving the codex in some parts a chronicle character and broader historical dimension. These reports relate mainly to the period of the Hussite wars. The introductory part of the book is richly decorated with large illuminations with figural motifs, one of them depicting the city council oath.[7] Its figures have been identified as Olomouc city council members and the scribe (city clerk) Wenceslas of Jihlava. An accompanying inscription reads: *Iuste iudicate filii hominum* (Fairly judge the sons of men).[8]

4. For further reading, see František Šmahel, *Die Hussitische Revolution*, 3 vols., Hannover, Hahnsche Buchhandlung, 2002 (MGH Schriften 43), vol. II, pp. 925-949.

5. VKOL, sign. M II 91, fol. 165v-167r: *Protestatio nobilium regni Boemiae et Moraviae marchionatus concillio Constantiensi missa ...*

6. SOkA Olomouc, AMO, Knihy, sign. 1540; *Památná kniha olomoucká (kodex Václava z Jihlavy) z let 1430-1492, 1528*, ed. by Libuše Spáčilová and Vladimír Spáčil, Olomouc, Univerzita Palackého, 2004.

7. For the descripton of the illumination, see: Josef Krása, *České iluminované rukopisy 13.-16. století*, Prague, Odeon, 1990, p. 396.

8. SOkA Olomouc, AMO, Knihy, sign. 1540, fol. 2v.

Figure 5: Václav z Jihlavy, *Liber civitatis*, city council, illumination, 1430.

The codex contains an interesting note about the trial of summer 1415. Two laymen were arrested for public support of Hus's teachings. This support was strictly against the Church's official position, especially after Hus's execution. The note says: "The two laymen, who preached the erroneous articles of Jan Hus, were ordered to be burned by the citizens of Olomouc, against the will of Laczko, the land captain of Moravia."[9] Both men were tried and burned at the stake by the municipal court. The note in the codex of Wenceslas of Jihlava clearly shows that the trial, judgement and execution were carried out against the will of Laczko of Kravaře. They were not handed over to ecclesiastical court. They did not get an opportunity to appeal to a higher court, nor did the city itself hand the case to the court in Wrocław (which usually happened in more trivial matters). Both men were burned for heresy without delay by the decision of the municipal court. The case is remarkable for the unusual speed with which the city council progressed with the trial (the men were arrested, tortured, sentenced and burned within one day) and for the disruption of jurisdiction. The heresy trial simply did not belong to the competencies and qualification of the municipal court. The city of Olomouc had no right to pass judgments on theological matters.

The trial and its brutal consequences did not go unanswered. The rector of Prague University, Briccius of Buda, sent a protest letter to the land captain of Moravia. He complained to Laczko, naming one of the sentenced men as a certain John, a student of Prague University. Briccius described the citizens and the court of Olomouc as tyrannical, "... real savage tyrants ...".[10] Nevertheless, the nature of the letter to land captain Laczko is merely a complaint; it contains neither advice for preventing such acts nor a punishment for the Olomouc city council by the land captain representing the king. The reaction of Laczko is not known, but it is clear that his ability to act decisively against the city council was limited. According to the law, Laczko could have exercised his power in the name of the margrave and the king, but the upcoming religious conflict overshadowed all previous legal practice and confidence. Religious conflict led the city into a sort of independence from existing structures of power. Nevertheless, the student John and his friend were not judged fairly in Olomouc. The tyrannical court of Olomouc, however, had allies as well as opponents. The Council of Constance praised the Olomouc court's decision and even celebrated the city in a letter addressed to the "... beloved sons of the Church ... councillors, and

9. *Ibid.*, fol. 5v: "Et quia ipsius civitatis Olomucensis cives duos laycos, qui Johannis Hus articulos erroneos predicabat, contra voluntatem domini Laczkonis, capitanei in Moravia, ... combuerre mandaverant ...".

10. *Documenta Magistri Ioannis Hus vitam, doctrinam, causam in Constantiensi concilio actam et controversias de religione in Bohemia, annis 1403-1418 motas illustrantia*, ed. by František Palacký, Pragae, F. Tempsky, 1869 (repr. Osnabrück, Biblio-Verlag, 1966), p. 561: "... quam non sine magno dolore cordis nostri recepimus, quomodo bonae memoriae Joannes, olim universitatis nostrae studii, nuper per Olomucenses, non veluti cives deliberate judicantes, verum immanissimos tyrannos, nostrae in eo linguae patentes inimicos, in civitate eorum cum socio suo captus, in spacio quasi unius mediae diei naturalis tortus, judicatus et ignis voragini traductus et combustus ..."; see also, *Dějiny Olomouce*, vol. I, p. 188 (Bohdan Kaňák).

the city Olomouc …". Thus the Council supported the court's decisive action against the Hussite heresy.[11]

Bishops of Olomouc

Olomouc had been for centuries the seat of a bishopric, and the problems incurred by the episcopal curia in the 1410s contributed to the escalation of religious controversies. The diocese was paralysed by a dispute over the occupation of the bishop's seat. Olomouc had no bishop during the crucial moments at the beginning of the Hussite era. The bishopric had only the administrator of the diocese and titular patriarch of Antioch Wenceslas Králík of Buřenice (1416), who belonged to the circle of King Wenceslas IV. The king himself cautiously supported the reform movement led by Hus until 1412 when after pressure from abroad he changed his position. Wenceslas of Buřenice acted accordingly. But he changed his position rather late, and the Council of Constance threatened him with possible legal proceedings for supporting or even promoting the heresy.[12] The administrator Wenceslas, as well as most of his successors in the bishop's seat, did not dwell in Olomouc. Rather, they resided in estates belonging to the bishopric, mainly in Vyškov (Wischau) or in Kroměříž (Kremsier) in central Moravia. Wenceslas's influence on the city and the city council was therefore limited due to both his support of reformers and practical reasons. The city started to act independently of both royal power represented by the land captain of Moravia and the diocese administrator, who was reluctant to obey the Council of Constance.

In Bohemia, however, there was a bishop who fully met Catholic standards and who became a favourite of the Council of Constance, and later of the pope. John, called John the Iron (Jan Železný), bishop of Litomyšl in eastern Bohemia and later cardinal of the Holy Roman Church, took the opportunity to become the bishop of Olomouc after the death of Wenceslas of Buřenice in 1416. The canons of the Olomouc chapter residing permanently in the city elected him as bishop just several days after the death of Wenceslas of Buřenice, asking the Council of Constance for approval of their election.[13] King Wenceslas did not agree with this development and especially with John the Iron, a fierce critic of the Hussites and the king's inability and reluctance to cope with them. Therefore the king forced his loyal canons of the Olomouc chapter living at the Prague royal court to elect his chosen candidate, Aleš (Alsso) of Březí.[14] That election happened two weeks after John the Iron's election and caused the schism in the bishop's

11. *Ibid.*; Berthold Bretholz, "Die Übergabe Mährens an Herzog Albrecht V. von Österreich im Jahre 1423. Beiträge zur Geschichte der Husitenkriege in Mähren", *Archiv für österreichische Geschichte*, 80 (1894), pp. 251-349: 310-311, "Sacrosancta et generalis synodus Constantinensis dilectis ecclesiae filiis … magistro civium, consulibus … civitatis Olomucensis …".

12. *Documenta*, p. 623, "… quia idem archiepiscopus in nullo defended clerum, et alienavit bona, et sic similiter dicitur de domino Wenceslao patriarcha Antiochensi etc.".

13. *Dějiny Olomouce*, vol. I, p. 218 (Petr Elbel).

14. Eduard Maur, "Příspěvek k biografii biskupa Aleše z Březí", in *Táborský archiv. Sborník Státního okresního archivu v Táboře*, Tábor, Státní okresní archiv, 1998, pp. 11-35.

office.[15] The sympathies of the Olomouc citizens and of the city council were on the side of Bishop John. But the king enforced his will and threatened them with force if the city obstructed Bishop Aleš's entrance to Olomouc.[16]

The episcopate of Aleš of Březí was marked with constant disputes with the supporters of Bishop John and the citizens of Olomouc. Aleš, on the other hand, utilised the backing of the Hussite Moravian nobility. The real scandal, which might illustrate the episcopate of Aleš, happened in the winter of 1416 when a certain priest John offered the Holy Communion under both kinds, i.e. wine and bread (the Hussite custom) during a service in the Olomouc cathedral in the presence of Bishop Aleš. The priest and the people who received Communion in such a way were immediately arrested by the Olomouc citizens. The bishop released them however. The event was immediately communicated to the Council of Constance by the canons supporting Bishop John the Iron.[17]

The Council of Constance supported Bishop John the Iron during the winter of 1416-17 with the Council bull declaring Bishop John the only administrator of the Olomouc bishopric. But that was the maximum help the Council could provide in John's case.[18] Also, the residing canons who were openly or secretly on the side of Bishop John opposed Bishop Aleš. After the winter incident with the Hussite priest they refused to participate in any activities in the Olomouc cathedral. They considered the cathedral desecrated and Bishop Aleš had to bring them back by force.[19] Those canons, unlike the bishop, actually lived in Olomouc, and it is very likely they had the support of Olomouc's Catholic citizens.

The schism was not resolved until the death of King Wenceslas IV in 1419. The new king of Bohemia and the new Margrave of Moravia (and King of the Romans) Sigismund promptly granted the Olomouc bishopric's properties to Bishop John. And Bishop Aleš, lacking royal support, had to leave and he was granted the bishopric of Litomyšl in exchange.[20] At that moment John the Iron, who in 1421 became administrator of the Prague archbishopric, was the mainstay of Catholics in Olomouc and Moravia and throughout all the Bohemian Lands. John became the most significant ally of King Sigismund and the Catholic Church against the Hussites. The king entrusted him with the administration of several royal cities in Moravia including Olomouc. Therefore, John was both the Bishop of Olomouc and a representative of the city's owner.[21] Bishop John took part in most of King

15. *Dějiny Olomouce*, vol. I, p. 219 (Petr Elbel).

16. *Ibid.*

17. *Ibid.;* Bretholz, "Die Übergabe Mährens", pp. 315-316, "… ita quod ex quadam presumcione in adventu domini proxime preterito quidam intraverunt in ecclesiam Olomucensem Husiste et ibidem sub utraque specie sacramentim a quodam presbytero nomine Iohanne presente dicto … electo Alssone … quam illi, quos communicavit, fuissent per cives Olomucenses katholicos detenti et dicto Alssoni presentati … fuerunt per dictum Alssonem absque aliqua punicione et pena libere dimissi …".

18. *Dějiny Olomouce*, vol. I, p. 219 (Petr Elbel).

19. *Ibid.*, p. 220; Jan Sedlák, "K činnosti Jana Železného", *Studie a texty k náboženským dějinám českým*, 3 (1919), pp. 92-104: 97-98.

20. *Dějiny Olomouce*, vol. I, p. 221 (Petr Elbel).

21. *Ibid.*, p. 223 (Petr Elbel).

Sigismund's military activities during the Hussite wars, which were, however, largely unsuccessful. In addition to Sigismund's Bohemian campaigns, John had to fight in Moravia against the Hussite nobility during the early twenties until the decisive defeat of his army by the Hussites in the battle near Kroměříž in June 1423. With the loss of Kroměříž he lost one of the bishopric's most important estates and his military power and political influence diminished.[22]

The Besieged City

The Catholic city of Olomouc as early as 1420 declared war against Hussite Prague.[23] City troops most likely participated even in the crusade against the Hussites. It is not surprising that the city filled with numerous Catholic refugees, not only from nearby areas but also from large Bohemian cities including Prague. Even a part of the canons of the Prague cathedral chapter found refuge in Olomouc.[24] The participation of Olomouc troops in the war in Moravia was initially successful. Olomouc and its bishop took part in the military campaign of Sigismund in central and southern Moravia. This episode of the war, successful for the Catholics, ended with the *landfrýd* (*Landfriede*, land peace) for Moravia, ratified in Brno in November 1421. This *landfrýd* was concluded for five consecutive years. All Moravian Hussites were commanded to give up their heresy and to do so in designated cities including Olomouc.[25] Olomouc did play just a passive role when the *landfrýd* of 1421 was concluded, as there was not a single Moravian city among signatories of the document. The peace agreement was signed only by members of the Moravian nobility, the Olomouc bishop and the king. This is significant because it is the last time such a situation occurred in Moravia. The following *landfrýd*s were negotiated with the strong (and almost essential) participation of the cities.[26] However, the Catholic armies of King Sigismund were defeated in Bohemia soon after, and the situation that seemed to be so promising for the Catholic side, and for Olomouc in particular, had changed.

The nearby territories of Olomouc became battlefields and constant targets of plundering by both sides of the conflict. During 1421 Olomouc experienced also the military presence of Sigismund's troops under the command of Pippo Spano. Spano, or rather Filippo Buondelmonti degli Scolari, was a famous condottiere of

22. *Ibid.*, p. 188 (Bohdan Kaňák).

23. *Archiv Český*, ed. by František Palacký, vol. IV, Prague, 1848, p. 380, "… my radda města Olomuckého i všechna obec … wystřiehámy se protiv wám. [… we the council of the city of Olomouc and all the community … shall refrain from you]".

24. Jaroslav Kadlec, *Katoličtí exulanti čeští doby husitské*, Prague, Zvon, 1990, p. 26.

25. *Archiv Český*, ed. by Josef Kalousek, vol. X, Prague, 1890, pp. 246-250; Josef Válka, *Husitství na Moravě. Náboženská snášenlivost. Jan Amos Komenský*, Brno, Matice moravská, 2005, pp. 33-34, Válka described the *landfrýd* as the first act of the "Counter-Reformation".

26. Jaroslav Mezník, "Markrabě a páni. (K mocenskému dualismu na Moravě v době předhusitské)", *Sborník prací filozofické fakulty brněnské univerzity. Studia minora facultatis philosophicae Universitatis Brunensis*, C 42 (1995), pp. 39-50: 48-49, Mezník expressed the idea of transition to the estate monarchy.

Florentine origin in the service of King Sigismund. Spano soon became well known on the Czech and Moravian battlefields in the long-lasting campaign against the Hussites.[27] He was not the only condottiere "at the gates" of Olomouc however.

In the course of the conflict the city was attacked and besieged by the army of the other side, the Lithuanian duke Sigismund Korybut who was acting on behalf of the Grand Duke of Lithuania Vytautas in 1422. He was temporarily recognised by the Hussites as the regent of Bohemia and his troops closely cooperated with the Hussites. Olomouc was defended only with the greatest of efforts, and Hussite troops in the region remained a constant threat. In such a situation King Sigismund decided to pass the rule over Moravia to his vigorous son-in-law Albert of Habsburg. Albert became the Margrave in 1423 and immediately started his efforts to fully control the land. Olomouc stood firmly on his side, which meant participation in the endless war in the region. Battles took place just a few miles outside the town. The countryside, the economic base of the city, was systematically devastated, causing direct damage to the city. Trade routes were unsafe or constantly interrupted, and the city accepted new waves of refugees. The monasteries situated outside the city walls were mostly destroyed and their monks found refuge in the city where they officially transferred their institutions. The abandoned monasteries, such as the Carthusian foundation in Dolany, became strongholds of the Hussite troops that engaged Olomouc military forces. The Dolany monastery was (after an unsuccessful siege) finally bought by the city of Olomouc from the Hussites and destroyed in 1425.[28] During the following years the situation became so critical that the city repeatedly had to negotiate with the Hussites for a short ceasefire.[29] The crisis culminated in 1432 when Hussite troops occupied the Premonstratensian monastery of Hradisko, situated just a few steps from the city on the opposite side of the river Morava. This meant an immediate threat to the entire city. The food supply was interrupted, which triggered a sharp rise in prices followed by local riots.[30]

Temporary relief came in 1435 when the peace agreement was concluded and the rule of Albert of Habsburg was accepted by all Moravians, both Catholics and Hussites.[31] This fragile peace was violated in 1437 when the remnants of the Hussite troops attacked the nearby town of Litovel. The attacking Hussites were defeated by Olomouc troops and troops of the new bishop Paul of Miličín. Olomouc residents then witnessed the mass execution of dozens of Hussite prisoners. The horrors of war in the besieged city were described in unique annotations made by

27. Gizella Nemeth Papo, *Pippo Spano. Un eroe antiturco antesignano del Rinascimento*, Gorizia, Edizioni della Laguna, 2006.

28. For example see: Jakub Vrána, "Kartuziánský klášter v Dolanech u Olomouce", in *Archeologické památky střední Moravy*, vol. XIII, Olomouc, Archeologické centrum Olomouc, 2007, pp. 19-22.

29. For example see the document issued by the city granting the Hussite lords secure stay in Olomouc during the negotiations: SOkA Olomouc, AMO, Knihy, sign. 677, sign. 95a, fol. 111r; *Archiv Český*, ed. František Palacký, vol. VI, Prague 1876, p. 414.

30. SOkA Olomouc, AMO, Knihy, sign. 1540, fol. 20v-21r.

31. *Archiv Český*, vol. X, pp. 250-254.

the priest Mach (probably Matthew) of Hnojice (Gnoitz).[32] Formerly an Augustinian canon, Mach was (after the destruction of his monastery in Prostějov) the chaplain of the town of Litovel. He eventually served the noble lady Elisabeth of Šternberk[33] and experienced the Hussite raid on his town in 1437. Mach fled from Litovel and survived. The marginalia on the Czech translation and the copy of the text by Gerhard of Liège *Liber de doctrina et preparatione cordis* – the texts Mach was at that time copying or translating – contain a number of Czech-Latin notes briefly describing the traumatic situations he experienced, including the mass hanging of Hussite prisoners in Olomouc[34] and the attack on Šternberk that he survived.[35] It seems that he wrote these notes for himself, out of a need to express his internal feelings. They are short sentences, sometimes just a few words. They touch upon the horrors of war, his fear and especially his solitude. Such sentences as "Mach, where could you go? Wolves and lions everywhere …",[36] or "Mach *bis sam* …" [Latin-Czech, "twice alone"],[37] "we are half dead half alive",[38] or even "Machu *abstine et bene vive* [Mach, do not drink and live well]",[39] show a man totally exhausted by war. At that time the war had been going on for seventeen years, in medieval perspective almost an entire generation.

King and Emperor Sigismund died in 1437 and Margrave Albert of Habsburg inherited his kingdoms – Hungary and Bohemia – and was elected King of the Romans a year later. His brief rule as king of Bohemia ended with his premature death in 1439, and the country, for such a long time affected by the religious war, was again without a king. Albert's son and heir to the throne Ladislas was born after his father's death, and therefore the Margravate of Moravia and the Kingdom of Bohemia were controlled by representatives of the estates – in both countries moderate Hussites. The maintaining of peace was performed by various regional *landfrýd*s.

Throughout that stormy period Olomouc remained an undisputed centre of Catholicism in Moravia, supported by its bishops, especially Bishop John the Iron, and even more so by the cathedral canons. Olomouc and the bishop remained allies for almost two decades when the country was deeply divided between Hussites and Catholics. However, the residing canons, unlike the bishops,

32. VKOL, sign. M I 10, Gerardi Leodiensis O.P. Liber de doctrina et preparatione cordis; VKOL, sign. M I 302.

33. VKOL, sign. M I 10, fol. 186r, "Hec Mach z Hnojicz, domine generose Elisabeth de Stermberg existens capellanus in castro supradicto. Item Tunkl sine difidacione dolose et infideliter in die Wenceslai martiris Christi expoliavit totum opidum Stermberg et multa dampna intulit toti confinio. Et fuit secunda feria in die Wenceslai me presente. Hec Mach anno Domini XXXIX.".

34. VKOL, sign. M I 10, fol. 186r.

35. VKOL, sign. M I 10, fol. 1r, "anno Domini M°CCCCXXXVII° Luthovia fuit acquisita per Pardus in die Animarum post Omnium sanctorum et ipso anno transimus in Sternberg ad castrum Elisabeth Mach sam [in Czech, Mach alone] cum Adam. In die Barbare feria IIII fuit et suspensi fuerunt XLVIII° una die in Olomouc.".

36. VKOL, sign. M I 10, fol. bs.

37. VKOL, sign. M I 10, fol. bs.

38. VKOL, sign. M I 10, fol. bs.

39. VKOL, sign. M I 302 fol 119v.

stayed mostly in the city. Almost all the chapter canons after the Hussite wars were members of local families. There were practically no outsiders, unlike in the previous and the following periods.[40] It seems that a canonry of the chapter in the besieged city was not a very desirable benefice and thus a position commonly occupied by clergy from local families.

Religious life generally suffered during the Hussite period. Almost all convents and monasteries in the Bohemian Hussite territories were destroyed and their communities dispersed.[41] The situation in Moravia was definitely better than in Bohemia – convents and monasteries situated in Catholic cities especially survived the stormy period. That was the case for Olomouc too where within its walls still stand the original convents founded in the city and the communities that received asylum in Olomouc – for example the Carthusians from nearby Dolany or Augustinians from the Moravian and eastern Bohemian towns of Prostějov (Proßnitz), Moravská Třebová (Mährisch Trübau) and Lanškroun (Landskron).[42] The number of religious institutions in the city had increased, which further strengthened the Catholicism of the city and its inhabitants.

Although the city had retained its Catholic faith the price was high. The long war, the number of refugees, the disruption of trade and the overall economic decline plunged the city into a protracted crisis. Economic crisis, or long-lasting stagnation, was evidenced by virtually zero growth in tax revenues during the Hussite wars.[43] Apparently the percentage of the non-economically active population in the city (for example monks and canons who found shelter there) increased significantly. Besides its Catholicism there was another characteristic of the city that made it markedly different from the surroundings: its language. It is estimated that the German-speaking majority reached at least two-thirds of the total population (compared to one-third of Czech-speaking inhabitants),[44] which at the beginning of the fifteenth century numbered about 3,500-5,500 inhabitants.[45]

The constant wars did not just affect the Catholics; Olomouc housed a Jewish community of as many as 200 people.[46] The Jewish settlement was situated near

40. *Dějiny Olomouce*, vol. I, p. 241 (Petr Elbel).

41. For general information about destruction of the Catholic institutions in the Bohemian lands and their representatives during the Hussite era, see Kadlec, *Katoličtí exulanti;* Howard Kaminsky, *A History of the Hussite Revolution*, Berkeley and Los Angeles, University of California Press, 1967, pp. 298-299; Michael D. Bailey, *Battling Demons. Witchcraft, Heresy, and Reform in the Late Middle Ages*, University Park, Pennsylvania State University Press, 2004, pp. 57-64.

42. For details on various Moravian monasteries, consult Dušan Foltýn et al., *Encyklopedie moravských a slezských klášterů*, Prague, Libri, 2005, ad indicem.

43. *Dějiny Olomouce*, vol. I, p. 206 (Roman Zaoral).

44. Jaroslav Marek, *Sociální struktura moravských královských měst v 15. a 16. století*, Prague 1967, pp. 19-26. These estimates were based on number of houses and tax records. For details on the particular history of the city houses of Olomouc consult: Wilhelm Nather and Friedrich Nather, *Die Olmützer Häuserchronik*, 2 vols., ed. by Vladimír Spáčil, Olomouc, Univerzita Palackého, 2005-2006.

45. *Dějiny Olomouce*, vol. I, pp. 141, 198 (Štěpán Kohout, Bohdan Kaňák).

46. The details about the Jewish population can be estimated on the basis of the Jewish lists of loans: Johann Kux, "Das Olmützer Judenregister vom Jahre 1413-1420", *Zeitschrift des Deutschen Vereines für die Geschichte Mährens und Schlesiens*, 9 (1905), pp. 385-423.

the office of the city reeve (*fojt, Vogt*). The local Jews, and the loans offered by them were – especially during the difficult period of the Hussite war – an important source of financing for both numerous individuals and the city council. It is likely that the Jews came under pressure as the city and its residents found themselves in increasing economic difficulties during the war. There is an illustrative example of anti-Jewish propaganda as early as 1425, in the form of a document describing an alleged conversion of Rabbi Moses of Olomouc and profanation of the host. The legend about his conversion ended with the building of a church in honour of the Corpus Christi, funded by former Jewish properties and money.[47] Although the narrative about the conversion and building of the church in Olomouc as a result of profanation of the host cannot be confirmed by other sources, it demonstrates (at least in rhetorical terms) the growing pressure on the Jewish community. From 1426 there is a contemporary example of Jewish persecution in another Catholic city – Jihlava. The local Jews were expelled for alleged collaboration with the Hussites and it was decided soon after to rebuild their synagogue as a chapel of Corpus Christi.[48] This pressure later culminated in the expulsion of the Jews from Olomouc. Economic reasons for the expulsion were heightened by emotional reasons provoked by the preaching of John of Capestrano. Capestrano, following the example of his teacher Bernardine of Siena, was a champion of Christian anti-Jewish sentiment. To blame the poverty of the city, exhausted during the Hussite wars, on the usury of the local Jewry was an easy and proven path. This seems to have gained him the favour of his Olomouc audience.

Capestrano in the City

St John of Capestrano's preaching mission north of the Alps happened between 1451 and his death after the celebrated Christian victory at the battle of Belgrade in 1456.[49] He visited Olomouc twice: during August and September of 1451, and during July and August of 1454.[50] Capestrano arrived in a city that had suffered a long period of war and religious tension. Initially he was invited by

47. Daniel Soukup, "The Alleged Conversion of the Olomouc Rabbi Moses in 1425. Contribution to the Host Desecration Legends in Mediaeval Literature", *Judaica Bohemiae*, 48, no. 1 (2013), pp. 5-38.

48. *Ibid.*, p. 29.

49. Gedeon Gál, Jason M. Miskuly and Ottokar Bonmann, "A Provisional Calendar of St. John Capistran's Correspondence II", *Franciscan Studies*, 49 (1989), pp. 255-345; Kaspar Elm, "Johannes Kapistrans Predigtreise diesseits der Alpen (1451-1456)", in Kaspar Elm, *Vitasfratrum: Beiträge zur Geschichte der Eremiten- und Mendikantenorden des zwölften und dreizehnten Jahrhunderts*, ed. by Dieter Berg, Werl, Dietrich Coelde, 1994, pp. 321-337; Johannes Hofer, "Zur Predigttätigkeit des hl. Johannes Kapistran in den deutschen Städten", *Franziskanische Studien*, 13 (1926), pp. 120-158; Johannes Hofer, "Die wiener Predigten des hl. Johannes Kapistran im Jahre 1451", *Jahrbuch der Österreichischen Leo-Gesellschaft*, 1 (1927), pp. 122-146; Norman Housley, *Crusading and the Ottoman Threat 1453-1505*, Oxford, Oxford University Press, 2012, p. 118.

50. Štěpán Kohout, "Pobyt Jana Kapistrána v Olomouci", *Ročenka Státního okresního archivu v Olomouci*, 3 (1994), pp. 117-140; František Šmahel, "Spectaculum fidei českomoravské mise Jana Kapistrána", *Z kralické tvrze*, 14 (1987), pp. 15-19.

the King of the Romans, Frederick III, and then received permission from Pope Nicholas V to preach in Austria. His goal was to convert the Hussites. Thereafter he responded to many invitations and visited several cities in Silesia and Moravia and even a few Catholic cities of Bohemia.

Capestrano's mission was made easier by the support of Olomouc bishop John Ház (bishop 1444-54). Ház was a strong opponent of the Hussites. On his way to Olomouc Capestrano was invited to the bishop's seat in Vyškov and while in Olomouc he stayed at the bishop's residence.[51] The next bishop of Olomouc, Bohuš (Bohuslav) of Zvole (bishop 1454-57), also supported Capestrano's mission. Bohuš probably met Capestrano during his first Olomouc visit in 1451 when he was dean of the chapter. He was elected bishop by the chapter in June 1454, a month before Capestrano's second visit. In July 1454 the Olomouc canons addressed a letter to Capestrano asking for his kind intervention with Pope Nicolas V in supporting confirmation of the Olomouc bishopric to Bohuš of Zvole. This happened immediately; the pope confirmed Bohuš in August 1454.[52]

Capestrano's preaching in 1451 took place at *Bělidla*, just outside the city walls. The friary of Observant Franciscans was founded at the site in 1453 to commemorate the event. Capestrano even had a chance to personally observe the construction of the convent during his second visit in 1454.[53] The monastery and the figure of John of Capestrano became significant once again during the later Olomouc visit of King Matthias Corvinus. However, there is no detailed information about the contents of Capestrano's Olomouc sermons (there must have been several due to his relatively long stay in the city). We can assume that the content of these sermons differed little from those delivered by Capestrano in other Bohemian cities because the Hussites were a key concern in this region and Capestrano's goal was to root out heresy. The only relevant sources that remain are the sermons Capestrano delivered in Silesian Wrocław (Breslau) during the spring of 1453. However, the period of the liturgical year spent in Wrocław was different; he always stayed in Olomouc during the summer. The Wrocław sermons were therefore preached during Lent and especially at Easter.[54] They were carefully recorded in several manuscripts, leaving no doubts about Capestrano's role in the Bohemian lands.[55] Gecser quotes that his position was denoted as "... the apostolic legate sent on the other side of the German mountains to inform Czechs about the unity of the Holy Mother the Church so that they would turn to the Catholic faith ..." or "inquisitor of heretics John of Capestrano, sent to preach the word of the Lord by the

51. *Dějiny Olomouce*, vol. I, p. 230 (Petr Elbel).

52. Ferdinand Tadra, *K pobytu Jana Kapistrana v zemích českých. Sedmnácte listův z rukopisu národní knihovny Římské*, Prague, Královská česká společnost nauk, 1889, pp. 40-41.

53. *Dějiny Olomouce*, vol. I, pp. 245-246 (Tomáš Černušák).

54. Ottó Gecser, "Itinerant Preaching in Late Medieval Central Europe. St. John Capistran in Wrocław", *Medieval Sermon Studies*, 47 (2003), pp. 5-20: 6.

55. Gecser used the manuscript published in Wrocław by Eugen Jacob, *Johannes von Capistrano*, vol. II, Die auf der Königlichen und Universitäts-bibliothek zu Breslau befindlichen handschriften Aufzeichnungen von Reden und Tractaten Capistrans, XLIV sermones Vratislaviae habiti a. D. MCCCCLIII, Breslau, Max Woywod, 1911.

order of the most holy Pope Nicolas V".[56] Although the Wrocław sermons focused on morality of believers, they contain several references to Hussites (to Utraquism and its doctrine on the Eucharist, and to John Rokycana, one of Capestrano's frequent preaching targets).[57] It is possible that the rhetoric of the Wroclaw sermons was very similar to those delivered in Olomouc. Both cities were Catholic and both experienced raids by the Hussites.

The activities of Capestrano and his preaching against the Hussites were well known in the Hussite areas of Bohemia. In 1452 John Rokycana[58] (c. 1390-1471), elected archbishop of Prague by the committee of the Bohemian Diet (but never consecrated), and the religious leader of the Hussite Church, invited Capestrano to a public disputation. Rokycana proposed to meet in Český Krumlov (Krummau), where the castle and the town were owned by a Catholic Czech magnate, Oldřich (Ulrich) of Rožmberk. It seemed to be a fair offer. Krumlov was a relatively safe place and was probably seen as a neutral locality for such a disputation. However Capestrano, who visited Český Krumlov before, refused to meet there and replied to Rokycana that he would not preach and debate in such a village in front of ignorant farmers and shepherds. Instead, he proposed large cities and university centres, some of them as far away as Naples, Bologna, Oxford and Cambridge. The closest locations suggested by Capestrano (from Rokycana's point of view) were Padua, Cracow and Vienna. Capestrano's suggestions meant in fact a refusal of any disputation with Rokycana. The Hussite religious leader – a heretic for most Catholics – could not freely visit such places, and it seems Capestrano knew that and wanted to avoid direct confrontation with him.[59]

So it is clear that the outcomes of Capestrano's mission to convert the Hussites were questionable. But his presence and his preaching had a considerable impact on the population of the Bohemian and Moravian towns and cities he had visited: Jindřichův Hradec, Český Krumlov, Tachov, Cheb, Most, Kadaň, Brno, Znojmo and Olomouc, to name just a few. All those places were inhabited by a Catholic majority, so the opportunity to convert Hussites was limited. Nevertheless, such a visit was an extraordinary event in the life of the city inhabitants. Capestrano was not sent to Olomouc (and to the other cities) to preach; he was invited by the local authorities who were impressed by his fame. As Ottó Gecser pointed out, Capestrano's fame "… like *fama sanctitatis* ..., was a constitutive element of … being recognised as elect or, at least, exceptional …".[60] A reputation as a "living saint" would explain Capestrano's immense popularity. His appearances were probably fascinating for the public. Even though he preached in Latin, which

56. Quoted in Latin by Gecser, "Itinerant Preaching", p. 6.

57. *Ibid.*, p. 7.

58. For details on the Catholic criticism of John Rokycana, see Jaroslav Boubín, *Žaloby katolíků na mistra Jana z Rokycan*, Rokycany, Státní okresní archiv, 1997.

59. Hofer, *Johannes Kapistran*, vol. I, p. 419.

60. Ottó Gecser, "Preaching and Publicness. St John of Capestrano and the Making of His Charisma North of the Alps", in *Charisma and Religious Authority. Jewish, Christian and Muslim Preaching 1200-1500*, ed. by Katherine L. Jansen and Miri Rubin, Turnhout, Brepols, 2010, p. 149.

most would not have understood,[61] Capestrano apparently used interpreters (in the case of Olomouc they had to translate into German). Nevertheless, not all of the huge crowds would have been able to hear the translation. Therefore Capestrano's physical gestures were very important, as were the objects he displayed and all the staged aspects of his preaching.

Memory of Capestrano's preaching lived on into the following generation. In 1462 a number of city councils in Central Europe, including the magistrate of Olomouc, sent letters to the papal curia requesting Capestrano's canonisation. Among the applicants was the Bishop of Olomouc, Prothasius (Tas) of Boskovice, who was himself, perhaps together with his father Beneš of Boskovice, converted by Capestrano to Catholicism.[62] The conversion of Prothasius of Boskovice and his petition requesting Capestrano's canonisation was later mentioned by A. S. Piccolomini in his brief description of Moravia.[63] The *fama sanctitatis* "materialised" in the cities with a Catholic majority where Capestrano spent time. In Brno, for example, they kept part of Capestrano's robe as a valuable relic. In Olomouc they had a well containing supposedly healing water sanctified personally by Capestrano.[64] This evidence of Capestrano's cult comes from a later period, but we can suppose that some tradition connected with his stay and devotion to his sanctity existed earlier at the places he visited and preached. Significant symbols of Capestrano's mission to Olomouc include Christograms – trigrams of the holy name of Jesus, IHS (yhs). These symbols connect Capestrano's Olomouc stay with St Bernardine of Siena (who was Capestrano's teacher) and with devotion to the name of Jesus, whose cult we can follow back to St Bernardine or even to Giovanni Colombini (1304-67), the founder of the congregation of Jesuates (Jesuati) and to Ubertino di Casale (1259-1330) and his *Arbor Vitae crucifixae Iesu*.[65] St Bernardine preached devotion to the name of Jesus and displayed a panel with the trigram of Jesus's name for public veneration. Adoration of the trigram appeared everywhere St Bernardine had preached, and similar symbols on public and especially private buildings signify the role of the cult. Capestrano's sermons followed the path of St Bernardine. He too preached devotion to the name of Jesus and his mission tour is marked with the trigrams.[66] There were at least three known sym-

61. On the practice of the mendicant preachers in the fifteenth century, see Maria Giuseppina Muzzarelli, *Pescatori di uomini. Predicatori alla fine del Medioevo*, Bologna, Il Mulino, 2005, pp. 15-95.

62. Martin Elbel, "Kult sv. Jana Kapistrána v českých zemích", *Acta Universitatis Palackianae Olomucensis. Philosophica – Aesthetica*, 16 (1998), pp. 81-99: 82.

63. *Enee Silvii Piccolominei postea Pii PP. II De Europa*, ed. by Adrianus van Heck, Studi e Testi 398, Città del Vaticano, Biblioteca Apostolica vaticana, 2001, pp. 108-109 (3130-3144).

64. Elbel, "Kult", pp. 82-83; Amandus Hermann, *Capistranus Triumphans. Seu Historia Fundamentalis de Sancto Joanne Capistrans*, Coloniae, B. J. Endterum, 1700 (repr. Nabu Press, 2011), pp. 799, 337.

65. Vincenzo Pacelli, "Il 'Monogramma' bernardiano: origine, diffusione e sviluppo", in *San Bernardino predicatore e pellegrino. Atti del convegno nazionale di studi bernardiniani* (Maiori, 20-22 giugno 1980), ed. by F. D'Episcopo, Galatina, 1985, pp. 253-259.

66. On the trigrams and Capestrano's mission to the Czech Lands, see Ivo Hlobil, "Bernardinské symboly Jména Ježíš v českých zemích šířené Janem Kapistránem", *Umění*, 44 (1996), pp. 223-234.

Figure 6: Olomouc, Ostružnická 22, house no. 333; IHS trigram, 1469.

bols of the name of Jesus on Olomouc buildings. One of them exists even today. It is a part of a sequence of four devotional plaques that are displayed on the façade of a burgher house and dated to 1469. This confirms the vitality of the cult, which was surely supported by the above-mentioned Observant Franciscan friary.

It is surprising that the Wrocław sermons, used as the comparative material in this occasion, had no references against Jews although Capestrano preached against this minority frequently in Austria.[67] But after Capestrano's departure from Wrocław local Jews were accused of profaning the host.[68] Capestrano was quickly back in Wrocław in July 1453 and personally participated as one of the judges. Forty-one of the arrested Jews were burned at the stake and those remaining were expelled from Wrocław.[69] It is noteworthy that the same scenario took place in Olomouc during Capestrano's second stay in 1454. The Jewish minority was expelled from Olomouc and three other Moravian royal cities (Brno, Znojmo and Uničov). The charter for Olomouc (and Uničov) was issued by King Ladislas on 22 July 1454 in Prague. Local Jews had to leave the city by the day of St Martin (11 November) 1454 and their properties were confiscated by the city, including the local synagogue and the Jewish cemetery. Nevertheless, the city had to continue paying the Jewish tax to the king.[70] Capestrano was almost certainly

67. Gecser, "Itinerant Preaching", p. 7.

68. Marek Derwich, "Jean Capistran et les Juifs. Exemple de Silésie", in *Les Chrétiens et les Juifs dans les sociétés de rite grec et latin: approche comparative*, ed. by Michel Dmitriev, Christian Tollet and Élisabeth Teito, Paris 2003, pp. 59-72.

69. *Ibid.;* Gecser, "Itinerant Preaching", p. 7.

70. SOkA Olomouc, AMO, Sbírka listin, inv. no. 206.

in the city at the time King Ladislas's charter was announced. It can be assumed, for example on the basis of the Wrocław events, that in Capestrano's Olomouc sermons he supported Jewish expulsion from the city in summer 1454. This expulsion initiated a long period of Jewish absence from Olomouc. Jews were not allowed to resettle in the city until the mid-nineteenth century.

Capestrano's Olomouc visits and the influence of his mission in the Olomouc Catholic environment show how deep the differences were between the Catholic and the Hussite regions. This can similarly be observed in Wrocław, Brno and even Vienna. The Hussite areas of Bohemia were isolated, standing outside current European spiritual trends. The popularity of John of Capestrano was one of them.

Conclusion

The city of Olomouc went through a turbulent period during the first half of the fifteenth century. The influence of the city's owner – the king himself – was weak. The city all the more rested on its allegiance to Catholicism, and this orientation was never questioned during the Hussite wars. The city had always been firmly against the Hussite Reformation, even at times when this attitude brought the city extreme economic troubles. Perhaps the most important reasons for such a firm attitude were the presence (at least symbolic) of the bishop, and especially the presence of the chapter during the most difficult years.

The allegiance of the city to Catholicism enabled Olomouc to remain linked to the main spiritual, intellectual and economic European trends. Olomouc, unlike the Hussite territories and cities, avoided international isolation. Such a position enabled the future development of the city, as we can observe in the second half of the fifteenth and the sixteenth centuries.

2. Between Hussitism and Reformation, 1450s-1520s

Antonín Kalous

On 6 June 1467 the mayor and magistrate of Olomouc concluded a defence alliance with their counterparts in three large Moravian royal cities – Brno, Znojmo and Jihlava – that felt it necessary to defend themselves against their legal king.[1] It was a deed of rebellion against the king driven not by loyalty of the cities to another king, but by the strong propaganda of papal diplomacy in the region. The accession of George of Poděbrady, king of Bohemia and an Utraquist, to the royal throne created an entirely new situation in the kingdom. King Sigismund was deprived of royal power during the Hussite wars. This power had been replaced by that of the city of Prague or the estates of Bohemia as the representatives of the land. But the throne itself was never transferred to anyone not of royal blood or who would not respect the Roman Church. When King George ascended the throne in 1458 he needed to make himself acknowledged in Moravia as well – a difficult but manageable goal. After a short period of resistance the cities started to respect him as their legal sovereign,[2] as well as that of all the country. And even though there was no official opposition by the Roman Church to the election, and even though the king was crowned with the blessing of the papal legate and the Hungarian bishops, the matter between the Kingdom of Bohemia and the papacy was unresolved. Problems started to manifest themselves quite early in the 1460s.

After the formal abolition of the Compacts (the treaty between the Council of Basel and the representation of the Kingdom, which legalised one of the main achievements of the Hussite revolution: communion in both kinds) the papal curia's advance against the king of Bohemia was noticeable on an international level, as was the activity of the king himself who was trying to support his cause.[3] What, however, was the result of such conflicts on the local level of the city?

1. SOkA Olomouc, AMO, Sbírka listin, inv. no. 265, similarly in the archives of Jihlava and Znojmo.

2. Rudolf Urbánek, *České dějiny*, part III, *Věk poděbradský*, vol. 3, Prague, Jan Laichter, 1930, pp. 379-384, 394-396.

3. Urbánek, *České dějiny*, part III, *Věk poděbradský*, vol. 4, Prague, Academia, 1962, pp. 464-770; Otakar Odložilík, *The Hussite King: Bohemia in European Affairs, 1440-1471*, New Brunswick, NJ, Rutgers University Press, 1965, pp. 135-189; Frederick G. Heymann, *George of Bohemia: King of Heretics*, Princeton, NJ, Princeton University Press, 1965, pp. 258-292 and passim; *The Universal Peace Organization of King George of Bohemia: A Fifteenth Century Plan for*

King George

After the disaster of the Hussite wars, which were drastic for the city of Olomouc, the 1450s and early 1460s was a period of recovery. There was an influx of newcomers from northern Moravia and elsewhere who supported Olomouc handicraft production in cloth, food, clothes and shoes.[4] In clear competition with Brno, another administrative centre, Olomouc was taking the lead in Moravian wealth and political significance during the second half of the fifteenth century.

The Hussite wars brought about almost total destruction. But the fact that Olomouc was never conquered by the Hussites and always strictly supported the Roman side (even in the clash of the two candidates over the episcopal seat of Olomouc in 1416-20) resulted in a reaffirmation of the city as a bulwark of Catholicism. That is why the city happily accepted the preaching of John of Capestrano and questioned the election of George of Poděbrady as king of Bohemia. The city representation was, however, placated by the official attitude of the Roman Church and the pope, who were planning to use Bohemian military expertise in the fight against the Turks, as seemed to be the plan of Pope Pius II.[5] As the conflict of the Utraquist king and the Roman Church accelerated in the 1460s, Olomouc was a loyal royal city with no aims to defect from its lord in Prague. Its Catholic nature, however, was always stressed. In the end of 1462 Pius II was writing to Olomouc to praise the burghers and "encourage them to persevere in the faith of their fathers".[6] Similarly, the papal legate Girolamo Lando wrote seven months later to urge the burghers to continue in what they began, meaning the tradition of loyalty to the Roman Church.[7]

These exhortations were not specific enough and did not attempt to entice the city to abandon obedience to the king. Nevertheless, the king felt that Olomouc might be a crucial location for keeping his government stable. In January 1464 King George organised the land diet of Moravia in Olomouc, the first opening of the land registers after sixteen years. There, he published an essential charter that stressed the formal inseparability of Bohemia and Moravia. It was, however, a legal deed soon to be forgotten.[8] And with other Moravian royal cities Olomouc then renewed its oath of obedience to the king.[9]

World Peace 1462-1464, ed. by Jiří Kejř and Václav Vaněček, Prague, Czechoslovak Academy of Sciences, 1964. The most recent treatment of the whole period is Petr Čornej and Milena Bartlová, *Velké dějiny zemí Koruny české*, vol. VI, 1437-1526, Prague and Litomyšl, Paseka, 2007.

4. *Dějiny Olomouce*, vol. I, ed. by Jindřich Schulz, Olomouc, Univerzita Palackého, 2009, p. 203 (Roman Zaoral).

5. Cf. at least Kenneth M. Setton, *The Papacy and the Levant (1204-1571)*, vol. II, *The Fifteenth Century*, Philadelphia, The American Philosophical Society, 1978, pp. 196-270.

6. SOkA Olomouc, AMO, Sbírka listin, inv. no. 237, 3 Dec 1462.

7. SOkA Olomouc, AMO, Sbírka listin, inv. no. 240, 3 Jul 1463.

8. František Kameníček, ed., "Jednání sněmovní a veřejná v markrabství moravském", in *Archiv český*, vol. X, ed. by Josef Kalousek, Prague, 1890, no. 28, pp. 274-275; cf. Josef Válka, *Dějiny Moravy*, vol. I, *Středověká Morava*, Brno, Muzejní a vlastivědná společnost, 1991, pp. 157-158.

9. Urbánek, *České dějiny*, vol. III/4, pp. 720-725.

Urging of the city to defect to the opposition came only after the open clash in 1465. Both the bishop and the city of Olomouc had long held to the side of the king, but the pressure was too strong for the burghers to resist. There is no direct source that describes the decision-making process of the city council; however, it is illustrated in the papal letters sent to the city. Pope Paul II was very active in organising the fight against George of Poděbrady, now treated as a heretic and a deposed king. In May 1466 the pope exhorted burghers to not help the king against the city of Plzeň in Bohemia and instructed them that their oaths of obedience to the king were invalid if he was a heretic and an adversary of the papacy.[10] The pope expressly called upon the city to abandon the service of King George in a bull that proclaimed him a heretic and deposed him as king.[11]

A remarkable document from the mid-1460s reveals the following. The city sent an envoy to the king to inform him of a few problems. They notified him that letters were coming to the city that defamed him, and they asked him to solve the matter and advise them on what to do. They also communicated that they had sent an envoy to the legate in Wrocław (Breslau) to ask him to refrain from any action in Moravia while they sent an embassy to Rome to prove they were still loyal to the Roman Church and the king in Prague. The burghers also asked the king for help against troops that were entering the province from Hungary and Austria and were pillaging the land. Finally, the burghers complained about a possible interdict that threatened faithful Catholics who were afraid that their children would be deprived of baptism and other sacraments including last rites (extreme unction), and that their bodies would be transported outside the city without proper funeral rites.[12] This rather lengthy report is recounted here because it shows that the interdict, despite all its late medieval relativisation,[13] still had power and negotiation potential. In Bohemia and Moravia it was the interdict that finally brought the Catholic nobles and Catholic cities over to the opposition against the Utraquist king.[14]

The history of relations between Olomouc and King George is thus a history of war that is well known.[15] For Olomouc it was particularly crucial that the opponent of the "heretical" king, Matthias Corvinus of Hungary, chose the city for his residence. Whether it be for its economic dynamism, trade connections, geographical position, church or political significance was of little importance. What mattered was the result. Matthias Corvinus visited Olomouc every year and was even elected in the cathedral as king of Bohemia on 3 May 1469. What preceded this act was first the strategic defeat of Matthias in the war against George

10. SOkA Olomouc, AMO, Sbírka listin, inv. no. 258, 26 May 1466.
11. SOkA Olomouc, AMO, Sbírka listin, inv. no. 252, 3 Jan 1467.
12. SOkA Olomouc, AMO, Zlomky registratur, inv. no. 4405.
13. Cf. Charles Trinkaus, *The Spiritual Power: Republican Florence under Interdict*, Leiden, Brill, 1974; William Kurtz Gotwald, *Ecclesiastical Censure at the End of the Fifteenth Century*, Baltimore, Johns Hopkins University Press, 1927.
14. For the relevance of the interdict in Bohemia at that time see Iohannes Rabensteinensis, *Disputacio*, ed. by Bohumil Ryba, Budapest, Egyetemi nyomda, 1942, p. 10; in another edition, Jan z Rabštejna, *Dialogus*, ed. by Bohumil Ryba, Prague, Matice česká, 1946, p. 42-44.
15. In English, Heymann, *George*, pp. 437-585; Odložilík, *The Hussite King*, pp. 161-262.

and subsequent negotiations. The talks between the two kings were conducted in a tent in the fields north of Olomouc. Talks between George's son Victorin on one side and the Catholic estates with Matthias on the other took place in the city. Matthias was open to negotiations, but according to a contemporary report the two papal nuncios, Lorenzo Roverella and Rudolf of Rüdesheim, were against the negotiations and even pronounced an interdict over the city when the "heretics" were present. When the leader of the Catholic estates Zdeněk of Šternberk was drinking with them, he felt it necessary to exclaim, "My lord and celestial father, forgive me that I drink with the cursed heretics".[16]

The new Catholic king was elected by the Catholic estates of the Bohemian lands on 3 May 1469 and the city rejoiced. According to the Wrocław scribe Peter Eschenloer there were fountains full of wine on that day and a huge celebration.[17] Furthermore, the burghers had the king confirm their privileges two months later, just as the other Moravian royal cities did following the election.[18] With this act they formally acknowledged the supremacy of a new lord and had a king once again. Transferring loyalty to a new king was problematic because King George was not pressing the city, not extracting more money in due payments and taxes and was overall a good king. But pressure from the papacy and papal diplomacy and the religious division of the country finally made the city acquiesce and accept an uncertain future with a king who was famous for his rigid rule.

Competing Catholic Institutions

The city as such was not the only loyal Catholic institution. There was also the bishop, the chapter and a number of monasteries and friaries within and without the city walls. As illustrated in the previous text, the situation on the Catholic side in the 1460s was not easy. A clear-cut division never existed, and the start of the confessional age was bringing confessional conflict in the dividing of religious and political loyalties as if they were mutually exclusive categories.

Such an attitude is revealingly described by one of the most famous contemporary authors, Jan of Rabštejn. In his *Dialogus* he had four Catholic noblemen (including himself) discussing the situation of the war between King George and the opposition led by Matthias Corvinus. The author concludes that obedience to the pope is crucial and decisive, but the four debaters represent various degrees of loyalty to the pope and the crusade efforts. It is mentioned in the argumentation that holy war cannot be commanded, that protection of the homeland (*patria*) is one of the duties of its inhabitants, that the strict position of the opposition leader

16. *Urkundliche Beiträge zur Geschichte Böhmens und seine Nachbarländer im Zeitalter Georg's von Podiebrad (1450-1471)* (Fontes rerum austriacarum II/20), ed. by Franz Palacky, Vienna, 1860, pp. 571-575, quotation p. 575: "Herr himmlischer vater vergieb mir, das ich mit den verfluchten ketzern tryncke."

17. Peter Eschenloer, *Geschichte der Stadt Breslau*, 2 vols., ed. by Gunhild Roth, Münster, Waxmann, 2003, vol. II, pp. 758-759.

18. SOkA Olomouc, AMO, Sbírka listin, inv. no. 278.

drives moderate Catholics towards King George, etc. The *Dialogus* distinctly represents a split within the Catholic side. Even papal diplomacy in the early 1470s identified two of the discussants – Zdeněk of Šternberk and Vilém of Rábí – as effective leaders of the conflict's two sides.[19]

This document speaks not just of the position of the nobility but of all the inhabitants of the land, mostly Catholics of course, and both individuals and institutions. It reflects the situation in České Budějovice, the later centre of Matthias' rule in Bohemia. This southern Bohemian Catholic city switched sides only in August 1468 when Matthias was already on the side of the opposition. The same was already described in the case of Olomouc itself and we might go even further to analyse the position of individual Catholic institutions in the city.

The signing of the treaty between the Moravian royal cities, mentioned at the beginning of this chapter, was preceded by a moment that is particularly revealing of papal policy. It was not only the above-mentioned threats of an interdict that helped the burghers make up their minds. Just outside the city walls the old Premonstratensian monastery of Hradisko stood, and as previously during the Hussite wars in the 1460s its abbot displayed a tendency to support the heretics. He was in favour of King George and thus was reprimanded by the pope and urged to stop any contact with the heretics. A few months later the monastery with all its property was transferred to the "loyal hands" of the burghers.[20] The papal nuncio Rudolf of Rüdesheim also got involved in the clash, and it was he who acted as mediator between the city and Rome, even asking the city to take the monastery by force and capture the abbot. This was already more than a month after the treaty of the Moravian cities when the inclinations of the city were secure and obvious.[21] Within a month the nuncio was communicating with the city again, praising their fight against the heretics and promising he would do his best to bring the Polish king to the Czech throne.[22] Two years later in a completely different situation the pope authorised his two representatives in the region, Bishops Rudolf of Rüdesheim and Lorenzo Roverella, nuncios and orators as he addressed them, to permit the destruction of the monastery.[23]

The bishopric was the most prominent Roman Catholic institution. In the fifteenth century there were four bishoprics in the Bohemian lands. But only two had properly appointed and consecrated bishops in the post-Hussite period: Wrocław in Silesia and Olomouc in Moravia. Bishop Prothasius of Boskovice was a member of an old and respectable noble family of Moravia, which, however, converted only in 1451 to Catholicism after the preaching of John of Capestrano in Brno.

19. Iohannes Rabensteinensis, *Disputacio;* Jan z Rabštejna, *Dialogus*. For the report of the papal diplomats for the new legate Marco Barbo in 1472, see Rome, Biblioteca Angelica, Ms. 1077, fol. 22r: "Inter Bohemos duos barones cognosco, quorum alter est imparte regis Ungarie et precipuus omnium, vocatur dominus Zdencho de Stella sive in lingua eorum de Staranberch, alius est imparte Polloni et vocatur dominus Guillemus de Rabi."

20. SOkA Olomouc, AMO, Sbírka listin, inv. nos. 255, 256, 263, 264.

21. SOkA Olomouc, AMO, Sbírka listin, inv. no. 267.

22. SOkA Olomouc, AMO, Sbírka listin, inv. no. 269.

23. SOkA Olomouc, AMO, Sbírka listin, inv. no. 277.

His father's conversion was crucial for Prothasius, as well as for the whole family and its role in fifteenth-century Moravia. Prothasius, who had studied in Vienna and Italy, was appointed as the bishop in Olomouc only six years after his father's conversion and remained in office until his death twenty-five years later. He was not yet properly consecrated in 1458 and thus could not exercise his privilege to substitute for the archbishop of Prague at the coronation of the king. It was performed by Hungarian bishops, but Prothasius remained a close collaborator of the Utraquist King George.

The situation started to change only with the conflicts between George and the papacy. When the king imprisoned a papal nuncio, Fantino Della Valle, the bishop left the king's court and fled to his home diocese, as Pius II reported in his *Commentaries*.[24] Nevertheless, Prothasius remained in the service of the king as a worthy diplomat even into the second half of the 1460s with the onset of pressure from papal diplomacy and the pope himself. Like the noblemen and the cities he was urged to abandon the king and prove his loyalty to the Roman Church by opposing the king and joining the anti-royal league.[25] In October 1466 Prothasius complained about the problems and injustice the Catholic opposition had caused him.[26] Not even a year later, in July 1467, Ctibor of Tovačov declared enmity against the bishop and reprimanded him for his action against the king.[27] As a Catholic bishop Prothasius probably had little choice. What is peculiar, however, is that it took him so long. At the end of 1467 he took part in the assembly of the Catholic estates in Wrocław. To get there he even had to ask for a loan from a Moravian nobleman, due to the destruction of his estates.[28] After the convention he left as an envoy of the Catholic opposition and went to Hungary to invite King Matthias to participate in the fight against the "heretical" king.

When the war started Prothasius was one of the crucial personalities that supported the cause of Matthias, who had been writing letters to all possible collaborators, including the Catholic cities of Moravia. The king had written a unique letter to the city of Olomouc praising the bishop and stressing that it was due to his activity and his singular merits that "we received his church and all of you into our particular guardianship".[29] The bishop himself was also writing a manifesto to the Catholics of the kingdom on behalf of the king, explaining that all was happening in concord with the decisions of the Catholic assembly in Wrocław, from where he had been sent to seek the king's support. Like the city, the bishop had to be pushed to switch sides. Nevertheless, there was no room for neutrality, as the

24. *Pii Secundi Pontificis Maximi Commentarii*, 2 vols., ed. by Ibolya Bellus and Iván Boronkai, Budapest, Balassi Kiadó, 1993, vol. I, pp. 442-443; *Pii II Commentarii rerum memorabilium que temporibus suis contigerunt*, 2 vols., ed. by Adrian van Heck, Città del Vaticano, Biblioteca Apostolica Vaticana, 1984, vol. II, p. 564.

25. For list of the references, see, Antonín Kalous, "Boskovice urai Mátyás király diplomáciai és politikai szolgálatában", *Századok*, 141 (2007), pp. 375-389: 380, n. 29.

26. *Archiv český*, vol. IV, ed. by František Palacký, Prague, 1846, no. 23, pp. 133-134.

27. *Ibid.*, no. 32-34, pp. 141-146.

28. ZAO-O, AO, Pergameny, sign. C I b 10.

29. *Mátyás király levelei, külügyi osztály*, 2 vols., ed. by Vilmos Fraknói, Budapest, Magyar tudományos akadémia, 1893-1895, vol. I, p. 207.

nuncio Rudolf of Rüdesheim remarked in the case of České Budějovice.[30] After Prothasius started to serve the new lord he became as important a diplomat as he had been for King George, and even more so because it was crucial for King Matthias to have the Church of Moravia on his side.

The bishop of Olomouc was then fundamental for Matthias' rule in Moravia. He had always tried to have him on his side and when Prothasius died the king secured the election of John (Jan) Filipec, his courtier and bishop of Oradea (Várad) in Hungary and later secret chancellor. Even though Bishop Filipec was never confirmed by the pope he was effectively guiding the diocese in the 1480s. The king, moreover, needed him in Moravia and Silesia as a supporter of royal policy. When the king died in 1490 Bishop Filipec resigned from all church and secular positions and became an Observant Franciscan friar. The bishopric was later held by two cardinals, who were never present in Olomouc, and thus the life of the diocese was organised by administrators.[31]

A bishopric is not only the bishop but also the cathedral chapter, which in Olomouc's case was quite sure of its own significance. The chapter had a years-old privilege of episcopal free election. In times of trouble for the Olomouc bishop the chapter, as in other bishoprics, was the maintainer of standards, keeping the cathedral liturgy and running the centre of the diocese.

As true and proper Catholics the chapter was the first to support the cause of the *res publica christiana.* On 19 August 1466, when the papacy was seeking loyalty from the city and bishop, Pope Paul II commissioned the nuncio and bishop of Wrocław Rudolf of Rüdesheim and the abbots of the monasteries of the Scots of Vienna and of Hradisko (still believed at this point to be a good contact) to protect the chapter against malefactors. They may have used ecclesiastical penalties or called upon the help of the secular arm. The bull itself might be considered too general, and indeed it is. Nevertheless, it clearly shows that the chapter was the first to be cooperative and answered positively to the calls of the *ecclesia militans*.[32] At the end of 1467 all three major Catholic bodies of Olomouc were on the same side again.

The Bishop, the Chapter and the City

It seems that the bishop, the chapter and the city were united again with the common goal of loyalty to the Roman Church and transferring that loyalty to the new king when he was elected in 1469 in Olomouc. The new king confirmed the rights and privileges of all three institutions within one week. On 21 July 1469 the charter for the Olomouc bishopric stated that in recent years the church of God in the Kingdom of Bohemia and the Margravate of Moravia was "shaken by

30. Reported by Eschenloer, *Geschichte*, pp. 690-691.

31. In detail see Antonín Kalous, "Spor o biskupství olomoucké v letech 1482-1497", *Český časopis historický*, 105 (2007), pp. 1-39; Tomáš Baletka, "Olomoucké biskupství v době sedisvakance. Osoby a instituce ve víru vzájemných interakcí (1482-1497)", in *Sacri canones servandi sunt: ius canonicum et status ecclesiae saeculis XIII-XV*, ed. by Pavel Krafl, Prague, Historický ústav AV ČR, 2008, pp. 540-544.

32. ZAO-O, MCO, Listiny, sign. A IV b 23.

the most damned heretics". On the request of the bishop, the deacon, the provost, the canons and the chapter, King Matthias confirmed all the old privileges of his predecessors, including his "immediate predecessor" Ladislas (thus disregarding King George completely) and accepted the church under his special protection. In his charter, the king even states:

> We have learned that it [the Olomouc church] was always strong when positioned among the heretics and pressed very hard by them, the only church decorated with the pontifical honour, and glowing red just as a sole rose among the thorns and a lantern tightly confined by the darkness; a church from which the light of the holy Catholic faith is again poured into faithless hearts.[33]

The tenor of the charter is quite special and demonstrative of the unique position of the church of Olomouc and the particular interest of the king or any potentate who needed to lean on the structure of the only steady Catholic institution. It was represented also by the cathedral chapter, which had its rights and privileges confirmed on the same day at the same occasion in one of the bishop's residences at the castle of Vyškov (and thus the phrasing of the confirmation is quite similar).[34]

Four days earlier the king resided in Brno where he confirmed the rights and privileges of the Olomouc burghers. As in the case of the Olomouc church, the king was openly affectionate toward the city and generous in his words. Apart from the confirmation, "the capital city of Olomouc in this our margravate" was generously endowed by the king, "so that after the cruel and terrible attacks of the heretics and the gaping chasms of the fire,[35] it could, joyful with our gifts, breathe under our peace in the former abundance".[36] The rhetoric of the charter is again centred on the fight with the heretics, and both the Olomouc church and the city are seen as a heart of this fight. All this clearly confirms the high standard of the "bulwark of Catholicism". Moreover, the charter twice describes the city as the capital of the Margravate of Moravia, which is an extraordinary achievement in the contest with Brno, Olomouc's main ally but also rival.[37]

For Olomouc it seemed to be a successful July of 1469. Strong cooperation with the new king meant a political and economic boost. Thus the long campaign against the "heretics" started to pay off. The city itself was divided into two historical parts. The older one, Předhradí, was the original early-medieval castle of the ruling dynasty. Since the fourteenth century it was used predominantly by the bishop and the chapter. The other part was the city itself, founded in the 1230s. The two parts were protected, but also divided, by a wall, modernised in the fifteenth century. A few new monasteries or friaries appeared in the city, some of them (Augustinians and Carthusians) run-away communities seeking refuge

33. ZAO-O, AO, Pergameny, sign. C I b 11.

34. ZAO-O, MCO, Listiny, sign. A IV c 4.

35. One third of the city burned down on 19 April 1469, i.e. before the election of the new king during negotiations with the side of King George.

36. SOkA Olomouc, AMO, Sbírka listin, inv. no. 278.

37. For details of the competition, see *Dějiny Olomouce*, vol. I, p. 194, n. 41 (Antonín Kalous).

in Olomouc because of the Hussite threat. They settled in the "ecclesiastical" part of the city. Others were modern orders related to city piety and devotion (Observant Franciscans) who settled just outside the walls of the city proper. All of them seemed to feel safe in the centre of Moravian Catholicism, but the physical division of the city meant also a division in minds. The common goal achieved, the older disagreements and discords among the individual Olomouc institution appeared again. One might even say they never, even in times of war, ceased to exist.

An illustrative case is that of the city parish school of St Maurice. The church of St Maurice in Olomouc, mentioned in detail later, was a centre for the religious life of the burghers. Like in many cities of fourteenth- and fifteenth-century Europe a city school seemed to be a good investment. There was, however, another school in Olomouc: St Wenceslas was established by the cathedral chapter and run purely as an ecclesiastical school. But the inhabitants of the city wanted their children's education in their own hands.

Documentation of the tension over the two schools starts in May 1457 when the papal legate Juan Carvajal confirmed the chapter's right to run the school. King Ladislas three days later published a similar confirmation that even stressed *expressis verbis* that the only school in Olomouc be the cathedral school run by the chapter.[38] Even though there are no sources that confirm it, it is possible that the burghers opposed the sole right of the chapter already before the 1460s. The city took action only in 1465 when two petitions were sent to Pope Paul II or to the Roman curia. The argumentation was carefully phrased and the same wording appeared in the later papal bull. The petitions (*supplicae*) stress that there were four parish churches in the city and too much to do in the care for the souls of the faithful. They ask the pope for the "apostolic licence to keep and assign the *scolasticus* and *magister scholarum* with the afore-mentioned church of St Maurice and to build and construct in the same parish church or near a school with perpetual duration for the youths and pupils who want to thrive in letters and virtues". The petition states that there should be four pupils at the church of St Maurice to help with the singing and the liturgy, that the number of those taking communion in the church was particularly high (some 12,000 communicants), and, most importantly, that St Wenceslas school was "an Italian mile or so" distant from the parish church and the road too difficult and dangerous in winter.[39] Pope Paul II consented to the establishment of the school in a bull in February 1466.[40]

Both the city and the chapter turned to Rome for help. Rudolf of Rüdesheim was appointed judge of the case, commissioned with the task of settling the quarrel. He decided that St Maurice school should be subordinated to St Wenceslas school,[41] but it seems he was unable to push through the decision

38. ZAO-O, MCO, Listiny, sign. A IV a 28, A IV a 29.

39. ASV, Reg. Suppl. 580, fol. 159rv; Reg. Suppl. 589, fol. 6rv.

40. SOkA Olomouc, AMO, Sbírka listin, inv. no. 247; ASV, Reg. Lat. 635, fol. 77rv

41. ZAO-O, MCO, Listiny, sign. A IV b 22 (=ASV, Reg. Lat. 629, fol. 35v-36v), 14 Aug 1466; SOkA Olomouc, AMO, Sbírka listin, inv. no. 275 – the appointment mentioned in Rudolf's charter, 9 Sept 1466.

since the commission was formed again after three years.[42] The aims of the apostolic see were clear: to settle any disputes among the Catholic adherents of the Roman Church so that their powers would not be wasted (as in the case of organising the crusades, the popes attempted to bring peace among the Christian rulers). Rudolf, the bishop of Wrocław and the papal nuncio, an important personality in the early stage of the struggle against King George, was more a protector of the chapter and the bishopric than the city. The city, however, was far more important for the king. In June 1473 King Matthias confirmed the construction of the new school at St Maurice, and taking into consideration the pope's permission he urged the chapter and the bishop not to hinder its implementation under threat of "our royal wrath".[43]

The establishment of the school of St Maurice – a process that lasted for a few years and involved both local players and the highest representatives of external secular and ecclesiastical powers – illustrates many contemporary phenomena. One was the manner in which topographically the two parties in the dispute – the city and the chapter – where represented by two distinct parts of the city. The burghers defined the city centre, from which the cathedral and its school were distant. The cathedral school is even described in one of the papal letters as "outside the city of Olomouc" (*extra civitatem Olomucensem*). These two topographical sectors represent two entities that were strictly Catholic but hesitant to cooperate. The situation also underscores the strength of the city's Catholic identity. The city directly communicated with the papal curia and even had an agent in Rome,[44] who might have been responsible also for the negotiations and petitions in the matter of the city parish school.

In this period between the Hussite and the German Reformations, the city was presented as the stronghold of Catholicism. When heretics were mentioned it was only in the villages and definitely outside the city itself;[45] even the Utraquist chronicle of Prague narrates an event in 1468, when the "Germans of Olomouc" murdered an Utraquist priest in a nearby village.[46] It was for further negotiations rather than military actions and fights, however, that the burghers presented their Catholic image. They used their Catholicism not only to approach the pope but also the new Catholic king, who identified them with the anti-heretical fight, or rather defence. While the pope aimed at compromises and a peaceful solution to the problem, the king supported his city against any secular or ecclesiastical power. Olomouc presented itself in the later 1460s as the most faithful Catholic city and the capital of Moravia.

42. ASV, Reg. Vat. 531, fol. 290rv, 22 Apr 1469.

43. SOkA Olomouc, AMO, Sbírka listin, inv. no. 284.

44. SOkA Olomouc, AMO, Sbírka listin, inv. no. 253, chaplain Paul.

45. SOkA Olomouc, AMO, Sbírka listin, inv. no. 273.

46. *Staré letopisy české z rukopisu křižovnického*, ed. by František Šimek and Miloslav Kaňák, Prague, SNKLHU, 1959, pp. 278-279: "In Moravia the Olomouc burghers attacked a village; a priest there, who was administering the blood of Christ sought refuge in church and took in his hands the monstrance with the body of God thinking the Germans of Olomouc would be discouraged and he will stay alive. But they took the monstrance out of his hands and cut him in pieces." (the author's translation).

Even though there were clashes between Catholics in the city there are no traces of heretics or conflicts with them. Catholic identity might have been a commonplace everywhere else in Western (i.e. Latin) Europe, but it was not so in the then confessionally divided Bohemia and Moravia. As shown earlier, the city of Olomouc paid close attention to its reputation. During the Hussite wars they did not hesitate to execute suspects of heresy, and later their troops even attacked priests who administered communion in both kinds. They had turned to Rome with their pleas and, apart from a conflict over the school, respected their bishop, who was later active in the organisation of the fight against heretics and, just like the city, supported opposition against King George.

This attitude is illustrated in textual documents, letters and charters, as well as in a more tangible material object: the parish church of St Maurice. The construction of the main city shrine started in 1414 and was protracted for over a century due to the city's economic stagnation during the Hussite wars and the high cost of the project, which was competing with the bishop's cathedral. It was the centre of the city's religious life, the burghers gave donations for the construction[47] and the church was endowed with indulgences linked to its construction and the liturgical operation of the parish.[48] The presbytery was vaulted in 1483. The exact date is inscribed on one of the keystones that decorate the vault. The programme of the decoration is, however, something more than just about dating. It entails a heraldic gallery that eloquently represents the deepest thoughts and highest aspirations of the city. Immediately above the high altar the pope is represented by the keys and tiara. Representing their ecclesiastical institutions, the Olomouc bishopric and chapter follow in the next keystone to the west. These follow here because of the crucial emphasis on the Roman Church and on the patron of the church itself which was the Olomouc cathedral chapter. Worldly powers are represented by the imperial eagle, followed by the Bohemian lion and Moravian eagle in a single field. Next is a complex coat of arms of the king of Hungary and Bohemia, the lord of the city who at the time happened to be King Matthias Corvinus. The heraldic gallery is completed by the symbol of the city itself, the chequered eagle with a crown.[49] The symbol of the pope is right above the high altar and the furthest from the faithful during mass. The coats of arms of Matthias Corvinus and the city are the closest (only preceded by a keystone with a figure holding a band with the date 1483) and were both well known to the people of the city. In 1483 Bohemia's capital Prague experienced the second defenestration during an uprising of the Utraquists against the new Catholic city elite. In contrast, the Moravian capital Olomouc clearly stated that its preference was traditional Roman Catholicism.

47. E.g. *Památná kniha olomoucká (kodex Václava z Jihlavy) z let 1430-1492, 1528*, ed. by Libuše Spáčilová and Vladimír Spáčil, Olomouc, Univerzita Palackého, 2004, passim.

48. E.g. ASV, Reg. Vat. 420, fol. 44v-45r (1452); ASV, Reg. Suppl. 957, fol. 10v (1492).

49. Cf. Ivo Hlobil, "Heraldické svorníky mořického kostela v Olomouci z r. 1483 a případná zpodobnění jejich autora", *Vlastivědný věstník moravský*, 33 (1981), pp. 214-218: 214.

Figure 7: Olomouc, St Maurice church, six heraldic key stones (pope; Olomouc bishopric/ chapter; Holy Roman empire; Kingdom of Bohemia and Margravate of Moravia; Matthias Corvinus, king of Bohemia; city of Olomouc), 1483.

King Matthias

As shown earlier, the Olomouc burghers had pledged obedience to a new and (most importantly) Catholic king in the time when another king was still alive. Matthias Corvinus, king of Bohemia, was elected in Olomouc thanks to the pressure of Catholic lords.[50] Originally he had made an agreement with King George after he was taken captive in his raid to Bohemia in February 1469. George was far better acquainted with the terrain in the mountainous region at the border between Bohemia and Moravia and the Hungarian raid ended in disaster. The two kings had met and reportedly agreed that Matthias would be set free, but in exchange he would negotiate with the Papal Curia to improve George's situation.[51]

Matthias then retired first to Brno and then to Olomouc where negotiations with the "heretics" and the papal nuncios were held. Even though one-third of the city was burned down during the talks, and even though an interdict was proclaimed over the city during the presence of George's son Victorin, it was a success, culminating with the election of the new king. The confirmation of rights that followed was not the only profit the burghers gained. Later on they were given (or confirmed to hold) a few villages in the vicinity. And they also secured a number of royal orders on arms production. The profit, however, is questionable; as late as seven years after Matthias' death his successor King Wladislas was still redeeming the royal debt of 417 florins.[52]

One of the crucial achievements of the city was the fact that it attracted the king himself. He was not only elected there and held his court sessions there, but the meeting in 1479 of the two kings of Bohemia, Matthias Corvinus on one side and Wladislas II, the successor of King George in Prague after 1471, on the other, was staged there – possibly one of the most lavish festivities ever held in the city. King Matthias planned the event for three weeks and the main characters were naturally not the burghers but rather persons with royal titles.

Surprisingly, the king arrived in the city with only a small retinue; his ceremonial entry was scheduled for another occasion. It was his wife, Queen Beatrix, who first entered the city ceremonially as a new queen of Bohemia. As described by Peter Eschenloer, the city scribe and chronicler of Wrocław, "she came later with the Hungarian lords, five thousand horses and an unutterable splendour, with decorations of gold, silver, pearls and gems, both people and horses embellished, the queen was sitting on a golden wagon as were her ladies-in-waiting." He goes on to even claim that a whole book should be written about the ceremonies in Olomouc.[53] In an eye-witness account Albert of Saxony reported the later entry of the two kings of Bohemia – Matthias invited Wladislas to talk and confirm the peace between them. This was an occasion for Matthias too. Both of the kings entering the city under a baldachin went straight to the cathedral where they listened to

50. For reports on the negotiations, see *Urkundliche Beiträge*, pp. 571-582.

51. A well-known event, cf. for example Heymann, *George*, pp. 515-521; Odložilík, *The Hussite King*, pp. 216-218.

52. SOkA Olomouc, AMO, Sbírka listin, inv. no. 367.

53. Eschenloer, *Geschichte*, pp. 1063-1064.

"Czech singing", then to the singing of the bishop himself. Finally the kings were accompanied to their respective residences in the city, close to the main square.[54] The rest of Eschenloer's descriptions deal with details of the celebrations.

What is missing in the account are the heretics. The kings visited the cathedral together and the bishop celebrated Mass, but there is not a single mention of the heretics over whom the clash started in the first place. The reason for this might be that the festivities in Olomouc were celebrating the final ratification of the peace treaty between the two kings of Bohemia. The confessional division was officially accepted; the two Catholic kings were in concord. Just as in Bohemia proper, the two confessions (if we may use this term) – Catholics and Utraquists – were to be respected and the only element that mattered was the land. Rule and obedience were to be divided according to the simple fact of geo-politics: all inhabitants of Moravia, Silesia or the two Lusatias had to pledge loyalty to King Matthias; King Wladislas was the lord of all belonging to Bohemia. Some of the royal cities were "exchanged": České Budějovice and Plzeň, two strong Catholic cities in Bohemia, were swapped for two royal cities of Moravia loyal to Wladislas: Uherské Hradiště and Uničov. The land principle seemed to be the strongest political factor.

How does this comply with the city itself? Did Catholic affiliation still count? It is not easy to guess the feelings of the city representatives, but it is clear they had to respect the division of power like everyone else. A year later King Matthias informed the city council that his representative in the land would be Ctibor Tovačovský of Cimburk, a man who was until 1479 loyal to King Wladislas, and who was a traditional Utraquist. As the land captain (*zemský hejtman, Landhauptmann*) he was the highest representative of both royal power and the estates and had to be respected. Unfortunately, there is no evidence of whether the city council considered this a problem for them. However, their Catholic feelings are suggested by the 1483 iconographic program of city self-representation in the church of St Maurice. In their reaction the city must have evoked all the strong Catholic powers that the burghers leaned on. A later case, on the other hand, shows the dependence of King Matthias on his representative, the land captain Ctibor. He acted in many causes of the king, and concerning Olomouc he was the one who had to mediate yet another conflict between the chapter and the city. In early 1487 there was a clash between the two bodies over income from some of the city houses, and the chapter used an ecclesiastical ban on the city, which would strike it especially hard during Easter. King Matthias asked them to refrain from this until the matter was decided by the Utraquist land captain Ctibor.[55]

This event prompts further questions about the problematic cooperation of two Catholic institutions. But most importantly it raises questions about the significance of religious, or confessional, affiliation. It was the Catholic king Matthias who was finally after years of war (provoked by him) bringing peace based on the decision of the land estates who believed it to be crucial for the country

54. *Urkundliche Nachträge zur österreichisch-deutschen Geschichte im Zeitalter Kaiser Friedrich III.* (Fontes rerum austriacarum II/46), ed. by Adolf Bachmann, Vienna, Tempsky, 1892, pp. 453-455.

55. ZAO-O, MCO, Listiny, sign. A IV d 3/6.

to stop war and discord and work on the basis of political land affiliation rather than religious sentiment. The city, or the city council, presented itself always as a Catholic city, but the response from outside powers was no longer so strong and positive. No more fighting took place in the name of religious truth. There were no more clashes with heretics. Peace seemed to deprive the city of a strong negotiation position that could not be recovered without a conflict. King Matthias never visited the city after 1479. His followers did so only very occasionally. The city had to wait for other religious discussions and discords in the sixteenth century.

Religious Orders

As already remarked, the city was a haven for a number of religious orders that had literally fled from the dangers of the outside world. The Hussites jeopardised even the existence of some of the communities, which had to find refuge within the city walls. The latest newcomers, however, were not those who fled from the Hussites, but those who wished to fight them. That was at least one of the programme points of John of Capestrano, who preached in Olomouc and in many other Moravian and Silesian cities. He never managed to discuss church matters in Bohemia with leaders there, but his mission in Moravia and Silesia was crucial for the spread of the Observant Franciscans and their spirituality.[56]

The house of the Observant Franciscans was founded outside the Olomouc city walls on a place where, according to tradition, John of Capestrano himself preached. As a relative newcomer, the order and the friary had to establish themselves. As mentioned in the previous chapter, the friary's foundation in Olomouc is connected with the activity of the Italian preacher and was built quickly, within some fifteen years. The church was dedicated to the Immaculate Conception of the Virgin Mary and to St Bernardine of Siena, the newest Franciscan saint and a teacher of Capestrano.

What is quite telling with reference to the friary's early history is the decoration of the original church. To stabilise their position in the city the Franciscans utilised the older tradition of the founding fathers of the order of St Bernardine of Siena and John of Capestrano, the founder of its Central European branch. The friars moreover stressed links to the patron of the city, King Matthias, and employed the new Franciscan piety so popular in Italy.[57] The necessary image of St Francis in the presbytery was complemented by some extraordinary depictions on the walls of the church. One of them is directly linked to a crucial event for Christendom in the second half of the fifteenth century. The drawing on the wall of the presbytery vividly depicts the greatest success of the struggle against the Ottoman Turks. After the fall of Constantinople in 1453 all of Christian Europe was looking for a proper response. The collateral effects of the collapse of the second Rome were peace treaties, talks and negotiations, but no military action

56. For details see the first chapter.

57. Cf. Maria Giuseppina Muzzarelli, *Pescatori di uomini. Predicatori e piazze alla fine del Medioevo*, Bologna, Il Mulino, 2005.

Figure 8: Olomouc, Church of the Immaculate Conception of the Virgin Mary, *Battle of Belgrade* (1456), wall drawing, 1468-79.

was taken. It was the Sultan who – as a follow up – led a campaign to the Northern Balkans. He was stopped by Hungarian defences and was finally defeated while besieging the stronghold of Belgrade.[58]

It is the defence of Belgrade that is depicted in the Olomouc Franciscan church. It was this event that was to be connected forever with the name of John of Capestrano and thus the Observant Franciscans, and with the name of János Hunyadi and his family and its most well-known scion, Matthias Hunyadi, or Corvinus, second son of János Hunyadi. Behind this depiction there seems to be a clear intention of connecting King Matthias to the idea of the long-standing and close cooperation of the Franciscan order and the Hunyadi family. The link with the family might have appeared in the church between 1468 and 1479, when Matthias was visiting the city often. One of Matthias' close collaborators, who accompanied Bishop Prothasius on his mission to the king in early 1468, was Observant Franciscan Gabriele Rangoni. Rangoni was a proponent of papal policy in Central Europe in the 1460s and 1470s and later even a cardinal and papal legate *de latere.* In Hungary the Observant

58. Cf. Setton, *The Papacy*, vol. II, pp. 161-195; Norman Housley, "Giovanni da Capistrano and the Crusade of 1456", in *Crusading in the Fifteenth Century: Message and Impact*, ed. by Norman Housley, Basingstoke, Palgrave Macmillan, 2004, pp. 94-115.

Figure 9: Olomouc, Church of the Immaculate Conception of the Virgin Mary, heraldic key stone, with the coat of arms of Matthias Corvinus, 1469-90.

Franciscans rose to royal favour. With royal support religious houses were handed over to the Observants, especially in the 1480s. In Moravia the friars used the same strategy. The favour of the lord of the country was always useful. The friars also planted a keystone in the vaulting of their cloister with Matthias' armorial bearings (which may have inspired or been inspired by the church of St Maurice). Thus the friars attempted to stabilise their position in the city with royal power.

Another strategy of the friars was to stress the city's spirituality. The Catholic city was, obviously, perfect for such a purpose. The spirituality of St Bernardine of Siena was key to the development of the order and key to the city as well. Monograms of the name of Jesus were even placed around the city (some visible even today), and like John of Capestrano and János Hunyadi, St Bernardine was painted on the walls of the church. There is a further trace of St Bernardine in the church: in the image of the Coronation of the Virgin Mary and the Franciscan rosary. The image is a rare representation of the special Franciscan rosary type, over which the Dominican version prevailed in later periods. Below the Virgin one can see two rows of seven images depicting the Virgin Mary's seven joys and seven sorrows (or more precisely the effusions of the blood of Christ). The image was not just a decoration, of course. Its usage was explained in a short text entitled *A*

Figure 10: Olomouc, Church of the Immaculate Conception of the Virgin Mary, *Coronation of the Virgin Mary and the Rosary*, wall painting, 1500.

short exposition on the Crown of the immaculate Virgin, in which special devotion to the Virgin is expressly attributed to St Bernardine with the help of described and explicated rosary prayers.[59]

With the popularity in Olomouc of Franciscan devotion, which mirrored the situation in other Moravian and Silesian cities, the burghers were catching up with the latest trends and tendencies in the spiritual and devotional development of Europe, which in the fifteenth century originated mainly in Italy. This was one way of keeping the city's Catholicity. Instead of retiring to the Hussite isolation typical for Bohemia, accepting European influences connected Olomouc and other Moravian cities to the general church and all its innovations. But also its problems. The situation in Moravia was not an easy one.

Even though the political and social elites were generally tolerant (a "forced tolerance" as it was called by a famous historian of the Hussite period[60]), and the clash between the Catholics and the Utraquists lost its urgency, there were other reformed groups in the Bohemian lands. Of these, the Unity of Brethren was the most significant and the one that most irritated orthodox Catholics since it was the first church in the region to break off from the Roman Church and officially reject apostolic succession and reverence for the pope.[61] It was founded in the mid-fifteenth century and grew steadily in the second half of the century. It did not have much effect on the city itself, but Olomouc – as the centre of orthodoxy – was a place of disputations. To understand them we must turn to the Dominicans.

Figure 11: Indulgence letter of Cardinal Pietro Isvalies, *St Wenceslas*, detail, 1501.

The well-established position of the Dominican friars in the city contrasted with that of the newly emerging Observant Franciscans. The Dominicans had been present at the church of St Michael since the 1240s at the latest. From the following century the Moravian land diets and land law courts were held there, alternating with the Dominican friary in Brno. The convent often burned down and was rebuilt with support of the cathedral chapter, the city and indulgences.[62]

59. See the first chapter, and also Antonín Kalous, "Declaratio brevis Corone immaculate virginis: A source for the late medieval popular piety", *Umění/Art*, 55 (2007), pp. 40-44.

60. See František Šmahel, "Svoboda slova, svatá válka a tolerance z nutnosti v husitských Čechách", *Český časopis historický*, 93 (1994), pp. 644-679.

61. Cf. in English at least *The History of the Unity of Brethren: A Protestant Hussite Church in Bohemia and Moravia*, ed. by Rudolf Říčan, transl. by C. D. Crews, Bethlehem, PA, Moravian Church, 1992.

62. For basic information: Dušan Foltýn et al., *Encyklopedie moravských a slezských klášterů*, Prague, Libri, 2005, pp. 468-469.

The Dominican friary was the scene of public disputations with the "Valdensians and Pickards" (the Unity of Brethren). New forms of media were used, especially in attacks on the Unity of Brethren, by printers of the diocese: Matthias Preinlein and Konrad Stahel in Brno, and later Konrad Baumgarten in Olomouc. The printing shop of the latter used the image of St Wenceslas that had been printed originally in Brno in *Psalterium Olomucense* in 1499, and even on the indulgence letters printed for the papal legate Cardinal Pietro Isvalies, among whose tasks was "dealing with Olomouc matters".[63]

The public disputations were held by none other than the famous Dominican inquisitor Heinrich Institoris, whose works based on the disputations with Vavřinec Krasonický and Tůma Přeloučský *Clypeus* and *Opusculum*, were printed by Baumgarten. Institoris was explicit about his feelings for Olomouc: in his eyes it was the centre of the struggle to regain the position of the Roman Church. Pope Alexander VI even stressed the need for the cooperation of the Olomouc bishop and city council.[64]

Along with the Dominicans, the polemics with the Brethren were led by Olomouc humanists Augustin Käsenbrod and Bernard Zoubek, who were members of the cathedral chapter.[65] Thus, Olomouc in times of political and – even more importantly – religious compromise was still presented as the centre of Catholic orthodoxy and stronghold of Catholicism.

The City and the German Reformation

In the 1519 long epic poem *Stauromachia*, an account of the Hungarian peasant revolt of 1514, Stephan Stieröxel (Taurinus) recounts the events of the war to King Louis, king of Hungary and Bohemia. In explanatory notes he describes also the places, rivers and cities of the region. Olomouc is one of them. In his account Olomouc is the capital of Moravia and even though its burghers are too prone to visit the local wine houses ("as if it were their conference room"), he praises them for their erudition. He names the famous and most educated people, the teachers of the afore-mentioned school of St Maurice and the members of the cathedral chapter. In reality most of the educated humanists were members of the chapter. Linking both the city and bishopric (the bishop is also celebrated for his erudition by Italian visitors to the city[66]) to international Christian humanism might be un-

63. Augustin Theiner, *Vetera Monumenta Poloniae et Lithuaniae gentiumque finitimarum historiam illustrantia*, vol. II, Roma, Typis Vaticanis, 1861, p. 275; for the indulgence letters BAV, Vat. lat. 3922, fol. 305r-v; VKOL, sign. II 39012; Budapest, MNL OL, DL 36087, DL 66756.

64. Amedeo Molnár, "Protivaldenská politika na úsvitu 16. století", *Historická Olomouc* 3, 1980, pp. 153-174: 156-159.

65. Oldřich Králík, "Dvě zprávy o olomouckých humanistech", *Časopis Matice moravské*, 68 (1948), pp. 283-327: 306-307.

66. E.g. *Acta nuntiaturae Poloniae*, tom. 2, *Zacharias Ferreri (1519-1521) et nuntii minores (1522-1553)*, ed. by Henricus Damianus Wojtyska, Roma, Institutum historicum Polonicum Romae, 1992, p. 262.

derstood as another scheme to bring Olomouc out of the limitations of the confessionally problematic, and thus enclosed and isolated, Bohemian lands. Olomouc humanists were active at the court of the kings of Hungary and Bohemia, and in Italy during and after their studies.[67]

Stauromachia's author also speaks of the monasteries, city walls, moats and towers with which the city protected itself from its enemies, the Hussites. In the explanatory notes he adds that Olomouc is full of monasteries and describes it as the only city that was spared the treacheries of the schismatics. It could not be more favourable and fortunate, he writes, because the pious life of the city's clergy surpasses the life of many monks, and the biggest vice of the burghers is drinking.[68] That is the characterisation of the city written right at the outbreak of the German Reformation; a characterisation intended for the king, along with the whole work dedicated to him. This account is telling, even though this is just one example of the absence in written documents of Utraquists or heretics in the city. The city was able to secure a favourable position at the beginning of the sixteenth century as the true and always faithful capital of Moravia.

The advance of the Reformation came relatively fast during the 1520s. Even though the city streets and house fronts were decorated with images of saints placed there in the early 1520s (Virgin Mary, St Christopher, St Laurence, St Florian and St Hedwig of Silesia are still visible today),[69] the ideas of the Reformation were spreading around Moravia. Olomouc experienced a public spectacle linked to the protection of the Catholic order and faith. In 1523 King Louis and Queen Mary visited the city to spend Easter there on their return from Prague to Buda in Hungary where they resided. The royal couple took part in the Easter liturgy (or the queen alone according to some sources) and reportedly washed the feet of the poor. Easter seemed to be popular with the royal guests of Olomouc. Bona Sforza, too, when travelling to Poland to her new husband King Sigismund, spent the Easter holiday of 1518 there.[70]

The purpose of the royal couple's visit in 1523 was, however, manifold. The king even released prisoners from the city prison to prove the ideal of a good king. Another characteristic of an ideal sovereign was the protector of faith. Louis, according to a later report, sent a letter to the city council (read in the council in August 1522) against Martin Luther and against a preacher in Jihlava, another Moravian royal city.[71] The Jihlava preacher, who was influenced by Luther's

67. Eduard Petrů and Ivo Hlobil, *Humanism and the Early Renaissance in Moravia*, Olomouc, Votobia, 1999, pp. 36-126 (by E. Petrů); Peter Wörster, *Humanismus in Olmütz: Landesbeschreibung, Stadtlob und Geschichtsschreibung in der ersten Hälfte des 16. Jahrhunderts*, Marburg, Elwert, 1994.

68. Stephanus Taurinus Olomucensis, *Stauromachia, id est Cruciatorum servile bellum*, ed. by Ladislaus Juhász, Budapest, Egyetemi Nyomda, 1944, pp. 27, 61-62.

69. These were uncovered in recent years on the houses in Ostružnická and Univerzitní streets.

70. Beda Dudik, ed., *Olmützer Sammel-Chronik vom Jahre 1432 bis 1656*, Brünn 1858, p. 4; *Acta Tomiciana*, 8 vols., ed. by Stanislaus Gorski, vol. IV, Poznań, 1855, pp. 266-267, 269, 270, 303-304.

71. Dudik, *Olmützer Sammel-Chronik*, p. 5.

Figure 12: Olomouc, Univerzitní 4, house no. 226, *St Hedwig*, on the façade, 1523.

ideas, was Paul Sperat. He intended to join the royal court at Buda where he was invited as a preacher in 1522. He never managed, however, to get there. After he preached against celibacy in Vienna he was excommunicated and he departed for Jihlava where he became the city preacher. Later he was imprisoned and held in Olomouc. During the king's stay in the city a public burning of "Lutheran books including the New Testament" (probably referring to Luther's translation, which was published in 1522) was staged on the main square. The preacher was spared the flames and released from prison. He later found his place at the court of Albert of Brandenburg.[72] The city council was then still one that protected the Catholic faith and the good name of the city.

The advancing Reformation is illustrated by other events of the 1520s that foreshadow later developments. There was not just public burning of Lutheran books. The Observant Franciscans were a stable factor in the protection of universal Catholicism, with links to other traditionally Catholic areas (Italy, Si-

72. *Ibid.*, p. 6; Orsolya Réthelyi, *Mary of Hungary in Court Context (1521-1531)*, PhD dissertation, Central European University, Budapest, 2010, pp. 177-178; Zoltán Csepregi, "Court Priests in the Entourage of Queen Mary of Hungary", in *Mary of Hungary. The Queen and Her Court 1521-1531*, ed. by Orsolya Réthelyi, Beatrix F. Romhányi, Enikő Spekner and András Végh, Budapest, Budapest History Museum, 2005, pp. 49-61: 51-52.

lesia). It was they, however, who produced another "heretic" who followed the German Reformation movement. According to later reports he had been taken by the friars to the friary but then set free by a crowd of 200. Had the people not been appeased by the city council they would have killed the friars.[73] Another institution, representing universal Catholicism, was the bishopric. It also ran into troubles connected with the Reformation. The auxiliary bishop, Martin Göschl, titular bishop of Nikopolis, accepted the new ideas and even sought to secularise the Premonstratensian nunnery of Dolní Kounice close to Brno. This event was noted by a papal nuncio Giovanni Francesco Cito who recounted the marriage of Göschl to a noble nun (*una monacha nobile*) and mentioned the remarks of the bishop of Olomouc, Stanislaus Thurzo, that almost the whole of Moravia was infected by the Lutheran faith.[74] Martin Göschl was imprisoned by the bishop and died in 1528 in Kroměříž, the bishop's residence.[75]

These events show the advance of the German Reformation in the predominantly German urban environment. However, in the first half of the 1520s the burghers (or at least the city representatives, if the report on the crowd fighting for the heretical Franciscan friar is to be taken seriously) still tried to be faithful to Rome and Catholicism. Another humanist description of the city published in 1528 in Vienna seems to corroborate that. German humanist Georgius Sibutus wrote a description of Olomouc as part of a larger work dedicated to King Ferdinand. The image that Sibutus conveyed, as a true Catholic opponent of the Lutheran Reformation, was perfectly clear. Olomouc was full of educated people (among others he mentions the bishop) but more importantly full of beautiful churches and monasteries. The city was protecting the faith even when all of Moravia was affected by heresy. He concludes: "So beautiful is Olomouc about which we sing in our songs; in the first place the religion beatifies that city."[76] Olomouc did – or wanted to – enter the European confessional age as a defender of the true Catholic faith after its own experience with confessionally divided society. The impulses of the German Reformation were, however, much stronger than the will of the city council, as is clearly seen from later developments.

73. Dudik, *Olmützer Sammel-Chronik*, p. 6.

74. Wojtyska, ed., *Acta nuntiaturae Poloniae*, tom. 2, p. 262, 1 March 1526: "Trovai il Vescovo Olumucense. Me tenne un giorno cum molta humanità. Et mi mostrò una lettera del Re di Hungaria che li imponeva che senza altra dilatione detenesse et ben custodisse il Preposito Cunicense, suo suffraganeo, per haver contracto matrimonio cum una monacha nobile. Et il dì partì io, partì anchora sua Signoria per fare dicto effecto. Più mi disse che quasi tutta la Moravia era infecta dila fece Lutherana, et praesertim Igla, castello assai insigne, che ad sugistione di un Paulo Sperato, haveva immuntato tutto il rito antiquo dili divini offitii, et che non se li poteva providere senza la presentia del Re".

75. Josef Macek, *Víra a zbožnost jagellonského věku*, Prague, Argo, 2001, pp. 221, 346, 353.

76. Georgius Sibutus, *Ad potentissimum atque invictissimum Ferdinandum Hungariae & Bohemię, Dalmatię et Croatiae &c. regem ... Georgii Sibuti medici poetae & oratoris Panegyricus ... Eiusem illustratio in Olomuncz*, Vienna, 1528, fol. [E iiii r]-G ii v.

Conclusion

The period between the mid-fifteenth and early sixteenth century was significant for Olomouc. During this time the city recovered from the destruction and economic hindrances of the Hussite period and accepted the impact of the general European popularity of Observant Franciscans and Christian Humanism. And even when war began again in the late 1460s the city secured its position as the leading centre of Moravia. Especially in competition with Brno, Olomouc utilised its political position within the country and in relation to the new Catholic king. Its strongest argument was, however, the ever-remembered fight against the heretics and the protection of the true faith, Catholic orthodoxy. In that sense, both of the other main Catholic institutions, the cathedral chapter and bishopric, shared the same principles but never evaded conflicts within the city. The clash of the city authorities and the bishopric (and chapter) was facilitated by the division of the city itself, which consisted of the two parts mentioned in the beginning of this chapter. Předhradí, the quarter where the bishopric, the chapter and a few monasteries were located, was administratively connected to the city only by King Louis during his visit in 1522 on his way to Prague.[77] In the early 1520s the bishopric, the chapter and the city were all on the side of orthodoxy, protecting the true Catholic faith. It seems that all these institutions cherished the idea of a common front against "heresy".

77. SOkA Olomouc, AMO, Listiny, inv. no. 528.

3. The Divided City, 1520s-1600

Ondřej Jakubec

Olomouc entered the sixteenth century as a denominationally united city with firmly established church institutions.[1] Laudatory humanistic texts from the beginning of the century exalted the faithful Catholic character of the city. But there were numerous, albeit traditional, conflicts smouldering beneath this veneer of normality. A large number of church institutions (bishopric, chapter, number of monasteries, several parish and hospital churches and, starting in the 1560s, even the Jesuit College) and the unmistakable presence of the Catholic clergy produced many social and institutional interactions. The spectrum of conflicts inside the city walls between the church and city officials exceeded any denominational controversy. These conflicts included economic and business issues, jurisdiction and criminal competence, pragmatic disputes over maintenance of the city walls on the grounds of the local monasteries and other similar issues.

From the 1520s the array of conflicts in Olomouc expanded the growing confessional division (i.e. the spread of Lutheranism among all classes of society) from the lowest up to the ruling elite. This period was marked by the partial weakening of Catholic institutions, especially monasteries with decreasing discipline, and the diocese, which in the 1570s suffered from the uncertainty resulting from a rapid succession of bishops. A number of bishops were the victims of premeditated murder in the competitive and ambitious environment of the chapter. The Jesuits, who contributed to the renewal of Catholic life beginning in the 1560s, were also in a difficult position, running into understandable problems. These problems were not just with the non-Catholic population and city administration. Catholic institutions themselves caused the Jesuits complications. For example, the chapter blocked financial support for the Jesuit College. Yet despite all the internal conflicts in Catholic church institutions a strong base for Catholic reforms was created in the post-Tridentine generations of bishops and canons. Of course, both sides developed a programme of confessional politics. The Olomouc bishops energetically represented Catholic policies in their residential and metropolitan city. The interests of the dominant Lutherans (other denominations were marginal in the city) were also promoted with alternating intensity by the city council and a distinct group of the most active non-Catholic burghers. This naturally produced dramatic conflicts.

1. *Dějiny Olomouce*, vol. I, pp. 284-299 (Ondřej Jakubec) summarises the relevant literature.

Figure 13: View of Olomouc, Master MC, 1597.

Conflict and Coexistence

Controversial situations vividly portray the character of confessional conflicts and the polarisation of city society. The most commonly preserved reports, however, must not be overrated since they reveal only the partial and most visible facet of many forms of societal coexistence inside the city. A compromising and pragmatic perspective undoubtedly prevailed in the urban burgher community, as the form of conflicts also suggests. Denominationally motivated conflicts between burghers are virtually undocumented, whereas similar disputes between the 'external' authorities of Catholic institutions, regional Catholic officials or the Catholic monarch are extremely common. Nevertheless, the precise denominational structure of the city in the sixteenth century and beginning of the seventeenth is difficult to define. On one hand the local bishops knew of many non-Catholics, including the details of their lives; on the other hand, one bishop, Mark Kuen (bishop 1553-65), reported in 1559 that with regard to religion, "he cannot look into the hearts of other people".[2]

2. Stanislav Zela, *Náboženské poměry v Olomouci za biskupa Marka Kuena (1553-1565)*, Olomouc, 1931, p. 66, n. 262.

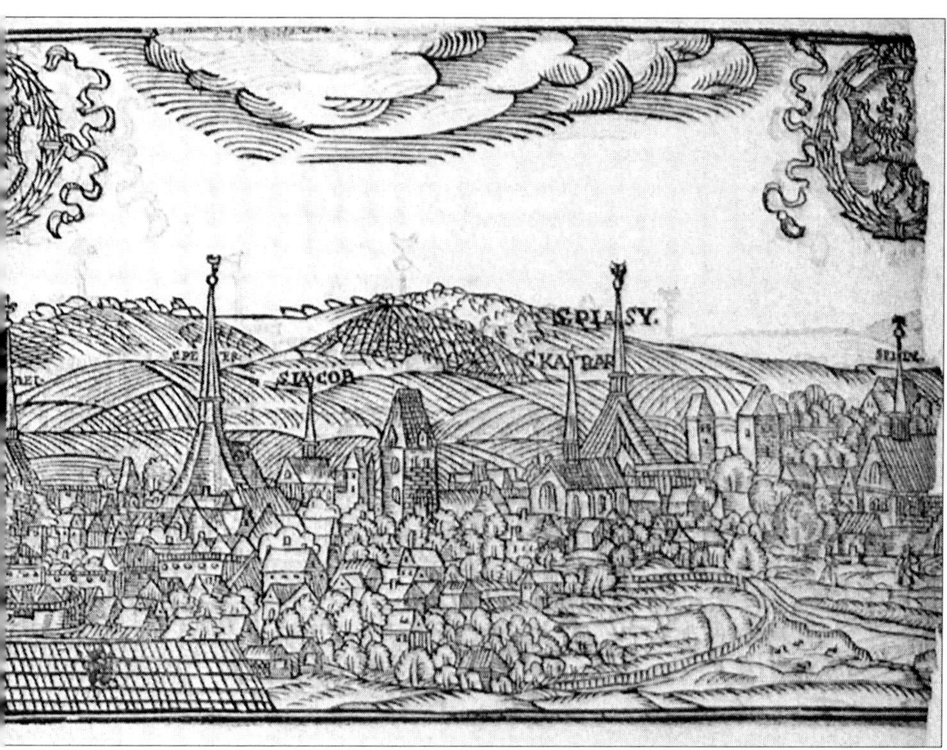

The denominational ambivalence in this complaint concerned the city council. From the mid-sixteenth century, councils were predominantly non-Catholic, as their "confessional policies" indicated. This is documented in particular by their official request for acceptance of the Augsburg Confession, the activities of non-Catholic clerics and their sabotage tactics aimed at the bishops' religious policies in the city. In contrast, thanks to the pressure of the local bishops, for a period of time around 1600 not a single non-Catholic sat in the city council. However, this situation did not last long, and beginning in 1610 non-Catholic burghers slowly returned to the council, albeit in a minority. Rare reports from this period document the character of the city population's confessional structure: in 1610 as many as 1,300 people reportedly visited in just three days the newly open (albeit illegal) non-Catholic chapel in the house of Friedrich Tiefenbach near the main square. Still other sources, referred to in the next chapter, prove that in Olomouc non-Catholics were in the majority in certain periods.[3] Providing an impression of

3. Cf. the following chapter. Also, František Hrubý, "Moravská šlechta r. 1619, její jmění a náboženské vyznání", *Časopis Matice moravské*, 46 (1922), pp. 107-169: 121, 128; Hans Kux, "Von der Reformation bis zur Gegenreformation", in *Aus der Geschichte des Protestantismus in Olmütz*, ed. by Friedrich Müller, Olmütz, 1927, pp. 4-15, 10-11; Zdeněk Kašpar, "Zplnomocnění olomouckých evangelických měšťanů roku 1610", in *Olomoucké baroko*, 3 vols., *Proměny ambicí jednoho města*, vol. I, *Úvodní svazek*, ed. by Martin Elbel and Ondřej Jakubec, Olomouc, 2010, pp. 52-56.

the denominational structure of the city at the end of the sixteenth century is the complaint by Olomouc bishop Stanislaus Pavlovský (bishop 1579-98) from 1580 that "there are very few Catholics in Olomouc".[4] In 1586 this same bishop curiously defined the character of the most radical Olomouc non-Catholics as being "much more Calvinist than Lutheran", which could be more of an expressive exaggeration than a factual description.[5] The increase of the Lutheran population in the city is also reflected in burghers' sixteenth-century wills; they reveal a marked decrease of pious bequests for church (Catholic) institutions.[6] Olomouc's confessional diversity and the clear presence of non-Catholics in the city were also evident to outside observers, as is documented in comments by the English traveller Samuel Lewkenor prior to 1600.[7] According to Lewkenor, Olomouc was a typical central European multi- or bi-confessional city.[8] The large Lutheran population was balanced by Catholic institutions and strong Catholic burgher personalities who, though forming a tight alliance with Catholic authorities (especially the bishops), took a compromise approach in the city, like non-Catholics.[9]

In studying the manifestations of denominational polarisation in Olomouc the situation should not be perceived as black and white or as a conflict of homogeneous and aggrieved Catholics against Lutherans. Beginning in the mid-sixteenth century part of the city elite certainly converted to the Lutheran faith. The large share of German-speaking citizens also played a role in the situation.[10] In addition, there was a class of influential Catholics strengthened by the presence of Catholic institutions and pressure from the vice-chamberlain (*podkomoří, subcamerarius*) as the representative of the Catholic Habsburg monarchs, to whom Olomouc as a royal city was subordinate. The confessional-social structure of the city was undoubtedly varied, as the spectrum of denominational conflicts also confirms. The position of radicals was balanced by the approach of compromise taken in particular by the city council, which attempted to eliminate the controversy and pressures from both sides. At the same time, the council kept in mind coexistence inside the city and with outside authorities, especially the monarch as the ruler of Olomouc.

The situation in Olomouc throughout the entire sixteenth century is reminiscent of the confessional coexistence that reigned in certain German and Swiss cit-

4. MZA, G 83, Kopiář (Cartulary) XVII, 1579-1580, cart. no. 43, inv. no. 169, fol. 68/7-8.

5. MZA, G 83, Kopiář nesign., cart. no. 42, inv. no. 168, fol. 67. Sometimes the term "Calvinist" referred to members of Unity of Brethren, a unique Church originating from radical Utraquists reformers.

6. Alžběta Steinerová, *Zbožné odkazy v testamentech olomouckých měšťanů v 16. století*, MA thesis, Department of History, Masaryk Univerzity, Brno 2014, pp. 80-82.

7. Otto F. Babler, "Ein englischer Reisender des 16. Jahrhunderts über Olmütz", *Mährisch-Schlesische Heimat*, 1 (1968), pp. 42-48: 47.

8. Ronnie Po-Chia Hsia, *Social Discipline in the Reformation: Central Europe 1550-1750*, London and New York, Routledge, 1989, pp. 82-84.

9. Tomáš Malý, "Confessional Identity in Moravian Royal Towns in the 16th and 17th Centuries?", in *Public Communication in European Reformation. Artistic and other Media in Central Europe 1380-1620*, ed. by Milena Bartlová and Michal Šroněk, Prague, Artefactum, 2007, pp. 323-334.

10. Jaroslav Miller, *Urban Societies in East-Central Europe: 1500-1700*, Aldershot, Ashgate, 2008, p. 203.

ies in the 1520s.[11] A large part of the city population and the elite was increasingly influenced by Lutheranism, which in Olomouc attempted to gain the position of a new denomination without threatening the stability of the city. Also evident are the activities of radical non-Catholics, who put great pressure on the political elite of the city to legalise the non-Catholic confession at any cost. This corresponded to the more general situation in Moravia where it was the goal of the non-Catholic estates to establish their own regional church administration.[12] Although it was often accommodating to public displays by non-Catholics, the city council's primary objective was to preserve order and limit further acceleration of unrest. These fears were often well justified. And it is the approaches and tactics of the city council that best demonstrate the character of the confessional conflicts in the city. As such, the council often became the pragmatic intermediary of compromise between the non-Catholic community and the political representatives of Catholicism, be it directly the sovereign or bishop or the vice-chamberlain. Although the council's opinion in matters of religion and its interests were also clearly connected to its denominational make-up, it often struggled to both balance political loyalty to the monarch and react to pressure from below (from the city itself).

One detail is telling about the confessional atmosphere and its transformation in Olomouc around the middle of the sixteenth century. In 1526 a local beggar was executed in Olomouc after having been caught eating meat during Lent.[13] The situation had changed completely a generation later. Prior to Easter 1557 Olomouc bishop Mark Kuen lamented the ostentatious behaviour of non-Catholic councilman Hans Knošpl who publicly consumed meat in his own house during Lent "to boast, to set an example and shock other people". The sale of meat and the consumption of alcohol during Lent were criticized by the bishop as fully tolerated by the "blaspheming" behaviour of Olomouc citizens.[14] In the environment of the non-Catholic community, "religious habits" had thus changed completely, and it had become the task of the bishops as the guarantors of Catholicism to confront this new situation.

1556-1558: Confessional Reversal

A change that occurred in Olomouc in the mid-sixteenth century was produced by a new generation that expressed less loyalty to Catholicism. The Reformation slowly seeped into the Olomouc community, as several anecdotal reports indicate. At

11. Carl C. Christensen, *Art and Reformation in Germany*, Athens, OH, Ohio University Press, 1979, pp. 35-39, 66-102; Lee Palmer Wandel, *Voracious Idols and Violent Hands. Iconoclasm in Reformation Zurich, Strasbourg and Basel*, Cambridge, Cambridge University Press, 1995 (the case of Zurich especially provides a good example of this slow process, pp. 53-101).

12. Jaroslav Miller et al., eds., *Konfliktní soužití: Královské město – šlechta – duchovenstvo v raném novověku. Edice. Knihy půhonné a nálezové královského města Olomouce (1516-1616)*, Olomouc, Danal, 1998, pp. 199-200; Josef Válka, *Dějiny Moravy*, vol. II, *Morava reformace, renesance a baroka*, Brno, Muzejní a vlastivědná společnost v Brně, 1995, pp. 50, 57-60.

13. Beda Dudík, ed., *Olmützer Sammel-Chronik vom Jahre 1432 bis 1656*, Brünn, 1858, p. 6, n. 2.

14. MZA, G 83, Kopiář 1557, cart. no. 34, inv. no. 158, fol. 28.

a city council meeting in October 1535 a delegation of Olomouc burghers requested "in the name of many fellow citizens" the preservation at the church of St Maurice of a non-Catholic preacher who had been removed by Bishop Thurzo.[15] Three years later a certain Carthusian who "preached the pure Gospel" gained the support of the city council.[16] As can be seen, the Reformation slowly began to be accepted even by members of the city political elite and, at least from the 1550s, became the "unofficial" religious ideology of many city council officials. In 1559 Bishop Kuen commented on this new situation. He saw the problem of supporting Lutheranism in the city council, which had only four Catholic members at the time (only a quarter of the entire assembly).[17] This development and gradual inclination of the city elite toward Lutheranism can also be observed in similar Moravian and central European cities.[18] Marking a distinct and exemplary turning point was a dispute in 1556-58 between two non-Catholic ministers – Jan Kyncl and Martin Adler – in the parish churches of the Virgin Mary in Předhradí and of St Blaise.[19] Both of these individuals were formally Catholic clerics; Kyncl was in fact an Olomouc canon.[20]

Yet both ministers were typical non-Catholic clerics, converts who quickly gained substantial popularity due to their work and agitation. Their sermons were heavily attended and they delivered Mass in German, administered both bread and wine during Holy Communion, led singing of Lutheran songs, simplified the sacramental rites and derided the Catholic clergy. Above all they refused to submit to the bishops' authority.[21] In both cases Bishop Mark Kuen's authority proved to be entirely negligible. His tactics were highly telling. When none of the clerics would respect his demands and he failed to gain even the city council's support, he turned to vice-chamberlain Přemek of Víckov and Emperor Ferdinand I with a request to intervene and rectify the situation in "their" royal city. The city council acted typically. At first it was restrained, seeking to balance pressure from the non-Catholic community and the bishop and sovereign authority. Both ministers had direct support in the council, and a chronicler wrote that the "entire community"[22] stood behind them (i.e. the most vocal citizens), and hence city council's main goal was to maintain peace in the city. This was the top priority both in respect to the size of the non-Catholic community and its significant radicalisation. In fact, a number of Catholics apparently left the city in fear. The acute atmosphere escalated from the singing of defamatory songs to hanging satirical leaflets to a raid by Lutheran journeymen on the Olomouc cathedral (perhaps with iconoclastic or merely disruptive

15. Hans Kux, *Geschichte von Olmütz*, Olmütz 1937, p. 151.

16. Dudík, *Olmützer Sammel-Chronik*, p. 9. Another controversial Carthusian, who came from Rome, is mentioned by Bishop John Dubravius in his letter to the Hradiště abbot in 1546.

17. Zela, *Náboženské poměry*, pp. 59-60.

18. Josef Válka, *Dějiny Moravy*, vol. II, p. 49; Karlheinz Blaschke and Siegfried Seifert, "Reformation und Konfessionalisierung in der Oberlausitz", in *Welt – Macht – Geist. Das Haus Habsburg und die Oberlausitz 1526-1635*, ed. by Joachim Bahlcke and Volker Dudeck, Zittau, Städtische Museen Zittau, 2002, pp. 121-128: 121-122; Miller, *Urban Societies*, p. 209.

19. For more on the dispute, see Zela, *Náboženské poměry*, pp. 18-52.

20. Zela, *Náboženské poměry*, pp. 18-19, 29-30.

21. Dudík, *Olmützer Sammel-Chronik*, pp. 22-29.

22. Dudík, *Olmützer Sammel-Chronik*, p. 22.

Figure 14: Olomouc, St. Wenceslas cathedral, monument of Mark Kuen, 1565.

motives), during which a priest was nearly killed. It was not long before physical attacks on the clergy began, and the bishop requested protection for the priests.[23] During the peak of the conflict the diocese official and pastor of the main city church (St Maurice) Jan Had (Hadius), who was involved in the dispute, became the target of attacks. Agitated Olomouc non-Catholics threw stones at him and his presbytery and shot out the windows of his house. If the bishops' documents are to be believed, fear spread among the Olomouc clergy after these violent attacks.[24]

As a result of the negotiations of vice-chamberlain Přemek of Víckov and an investigation by imperial commissioners, Martin Adler was expelled from the city and country. He nevertheless remained active in Olomouc. The situation came to a head in January 1558. The city council requested the legitimisation of Adler's work as a "new preacher". The vice-chamberlain curbed these council activities, pointing out the necessity to obey the monarch's ruling.[25] At the same time, secret meetings of Olomouc non-Catholics were organised, and the bishop remarked on the threat of riots. The tense situation climaxed with open rebellion against the royal decree banishing the two clerics from the city. An armed mob even attacked the city hall. The city council at this moment supported the radicals, perhaps out of sympathy for the ministers, but also in an effort to limit unrest. The city council's revolt against the monarch and bishops had its consequences, however. The monarch's concentrated pressure led to the issue of mandates forbidding all non-Catholic ceremonies in the city. Non-Catholic clerics were driven out, and burghers involved in the situation and the participants of the revolts were severely punished.

These measures included the execution of three leaders of the unrest, the flight of burghers under investigation, the expulsion of some of them from the city and monetary fines. One of the expelled individuals was city procurator Urban Kremer, which is proof that part of the city's political elite truly had converted to Lutheranism, regardless of the possible consequences. In the end the city's political representatives expressed their loyalty to the monarch, including in religious matters. Pledges of this type were also given in the following period, though often merely formally.[26] This was related to the fact that the sovereign was not all that active in promoting his "interests" in the city, and if the local bishops did not ask for help in these matters, he did not interfere in religious issues on his own accord. As a result, the city council was able to continue to realise its relatively liberal "religious policies" in favour of Lutheranism. Also contributing to this situation was the failure of Catholic institutions for years to find effective tools to limit displays of Lutheranism in Olomouc.

The Olomouc Bishops and Their Confessional Politics in a Divided City

The Olomouc bishops persecuted any confessional diversity in the city and diocese as early as the turn of the sixteenth century. Due to the weak position of Utraquism their main adversaries were members of the Unity of Brethren. Be-

23. MZA, G 83, Kopiář 1557, cart. no. 34, inv. no. 158, fol. 456.
24. MZA, G 83, Kopiář 1557, cart. no. 34, inv. no. 158.
25. Dudík, *Olmützer Sammel-Chronik*, pp. 27-28.
26. For more on the conflicts in 1556-58, see Zela, *Náboženské poměry*, pp. 18-52.

tween the 1520s and the 1530s their numbers occasionally expanded to include others, especially Lutherans, against whom the humanistically-cultivated bishops Stanislaus Thurzo and John Dubravius took sharp measures. Only in the middle of the sixteenth century were contemporaries explicitly informed of the confessional schism in Olomouc – "during the time of Bishop Mark the faith was split here in the city".[27] The aforementioned Mark Kuen (1553-65) was the first bishop who openly acted against the threatened hegemony of the Catholic Church in Olomouc and Moravia as a whole. The conflict from 1556-58 showed the extent to which his authority was limited and shaken. This included his authority over the clerics under his control but over which the city community held a protective hand. Hence political and religious perspectives continued to influence the city council's decision-making. This ambivalence also appeared in the future, when the council was forced to balance pressure from the local non-Catholic community and the Catholic authorities of the bishop, chamberlain and Habsburg monarch.

Therefore, the greatest point of conflict was naturally the relationship between the bishop and city representatives. At the same time, the city council's opposition to the bishop need not only have been motivated by religious issues, even though they were often lurking in the background. A primary factor was the city council's evident displeasure over the monarch's frequent interference resulting from complaints by the bishop. As a result of the sovereign's encroachment in city matters the council naturally viewed the bishop as a disruptive element in the city. It is therefore not surprising that following the end of the conflict from 1556-58 the agreement concluded between the city council and the bishop emphasised that in the future neither party would turn to the monarch with its complaints. However, this condition proved naive since involving the monarch in the confessional-political matters of the city became the main feature of the bishop's religious policy, an approach already taken by Mark Kuen. Despite the ineffectiveness of many of his measures he recognised the necessity of building a network of political ties between Catholic politicians, aristocrats, institutions and the monarch. He defined his own weakness in a letter to Emperor Ferdinand I from 1561: "therefore, unless you, Your Imperial Majesty, attempt to suppress such heresy in the church, my efforts alone will fail".[28] It therefore appears that a stronger and conspicuous spread of the Lutheran Reformation in Olomouc was enabled precisely by the submissive and passive policy of the bishop, who was already known at the time as being a "very simple-minded politician".[29]

Catholic reform took on a new dynamic under Kuen's successor, William Prusinovský of Víckov (bishop 1565-72), a member of an old Moravian noble family (Kuen was not of noble blood, which could have also contributed to his weak authority). He was well aware that the sluggish policies of his predecessors caused *ecclesiae calamitates*.[30] As a typical post-Tridentine bishop he supported

27. Zela, *Náboženské poměry*, p. 15.

28. MZA, G 83, Kopiář III, 1561, cart no. 37, inv. no. 161, fol. 104-105.

29. Bartoloměj Paprocký, *Zrcadlo Slavného Markrabství Moravského*, Olomouc, 1593, fol. 183v; ZAO-O, MCO, sign. C.O. 538, Magnoald Ziegelbauer, *Olomucium Sacrum quo Historici Ecclesiastica Moraviae et eius Episcopatus exponitur*, vol. II, 1798, p. 109.

30. Vladimír A. Macourek, "Počátky katolické restaurace na Moravě za biskupa Prusinovského (1565-1572)", *Sborník historického kroužku*, 28 (1927), p. 99, n. 31.

pastoral care and Catholic education, culminating in the founding of Olomouc's Jesuit College (1566) and the university (1573). Bishop Prusinovský organised visitations and secured censorship authority over all book production in Moravia. But even his policies had their limits. In 1566 the bishop was authorised to oversee church administration of legally-permitted Utraquists, to whom all non-Catholics (Lutherans and members of the Unity of Brethren) professed loyalty for logical reasons. Hence, the bishop planned to conduct a Reformation from above and to subordinate all of these Utraquists (or non-Catholics) within a diocesan synod and visitation. This project failed however; the synod did not end in success and the bishop was not allowed visitation rights in non-Catholic domains at this time or in the future. Although the diocesan synod in April 1568 adopted the decrees of the Council of Trent, the documents could not be published due to Emperor Maximilian II's reluctance and also resistance from non-Catholic nobles. In fact, Prusinovský's authority was only loosely respected on the bishop's own estates, and it is highly telling that in this period even non-Catholics served in the offices of bishop's towns.[31] Prusinovský was the first bishop to base his own confessional policy, even in Olomouc, on the programmatic engagement of "external" political actors and the intervention of friendly regional and royal officials, including Jesuits, papal nuncios, the land captain, the vice-chamberlain, the high chancellor, the high burgrave, the high Bohemian hofmeister and the judge of the land court.

Hence, these intricate diplomatic games began in the 1570s to transfer political activity to the Catholic side.[32] This was also related to the generational exchange of individuals in the bishop's office and chapter beginning in the 1570s when positions were filled by persons connected with the post-Tridentine programme with experience of studies at the *Collegium Germanicum* in Rome. After the middle of the sixteenth century, in addition to the bishops, the chapter itself created the foundations for Counter-Reformation policies in a system of "electoral capitulation" (i.e. of binding requirements for future elected bishops). This included, for example, respecting the Tridentine decrees, the founding of an inquisition, a diocese visitation, the establishment of a seminary for priests, authority over monasteries and support for pastoral activities. However, the confessional policies of the bishops had their limits, in part because of the reserved nature of the Habsburg rulers who, due to their own interests, could not aggressively defend Catholicism and their confessional-political partners.[33] In the same way, the Olomouc bishops were in many cases bound to political "correctness" or caution preventing them from taking radical steps in their religious policies.[34] An ambitious religious policy was then pursued fully by bishops Stanislaus Pavlovský and

31. Válka, *Dějiny Moravy*, vol. II, p. 50; ZAO-O, AO, Kopiář 1570, fol. 4.

32. On this Catholic coalition around the Olomouc bishops, see Válka, *Dějiny Moravy*, vol. II, pp. 51-52.

33. Miller, *Urban Societies*, pp. 209-210.

34. This confessionally ambivalent attitude is well illustrated by the example of the Wrocław bishops in the period around 1600. See Aleksandra Szewczyk, "The Bishop as Shepherd and as Duke: Some Aspects of the Patronage of Art by the Bishops of Wrocław in the Sixteenth Century", in *Public Communication in European Reformation. Artistic and other Media*

Figure 15: Olomouc, Jesuit church of the Virgin Mary of the Snow, monument of William Prusinovský of Víckov, 1572.

Francis of Dietrichstein (bishop 1599-1636), who were key protagonists of the Reformation and Counter-Reformation in Moravia. Their activities involved activist political steps and confrontational measures against non-Catholics, as well as "positive" Catholic reforms of the diocese (support for parish administration, education, monastery reform, pastoral care, artistic patronage, etc.).

Prior to 1600 the bishops' political capital rose significantly. The victory of Bishop Pavlovský in a dispute with the land court regarding his exclusive jurisdictional authority over the clergy in 1588 represented a symbolic triumph. At the same time, Emperor Rudolf II confirmed the princely title for the Olomouc bishops, introducing an entirely new title among the estates and making the bishops the formally highest ranking nobles in the Bohemian lands. The bishops confirmed their extraordinary position as political and ruling players with enormous assets and land, their own army and a feudal system with its own institutional court and assembly. In this sense, the bishopric essentially formed a state within the state or, to a certain extent, an independent or parallel protagonist to Moravian estates institutions. This was in line with the status of the Olomouc bishops, who in Moravia were both representatives of church administration and formally the highest estate, as Polish historian Bartołomiej Paprocki pointed out in 1593: "[the bishop] is not only *Princeps Ecclesiae Dei*, but *Princeps et senator supremus* of Moravia, as well".[35] The bishops also entered the religious situation in Olomouc in this position and with high ambitions, prepared to promote their re-Catholicisation policy from both inside and outside church institutions.

How did the Olomouc bishops solve the problem of confessional fragmentation in Olomouc? And what conflicts did this fragmentation produce? The spectrum of conflicts and their resolution essentially remained unchanged throughout this period and can be followed on two basic levels: first, among the internal residents of the city (individuals, the city council, the bishop and other Catholic institutions and authorities); and second, in the engagement of external protagonists at the request of both parties (vice-chamberlains, the monarch, etc.). Several basic conflicts typical for the entire period played out in this environment. They move between levels, from complicated political and diplomatic dealings with the monarch to the sphere of the everyday religious behaviour of individual Olomouc burghers.

The Olomouc City Council versus the Olomouc Bishops

"The elders of Olomouc turn their back on the activities of the non-Catholic ministers and ignore the services and the word of God and other sacraments at churches".[36] This was Bishop Kuen's response to city council members at the end of the 1550s. Thus he pointed out the primary problem of the confessionalisation policy of the Olomouc bishops: the confessionally indifferent or directly non-Catholic

in Central Europe 1380-1620, ed. by Milena Bartlová and Michal Šroněk, Prague, Artefactum, 2007, pp. 219-227.

35. Paprocký, *Zrcadlo Slavného*, fol. 383r.

36. MZA, G 83, Kopiář I., 1559, cart no. 35, inv. no. 159, fol. 14v.

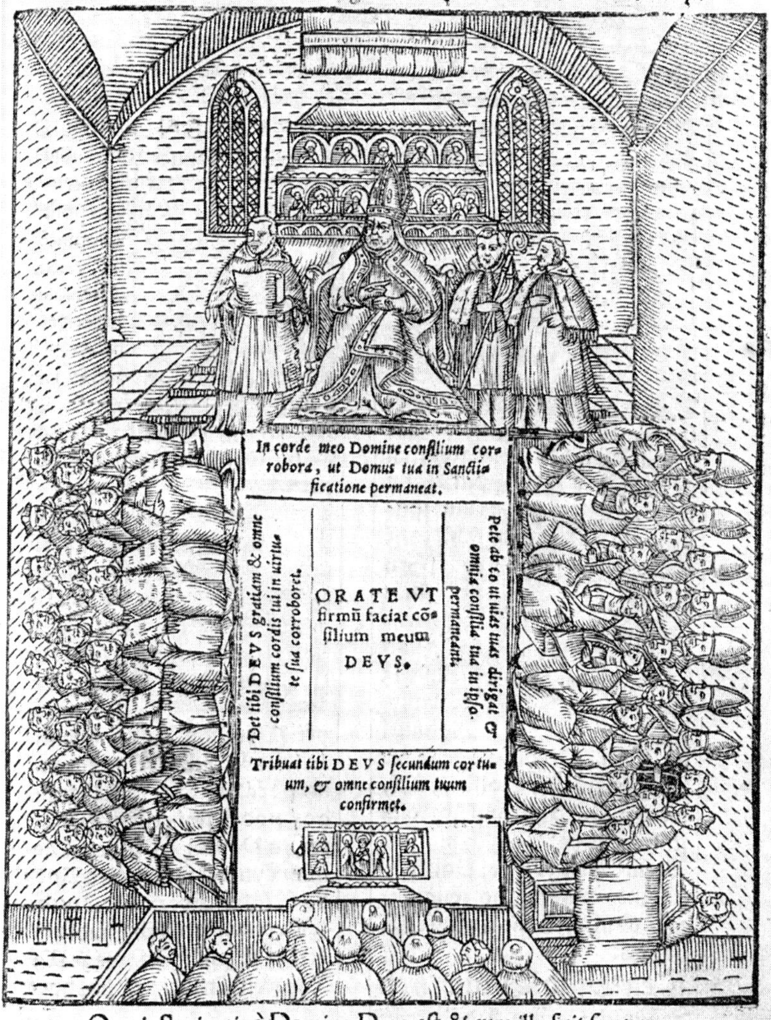

Figure 16: Synod in Olomouc in 1591 chaired by Bishop Stanislaus Pavlovský, 1593.

city council, which more or less supported the needs of the non-Catholic population. Although the mandate of Rudolf II limiting the membership of non-Catholics on city councils in royal cities had been in effect since 1577, it had been issued under the influence of the Catholic vice-chamberlain, Hanuš Haugvic of Biskupice. Of course, in 1586 Bishop Stanislaus Pavlovský complained to High Chancellor Adam II of Hradec that the mandate was not being respected.[37] He had clearly stated earlier that the membership of non-Catholics on the council would always be "an affront to the Catholic religion" in Olomouc.[38] Bishop Pavlovský then took concentrated political efforts to place exclusively Catholic burghers on the city council in order to "subdue" the Olomouc population.[39]

The tool for accomplishing this objective was the vice-chamberlain, a representative of the monarch in royal cities who formally confirmed city council members. This function was performed well by the bishop's close friend, Nicolas (Mikuláš) of Hrádek, originally a member of the Unity of Brethren who converted to Catholicism. The criterion for a suitable Catholic candidate for the council was his active participation in Catholic services.[40] This concentrated tactic was successful and some city councils were predominantly (if not exclusively) Catholic. On the other hand, Bishop Pavlovský was aware that the non-Catholic burgher elite was not only a large group but also effectively blocked the placement of Catholics on the city council in favour of promoting members from their own ranks. Testifying to merely relative success are the bishop's appeals to the vice-chamberlain in 1590 to ensure that "seats on the council were filled with good Catholic people so that the [Catholic] religion could slowly spread in this city". The bishop also pleaded for a Catholic to be elected reeve. The size and standing of the non-Catholic community was therefore significant, and its short-term displacement from political life had no lasting effect. Hence, when non-Catholics appeared again in the council for a certain period (in the beginning of the seventeenth century) they immediately acted in favour of the non-Catholic community, especially with respect to their religious demands. The Catholic city council maintained by the bishops (or the vice-chamberlains who approved the members in the name of the monarch) could not ensure the predominance of Catholicism in the city, not even over the long-term. The powerful non-Catholic community and important members of its elite continued to wait for their opportunity, attempting to advance their interests through both legal and covert means.

Disputes between the bishops and city council also involved problems that were not openly denominational. These predominantly concerned the power of town law over church institutions and the effect of canon law, especially in marital disputes,[41] the administration of ecclesiastical benefices and endowments estab-

37. MZA, G 83, Kopiář nesign., inv. no. 168, cart. no. 42, fol. 67.

38. MZA, G 83, Kopiář XVII, 1579-1580, inv. no. 169, cart. no. 43, fol. 68/7-8.

39. MZA, G 83, Kopiář XXIV, 1586, inv. no. 177 cart. no. 50, fol. 675.

40. MZA, G 83, archive copies (Prague Archive), inv. no. 199, cart. no. 64, 13 July 1589; *ibid.*, Kopiář XXVIII, 1590, inv. no. 181, cart. no. 54, fol. 349.

41. Zdeněk Kašpar, "Prameny k dějinám Olomouce 16. století v kopiářích olomouckých biskupů I", *Ročenka Státního okresního archivu v Olomouci*, 8 (1999), pp. 179-196: 192-193. On the difficulty of enforcing the bishops' jurisdiction in matters of marital law, see František

lished by burghers. This was merely a consequence of the close connection between the city and church institutions.[42] One example is the Olomouc Augustinian All Saints' Monastery, whose administration had been under the authority of the city council since the end of the fifteenth century, based on a ruling by diocese administrator John Filipec and King Wladislas II.[43] The monastery suffered a major decline after the mid-sixteenth century, and the city council primarily attempted to guarantee its economic stability. The magistrate therefore secured confirmation of its patronage over the monastery from Emperor Maximilian II. Although the monastery's internal relationships and monastic discipline fell under church competence,[44] the bishops greatly resented the city council's control over the monastery. Bishop Kuen also made no secret of his indignation that the city council held the key to the monastery's treasury, which contained valuable relics.[45] Moreover, the council sabotaged the plan of several bishops to use the monastery building for the Jesuit College.[46] The council's intervention in the monastery's matters (e.g. the election of provosts) also led Bishop Prusinovský to attempt (unsuccessfully) to wrest control of the monastery from the city.[47]

Although similar conflicts between city council and Catholic institutions arose throughout the entire period, their confessional character was probably not the only factor at play. There were also disputes between the city and Jesuits over maintenance of a section of the city walls by the Academy and jurisdiction conflicts between city and academic law in the case of transgressions by local students. These conflicts could have been aggravated by the animosity between councillors (Lutherans) and Jesuits, but that was not always the case. From the point of view of Catholic institutions, any non-Catholic element in the city council was a major obstacle to their successful religious policy in Olomouc. The bishops persisted in their efforts to ensure the Catholic uniformity of city council until 1618.

The City School at the Church of St Maurice

The previous chapter demonstrated that even in a Catholic city the Catholic school at the parish church of St Maurice became the subject of dispute between the city council and the chapter, which sought hegemony over city education. The establishment of a city school in the 1460s and 1470s, promoted against the will of the bishop and the chapter with support from King Matthias Corvinus, proved to be quite problematic in the post-Reformation period. This school became one

Hrubý, "Luterství a kalvinismus na Moravě před Bílou horou", *Český časopis historický*, 40 (1934), pp. 265-299: 272.

42. Miller, *Urban Societies*, p. 206.

43. Dušan Foltýn, ed., *Encyklopedie moravských a slezských klášterů*, Prague, Libri, 2005, p. 490.

44. Zela, *Náboženské poměry*, appendix no. 14, pp. 184-185.

45. MZA, G 83, Kopiář I, 1559, cart. no. 35, inv. no. 159, fol. 138.

46. Zdeněk Kašpar, "Prameny k dějinám Olomouce 16. století v kopiářích olomouckých biskupů V", *Olomoucký archivní sborník*, 3 (2005), pp. 176-186: 178-186.

47. *Ibid.*, pp. 180-186.

of the main centres of Lutheranism in Olomouc, one that was steadfastly protected by the city council from control by the local bishops. Moreover, despite competition from the Jesuits starting in the 1570s, the city Latin school maintained a high level of education and hence also popularity. The non-Catholic character of the school, as was the case with the conventional studies of students at Lutheran schools in Wittenberg, Leipzig and Frankfurt an der Oder, shaped and disciplined future generations of Olomouc citizens from an early age. The local bishops were keenly aware of the danger of infiltration by an emerging burgher generation.

Since the city council was in charge of the school's faculty it is not surprising that the school had a Lutheran profile beginning in the mid-sixteenth century.[48] It had a "school master with Lutheran sympathies" as early as 1533, and the city council installed Lutheran schoolmaster Jakob Kaucz in 1538. This was despite the fact that the city school's teaching candidates were to be presented and approved by the diocese official "regardless of whether or not they are Catholic".[49] Given the Lutheran orientation of the city council after the middle of the sixteenth century, John Mezon's (bishop 1576-78) complaint directly to Rudolf II over the replacement of the Catholic schoolmaster with an individual of "confused faith" was also not surprising.[50] Similarly, the chapter warned Emperor Ferdinand I in 1560 that the local school was being led toward "new and strange errors" and that it was neglecting "true piety".[51]

Denominational conflicts over the school culminated in the 1580s under Bishop Stanislaus Pavlovský. In 1586 the city council rejected the bishop's candidate, Johann Lindl, for the post of schoolmaster, and ignored his request for the introduction of the Catholic catechism of Peter Canisius. The bishop realised the refined form of the covert confessionalisation of the Olomouc students when he complained about local Lutheran teachers to High Chancellor Vratislav of Pernštejn in 1589: "During lessons in writing and arithmetic they teach them a heretic catechism so that it becomes ingrained at an early age".[52] He also complained in 1592 that "numerous heresies also appear" in their new textbooks.[53] However, the bishop failed in his efforts to influence the selection of teachers and lessons, thanks to an effective boycott by the city council. Even when the bishop stressed their mandatory loyalty to the Catholic monarch the city council employed its traditional tactic.[54] It stonewalled the bishop's complaints and during its sessions obscured or hypocritically (sometimes almost ironically) denied that they were aware of the activities of

48. Jiřina Holinková, *Dvě studie z dějin městské školy na Moravě v předbělohorském období*, Olomouc, Univerzita Palackého, 2005, p. 151.

49. Zela, *Náboženské poměry*, p. 17; MZA, G 83, Kopiář XXIV, 1586, cart. no. 50, inv. no. 177, fol. 80.

50. Holinková, *Dvě studie*, p. 37.

51. Zela, *Náboženské poměry*, p. 74.

52. MZA, G 83, Kopiář XXVII, 1589, inv. no. 180, cart. no. 53, fol. 189-190v; Kopiář XXVII, 1589, inv. no. 180, cart. no. 53, fol. 189-191.

53. Bishop Pavlovský interpreted the "tolerant" approach of the town council toward the distribution of textbooks as clear "insubordination and disorder", defying the bishop's censorship authority granted by the imperial mandate, i.e. as an expression of disloyalty to the emperor. MZA, G 83, Kopiář XXX, 1592, inv. no. 183, cart. no. 56, fol. 350-351.

54. MZA, G 83, Kopiář XXIV, 1586, inv. no. 177, cart. no. 50, fol. 80, 100, 743.

non-Catholics in the school. At the same time, the councillors were not afraid to admit their confessional convictions, and in response to the bishop in 1587 openly declared their allegiance to the Augsburg Confession.[55]

The council responded in similar fashion to the controversies in which the bishops raised the issue of private schools in burgher homes and the "German heresy" of the teachers.[56] The Olomouc chapter complained to the emperor about these Lutheran teachers as early as 1560, and the protests continued until the 1580s.[57] The primary interest of the bishops in this subject was natural and reflected an awareness of the role of "confessional education" in the denominational identification and discipline of the young. Despite efforts to engage Catholic political partners, these attempts were thwarted by the council's effective strategy secretly supported by the Lutheran teachers; outwardly, however, the council always made a show of its servile loyalty to the monarch.

Lutheran Preachers and "Agitators"

The Olomouc bishops were naturally agitated by the activities of non-Catholic preachers in the city. After the middle of the sixteenth century their random appearance in Olomouc was replaced by the targeted efforts of the non-Catholic council to gain official and permanent ministers. The council first tried to install a suitable candidate at the free parish church of the Virgin Mary in Předhradí and at the church of St Blaise (from where the aforementioned ministers Adler and Kyncl had been expelled). This effort was not just made towards the bishops; prior to 1560 the council also turned to the vice-chamberlain, Governor Ferdinand of Tirol and Emperors Ferdinand I and Maximilian II. A delegation "from the mayor, councillors and community" dispatched from the Olomouc land diet was sent directly to the emperor to request permission for a non-Catholic minister.[58] The city council had earlier rationalised this effort, pointing to the poor quality of the Catholic clergy who "prefer pubs and village taverns over the church ... and because of their bad example do no good". Olomouc Bishop Mark Kuen rejected these plans by the city council and labelled non-Catholic candidates "not preachers but debauchers and agitators". Moreover, he designated all of the requests by city council manifestations of insurrection against the monarch, warning that they would be "broken" for their disloyalty.[59] City representatives did not care for the bishops' steadfast approach any more than their persistent complaints to the vice-chamberlain and monarch. They logically saw it as misguided interference

55. MZA, G 83, Kopiář XXV., 1587, inv. no. 178, cart. no. 51, fol. 90/3-4; Holinková, *Dvě studie*, p. 39.

56. MZA, G 83, Kopiář XXIV, 1586, cart. no 50, inv. no. 177, fol. 80.

57. Stanislav Zela, *Náboženské poměry*, p. 74; MZA, G 83, Kopiář XXVII, 1589, inv. no. 180, cart. no. 53, fol. 189-191.

58. Zela, *Náboženské poměry*, appendix no. 7, pp. 168-169.

59. *Ibid.*, pp. 58-62, 65, n. 258; MZA, G 83, Kopiář II, 1560, inv. no. 160, cart. no. 36, fol. 52-54, 67.

into internal city matters with the aim of "dragging them before the emperor with hatred". The bishop deemed city council's behaviour as "mocking, unchristian defamation".[60] The legal framework of these demands was accompanied by unrest. As a result of the bishop's rejection of the request for a non-Catholic preacher, Olomouc Lutherans raided the church of St Blaise and the church of the Virgin Mary in Předhradí several times in 1564, disrupting Mass by singing Lutheran songs and other disorderly conduct. The raiders were not just lower class radicals; they also included members of the city council.[61]

After 1560, following unsuccessful negotiations with the bishop over use of several parish churches, the city council's attention focused on the construction of a new cemetery church outside the city walls. They declared that the church would be "their own", meaning beyond the control of the bishop. They openly anticipated that their "evangelical preacher" would be able to work unhindered. The city council submitted this request to practice the Lutheran faith during Emperor Maximilian II's visit to Olomouc in 1563.[62] Similarly, in 1574, Bishop John Grodecký (bishop 1572-74) anxiously informed the vice-chamberlain that Olomouc citizens had asked him for a minister who would "adhere to the Augsburg Confession during church services and preaching".[63] Eleven years later Bishop Pavlovský warned the vice-chamberlain of the misguided intention of Olomouc citizens to build a cemetery church in one of the suburbs and to install a preacher of their own.[64] It is interesting how the city council continued to try to achieve these aims by legal means, as documented by the same requests to the bishops between 1587 and 1608 to practice their non-Catholic faith.[65] This was in fact the strategy taken by non-Catholic communities in many central European cities. A cemetery church of this kind could thus become the lone tolerated space for the religious practices of non-Catholics. Due to strong opposition from Bishop Pavlovský and Bishop Dietrichstein, however, this never occurred in Olomouc.[66]

Olomouc non-Catholics compensated for the absence of a permanent preacher by travelling to services in nearby cities and villages with non-Catholic owners (Šternberk, Prostějov, Tršice, Velká Bystřice).[67] The bishops were naturally not pleased. Bishop Kuen described a Lutheran convert and priest Havel of Mohelnice who was serving in Šternberk: "the Lutherans steal many people from Olomouc and from our flock". The appeal of these preachers energised the

60. Zela, *Náboženské poměry*, pp. 58-62, 67.

61. MZA, G 83, Kopiář II, 1560, cart. no. 36, inv. no. 160, fol. 71; Zela, *Náboženské poměry*, pp. 112, 116-117.

62. Dudík, *Olmützer Sammel-Chronik*, p. 31; Válka, *Dějiny Moravy*, vol. II, p. 54.

63. ZAO-O, AO, Kopiář 1576, sign. 14, inv. no. 77, fol. 6r-v.

64. MZA, G 83, Kopiář XXII, 1585, inv. no. 175, cart. 48, fol. 599.

65. MZA, G 83, Kopiář XXV, 1587, cart. no. 51, inv. no. 178 fol. 90; ZAO-O, MCO, documents, inv. no. 1090, sign. B II b 17/2.

66. Václav Nešpor, *Dějiny Olomouce*, Brno, Muzejní spolek v Brně, 1936 (repr. Olomouc, Votobia, 1998), pp. 130-132; Jan Tenora and Josef Foltynovský, *Bl. Jan Sarkander. Jeho doba, život a blahoslavení*, Olomouc, 1920, pp. 87-88.

67. Dudík, *Olmützer Sammel-Chronik*, p. 31.

Olomouc non-Catholic community and Kuen warned against "discord" and possible unrest in Olomouc.[68] Bishop Francis of Dietrichstein also struggled against the practice of travelling to non-Catholic services outside the city.[69]

Olomouc non-Catholics could also attend services performed by secretly practising non-Catholic clerics. In 1560 two ministers from Hungary held services and baptisms (including for large numbers of children) in a city house, despite protests by the bishop and vice-chamberlain. As usual, city council denied that the ministers were active in the city.[70] Non-Catholic preachers were active even in Catholic institutions – at the Hradisko Monastery and with the Dominicans, where the prior was allegedly forced by the city council to allow the preaching.[71] The secret activities of Lutheran clerics can be followed throughout the second half of the sixteenth and beginning of the seventeenth century. Burghers housed the preachers and took collections on their behalf. Preachers were also introduced to city council along with requests for permission to stay in the city. The bishops continually appealed to the emperor for obedience among the burghers, referencing the imperial decree forbidding non-Catholic preaching in the city.[72] Nevertheless, secret worship and preaching in the homes of burghers continued, as is evident in the complaint by Bishop Pavlovský to the vice-chamberlain in 1580: "several individuals from this Lutheran sect hold meetings and preach in one townhouse in Olomouc".[73] This activity could never be eliminated, and the city council in its letters to the bishops always denied its existence and trivialised the situation despite their threats that, as was the case in 1556-58, they would again fall into the disfavour of the monarch.[74] On the other hand, the city council never officially accepted these wandering preachers without permission from the bishop, so as to avoid possible prosecution.[75] Preserved reports document that the activity of non-Catholic clerics was continual in Olomouc and that the bishops were essentially powerless to do anything against it. Despite the secret character of non-Catholic worship and the occurrence of preachers, it is evident that the bishops had a good grasp of the situation thanks to a network of Catholic informers in the city.

68. MZA, G 83, Kopiář I, 1559, cart. no. 35, inv. no. 159, fol. 30, 94; *ibid.*, Kopiář II, 1560, cart. no. 36, inv. no. 160, fol. 166-168.

69. Cf. the next chapter. Also, Nešpor, *Dějiny Olomouce*, p. 126. For an exemplary description of this practice in Austria, see Benjamin J. Kaplan, *Divided by Faith. Religious Conflict and the Practice of Toleration in Early Modern Europe*, Cambridge, MA and London, Belknap, 2007, pp. 144-171.

70. Zela, *Náboženské poměry*, pp. 68-69; MZA, G 83, Kopiář II, 1560, cart. no. 36, inv. no. 160, fol. 423.

71. Zdeněk Kašpar, "Prameny k dějinám Olomouce 16. století v kopiářích olomouckých biskupů IV", *Olomoucký archivní sborník*, 2 (2004), pp. 190-203: 191; MZA, G 83, Kopiář VI, 1564, cart. no. 39, inv. no. 164, 12 December; Zela, *Náboženské poměry*, pp. 118-119.

72. ZAO-O, AO, Kopiář 1567, inv. no. 60, sign. 8, fol. 2v.

73. MZA, G 83, Kopiář XVII, 1579-1580, cart. no. 43, inv. no. 169, fol. 68/7-8.

74. MZA, G 83, Kopiář XXIV, 1586, cart. no. 50, inv. no. 177, fol. 119.

75. Alois Vojtěch Šembera, *Paměti a znamenitosti města Olomouce*, Vienna, 1861, no. XXVII, pp. 141-142.

The Death of Georg Thaller in 1570 and non-Catholic Burials in Olomouc

The burial of non-Catholic burghers was another point of contention in bi-confessional Olomouc that collided with the bishop's authority.[76] The situation was expressed by Bishop Stanislaus Pavlovský at the beginning of his time in office in 1580, when he emphatically requested that non-Catholics "be separated from us after death and that they not be buried at our sacred sites".[77] Pavlovský was referring to the customary burial of non-Catholic burghers at local parish churches, especially the church of St Maurice. The Lutheran community tried through the city council to acquire other land for burial, primarily in the garden of the Observant Franciscan friary. Nevertheless, the main interest of local non-Catholics remained their own cemetery church with a pastor in the suburb. This request was entirely unacceptable for the bishops and was rejected by Francis of Dietrichstein.[78]

A greatest conflict arose in October 1570 when Bishop Prusinovský prohibited the burial of a prominent Lutheran burgher, merchant Georg Thaller, at the church of St Maurice.[79] Thaller made no secret of his Lutheran faith. A year before his death he invited Jan Kyncl, a cleric expelled from the city, to the wedding of his brother-in-law, much to the disdain of the bishop.[80] Following Thaller's death the bishop therefore ironically informed the city council that if they wished, they could bury anyone they liked at the city hall or in their home, but "churches, graveyards and sacred places under the administration of the bishop do not belong to the mayor and the city councillors".[81] The city council again viewed the attitude of the bishop as an entirely unacceptable violation of order and general peace and sent its own delegation to his residence. The talks must have been dramatic and city council representatives warned the bishop against unrest in the city. The bishop himself commented on the process by saying that the non-Catholics threatened his life: "I patiently endured everything from them. Whereupon I said that it is easier for me to fall into the hands of man than of God. They wanted to chop me to pieces for not allowing Thaller's burial, and if killing me is what they wish, they have the power to do so".[82] It is clear at this point that as a proper post-Tridentine bishop he saw the situation as an (unutilised) opportunity for martyrdom and his transformation into a typical Counter-Reformation saint. All the same, Thaller was buried at the church of St Maurice. Bishop Prusinovský immediately ordered the exhumation of the body (which was not done) and declared an interdict over Olomouc. For the city it meant a nearly year-long ban on the burial of non-Catholics. The situation was only calmed by the

76. In general Craig Koslofsky, "Honour and Violence in German Lutheran Funerals in the Confessional Age", *Social History*, 20 (1995), pp. 315-337; Penny Roberts, "Contesting Sacred Space: Burial Disputes in Sixteenth-century France", in *The Place of Dead: Death and Remembrance in Late Medieval and Early Modern Europe*, ed. by Bruce Gordon and Peter Marshall, Cambridge, Cambridge University Press, 2000, pp. 131-148.

77. MZA, G 83, Kopiář XVIII, 1580, inv. no. 170, cart. no. 44, fol. 274.

78. Nešpor, *Dějiny Olomouce*, pp. 130-132; Tenora and Foltynovský, *Bl. Jan Sarkander*, pp. 87-88.

79. Kašpar, "Prameny k dějinám Olomouce V", pp. 178-192: 185-186.

80. *Ibid.*

81. *Ibid.*, pp. 188-192.

82. ZAO-O, AO, Kopiář, sign. 10, inv. no. 66, fol. 219v.

efforts of an imperial commission.[83] During this time non-Catholics were buried outside the city walls and at surrounding sites, often distant.[84] Customary burials were not re-established in Olomouc until 1571. According to the testimony of a Lutheran chronicler the lifting of the ban was also welcomed by the Catholic clergy, who could again "ring the bells and bury, regardless of whether it was a Lutheran or a Zwinglian, just as long as they were paid".[85] Bishop Prusinovský did not change his attitude towards the council. He informed city council that he would continue to block the burial "of individuals confused in faith who despised us and the priesthood during their life in Olomouc". He called for council members to follow the correct (Catholic) faith of their ancestors.[86] It is remarkable that the only important surviving sepulchral monument from the non-Catholic burgher community of the sixteenth century in Olomouc is precisely Thaller's epitaph with its distinctive Lutheran iconography. The monument, still preserved inside the church of St Maurice, is a visible manifestation of how even the power of the strongest bishop was limited in the urban environment.[87]

Figure 17: Olomouc, St Maurice church, epitaph of Georg Thaller, 1572.

The bishops continued to cautiously follow attempts to bury non-Catholics at the church of St Maurice. Their familiarity with the faith of individual burghers is interesting. In July 1577 Bishop John Mezon informed the vice-chamberlain that the chapter had told him of the intention to bury burgher Hans Hirsch, "one great and confused heretic". The bishop urged the vice-chamberlain to pacify city council to prevent unrest in the city.[88] Non-Catholic burials in the city continued in the garden of the Franciscan friary, where they were tolerated even by the bishops. The deceased were also transported to nearby Šternberk, to the Lutheran domain of the lords of Berka of Dubá.[89] The situation for local non-Catholics remained unsatisfactory

83. Kux, *Geschichte von Olmütz*, p. 8.
84. Kux, "Von der Reformation bis zur Gegenreformation", p. 8.
85. Dudík, *Olmützer Sammel-Chronik*, p. 35.
86. ZAO-O, AO, Kopiář 1571, sign. 11, inv. no. 68, fol. 31r-v.
87. Hana Myslivečková, "Epitafy v renesanční sepulkrální sochařské tvorbě Moravy a českého Slezska", in *Ku věčné památce. Malované renesanční epitafy v českých zemích*, ed. by Ondřej Jakubec, Olomouc, Muzeum umění Olomouc, 2007, pp. 73-81: 78.
88. ZAO-O, AO, Kopiář 1577, inv. no. 79, sign. 15, fol. 68v-69r.
89. MZA, G 83, Kopiář XXVI, 1588, inv. no. 179, cart. no, 52, fol. 133.

however. Their request to the monarch at the land diet in Olomouc in 1610 sought permission for burials at the church of St Maurice and tolerance for non-Catholic funerals with the singing of psalms and other specific rituals.[90] The hostile attitude of the Olomouc bishops toward non-Catholic burials also produced tension and difficult circumstances at city churches. However, this was understandable; a funeral was a public ceremony that according to the expectations of the bishops had to be conducted according to Catholic ritual in a royal city.[91]

Disciplining of Religious Life in Olomouc

The bishops' confessional policies included more targeted and detailed measures focused on the religious life of city residents, especially its public presentation. The bishops came closest to the principle of confessional discipline in requiring of the local burghers a proper "Catholic life" concerning: participation in Mass, celebration of feast days, fasting and active participation in Catholic religious life. Given the large non-Catholic community it is not difficult to imagine how many forms of religious non-conformist behaviour of individuals and groups (guilds) provided a pretext for the bishops' frequent complaints. Even in this case the main line of the bishops' religious policy involved negotiation with vice-chamberlains and other Catholic officials (high chancellor, vice-chancellor, high burgrave) so that pressure on the Olomouc council led to the punishment of local burghers who defied Catholic religious customs. At the same time, the bishops' close familiarity with conditions in the city meant that; they were often able to present lists of problematic individuals against whom the city council was then asked to intervene. During the period in which its denominational profile was non-Catholic the city council reacted with the same tactic of denial.

The bishops were especially displeased by the weak attendance of burghers at Mass and, conversely, their participation in non-Catholic ceremonies. They were also annoyed by the decline in mandatory payments, especially from guilds, for various liturgical activities and ceremonies. The defection of part of the city community to the Reformation was also accompanied by a loosening of fasting rules during Advent and Lent. The Olomouc bishops sharply criticised the frequently ostentatious and provocative transgressions against Catholic rules – not observing a fast and inappropriate behaviour during fasting periods such as weddings and other celebrations.[92] They exhorted the city council to take action against drunks "who are a new, angry sect screaming against God's services" and who not only publicly offended during religious feast days but also commited blasphemy and slander against Catholicism.[93]

90. Nešpor, *Dějiny Olomouce*, p. 128, n. 3.
91. Kux, "Von der Reformation bis zur Gegenreformation", p. 13.
92. MZA, G 83, Kopiář nesign. 1556, inv. no. 157, cart. no. 33, fol. 257.
93. MZA, G 83, Kopiář II, 1560, inv. no. 160, cart. no 36, fol. 205-206.p

The most blatant expression of confessional disobedience by Olomouc residents was the collective boycott of key Catholic celebrations, especially processions during the feast of Corpus Christi. Many burghers, councillors and guilds stopped participating from the middle of the sixteenth century, drawing a sharp reaction from the bishops. This culminated in the 1580s with a sophisticated political campaign by Bishop Pavlovský involving land and court officials. The resulting pressure and orders from the vice-chamberlain induced many burghers to at least attend the processions. Based on the bishops' reports the number of participants rose, though many citizens still refused to attend. Stanislaus Pavlovský made no secret of his radical position when High Burgrave Vilém of Rožmberk suggested the demonstrative expulsion of the main culprits from the city and insisted on their harsh punishment.[94] Some non-Catholic radicals refused to obey, including city scribe Štěpán Kučera, who "apparently said that he would rather lose his property and neck than attend the procession".[95] It is not surprising that the bishop again took an individual's absence as a trivialisation of the monarch's authority, i.e. as a revolt against the establishment. This traditional argument provoked legitimate concerns and compelled many non-Catholics to conform religiously. These conflicts are a good indication of how ritualised forms of religious behaviour – in the sense of participation or refusal of participation – became the cornerstone of confessional identity.

The Confessional Topography of Olomouc and Its Visual Manifestations

The issue of confessional conflict is enriched by sources that expand on official documents and personal correspondence. These include works of art, architecture and other visual representations. In some artistic monuments it is possible to perceive expressions of a joint identity in a specific community or, contrast, differentiation from other "confessional cultures", to borrow a term from Thomas Kaufmann.[96] The role of urban artistic monuments and "confessional spatial structures" is of great symbolic and practical importance. After all, works of art and spatial topographies are not merely passive illustrations of historical texts or reflections of the socio-cultural and religious context; they are an autonomous agent in the formation of this context. As such, they are useful sources for interpreting the confessional situation in Olomouc. If, as for example, Heinz Schilling claims that "architectural sterility and invariability" prevailed in Protestant towns while Catholic sacred architecture represented distinctive islands with imaginative new forms,[97] then it would seem that Olomouc confirmed this definition. A

94. MZA, G 83, Kopiář XXXIV, 1597, inv. no. 187, cart. no. 59, fol. 496; *ibid.*, Kopiář nesign., inv. no. 168, cart. no. 42, fol. 103.

95. MZA, G 83, Kopiář nesign., cart. no. 42, inv. no. 168, fol. 67.

96. Thomas Kaufmann, *Dreißigjähriger Krieg und Westfälischer Friede. Kirchengeschichtliche Studien zur lutherischen Konfessionskultur*, Tübingen, Mohr, J.C.B., (Paul Siebeck), 1998.

97. Heinz Schilling, "Die konfessionelle Stadt – eine Problemskizze", in *Historische Anstöße. Festschrift für Wolfgang Reinhard zum 65. Geburtstag am 10. April 2002*, ed. by Peter Burschel, Berlin, Akademie Verlag, 2002, pp. 60-83.

certain "confessionality" of the architectural topography is apparent in Olomouc, especially in the Catholic environment.[98]

It is noteworthy that from the very beginning there was a duality of the actual city and Předhradí, a section fully dominated in the Early Modern period by its ecclesiastical function. This function was demonstrated by several monasteries, the Jesuit Academy, the bishop's and canons' residences with their yards, dwellings for the lower clergy and St Wenceslas Cathedral, all grouped in a small area. In this environment the church's role was not just applied practically; local construction also acquired substantial symbolic potential in the pre-White Mountain period.[99] The Olomouc Předhradí actually bolstered its insular character in this period. The symbol of this city section was the tall St Wenceslas Cathedral, which underwent substantial reconstruction around the year 1600. Bishop Pavlovský built an ostentatious family funeral chapel, and the cathedral acquired a monumental façade imitating, in a three-tower form, a Romanesque façade. The inscription above the main entrance directly beckoned local Lutherans to convert: "As a kind mother opens her arms to converts, let the lost souls return to the Church of Christ".[100] The monumental crown set on the tower also vividly celebrated the symbolic triumph of Catholicism.

Cardinal Francis of Dietrichstein proceeded similarly by building a new monumental chancel in the cathedral intended to include space for relics of Sts Cyril and Methodius, the ninth-century missionaries believed to have brought Christianity to Moravia. The reference of Catholic authorities to this historical legitimacy and Catholic tradition became a significant argument in confessional debate. An interesting augmentation of this historicising sense was St Anne's church near the cathedral, reconstructed in a mannerist vein by Provost Martin of Greiffenthal in cooperation with Bishop Francis at the beginning of the seventeenth century.[101] It was more than just an interesting building impressively dominating the adjacent space of the square on the cathedral hill with a consciously preserved historicising form. The "life" and function of this building were leading forces in the renewal of the cult of traditional local saint, St Anne, which had taken hold at the site in the

98. Anna Ohlidal, "Kirchenbau in der multikonfessionellen Stadt. Zur konfessionellen Prägung und Besetzung des städtischen Raums in den Prager Städten um 1600", in *Stadt und Religion in der Frühen Neuzeit. Soziale Ordnungen und ihre Repräsentationen*, ed. by Vera Isaiasz, Frankfurt am Main, Campus, 2007, pp. 79-80; Kai Wenzel, "Abgrenzung durch Annäherung – Überlegungen zu Kirchenbau und Malerie in Prag im Zeitalter der Konfessionalisierung", *Bohemia*, 44 (2003), pp. 29-66.

99. Ondřej Jakubec, "Confessional Aspects of the Art Patronage of the Bishops of Olomouc in the Period before the White Mountain Battle", *Acta Historiae Artium*, 47 (2006), pp. 121-127.

100. The inscription read: "Reddat aberrantes ut Christo ecclesia natos pandit conversis mater amanda sinum. MDXCV". Mořic Kráčmer, *Dějiny metropolitního chrámu sv. Václava v Olomouci*, Olomouc, R. Prombergr, 1887, p. 66.

101. Ondřej Jakubec, "Kaple sv. Anny na Olomouckém hradě a svatoanenský kult na Moravě kolem roku 1600", in *Arcidiecézní muzeum na Olomouckém hradě / The Archdiocesan Museum at Olomouc Castle. Articles from the International Conference*, ed. by Ondřej Jakubec, Olomouc, Muzeum umění Olomouc, 2010, pp. 197-209.

Figure 18: Olomouc, St. Wenceslas cathedral, 1593.

fourteenth century. The chapel also created an environment for numerous Catholic ceremonies (with conversions) and festivities, especially pilgrimages to Staré Město u Libavé near Olomouc, organised by the local Jesuits.[102] At the same time, remarkable buildings of this type, impressive in both in their architectural form and religious life, support Schilling's aforementioned theory on the ostentatious character of Catholic construction.

The promotion of faith is also reflected in the number of sacred buildings meant to cover an area identical to the scope of bishop's power. This is evident in the bishop's construction strategy. At the end of his time as bishop, Pavlovský evaluated his support for the renewal of churches in the diocese: "holy religion is being renewed in this region through the gift of God, and new churches are being built".[103] Consecration became a forum for confessionally distinctive and

102. Ondřej Jakubec, "Poutní místa, poutě a milostné obrazy v mecenátu a politice olomouckých biskupů raného novověku. Několik poznámek k poznání konfesionalizačních praktik na předbělohorské Moravě", in *Pielgrzymowanie i sztuka. Góra Świętej Anny i inne miejsca pielgrzymkowe na Śląsku*, ed. by Joanna Lubos-Kozieł, Wrocław, Uniwersytet Wrocławski, 2005, pp. 307-321; Ondřej Jakubec, "Konfesionalizace a rituály potridentského katolicismu na předbělohorské Moravě", in *Per saecula ad tempora nostra. Sborník prací k 60. narozeninám prof. Jaroslava Pánka*, ed. by Jiří Mikulec and Miloslav Polívka, Prague, Historický ústav AV ČR, 2007, pp. 360-366.

103. MZA, G 83, Kopiář nesign., fol. 279, 287. On the construction strategy of the bishops, see Ondřej Jakubec, *Kulturní prostředí a mecenát olomouckých biskupů potridentské doby: Umělecké objednávky biskupů v letech 1553-1598, jejich význam a funkce*, Olomouc, Univerzita Palackého, 2003, pp. 110-115, 134-139. On the consecration of buildings by Bishop Dietrichstein, see their listing, ZAO-O, ACO, ms. 109b, pp. 437-444.

promotional acts – pilgrimages, confirmations, preaching and the activity of Jesuits. There is a great deal of evidence for the consecration of sacred buildings, especially by Bishop Pavlovský, and it is possible that their ceremonial consecration combined with the announcement of indulgences was used as a convenient form of propaganda.[104]

One of the most visible new Catholic institutions in the city was the Jesuit Academy founded in the 1560s with strong support from Bishop William Prusinovský. In 1573 it acquired the status of a university. Funded by the bishops and constructed by Italian builders, the academy's monumental form and architectural quality were new and impressive. An equally visible part of the Jesuit strategy was their educational, pastoral and religious activities. Therefore, when Bishop Pavlovský wrote to Jesuit Superior General Claudio Acquaviva about the local academy in 1586, he emphasised in particular its importance for *propaganda Catholica Religione*.[105] It is therefore not surprising that even in Olomouc the Jesuits became a pillar of the bishops' confessionalisation policy, along with being a source of tension in the city.[106] The local Lutheran chronicler noted with concern the arrival of the Jesuits in 1566: "they have suddenly spread like weeds through the land".[107] The city council opposed the expansion of the Jesuit complex of buildings, and construction work resulted in numerous problems.[108] For example, the city refused to sell certain neighbouring houses and land in the bailey, and Bishop Pavlovský was forced to turn to both the vice-chamberlain and Emperor Rudolf himself.[109] The bishops also defended the freedom of the academy; for example, Bishop Pavlovský protested against the imprisonment of a student on orders from the mayor, which apparently was in conflict with university privileges. The bishop felt that the "council was mocking us as the head of the academy".[110] In fact, similar conflicts arose between the academic and city communities throughout the academy's history.

In addition to the established academy and the broad activities of the Jesuits in Moravia, their "mission" produced entirely new forms of post-Tridentine proto-baroque culture with a special "Jesuit style" or approach. The basic feature of this new style was its distribution of religious work to the community of lay

104. ZAO-O, ACO, ms. 109a, fol. 487-516.

105. ZAO-O, AO, Kopiář 1586, inv no. 97, sign. 23, fol. 49r-50r.

106. Most recently on the Jesuit Academy, see *Jezuitský konvikt. Sídlo uměleckého centra Univerzity Palackého v Olomouci. Dějiny – Stavební a umělecké dějiny – Obnova a využití*, ed. by Jiří Fiala, Leoš Mlčák and Karel Žurek, Olomouc, Univerzita Palackého, 2002. On the relationship between the Olomouc bishops and the academy and their support for its exhibitions, see Ondřej Jakubec, *Kulturní prostředí a mecenát*, pp. 225-229, 261-264; Zdeněk Kašpar, "V době předbělohorské", in *Olomouc. Malé dějiny města*, ed. by Jindřich Schulz, Olomouc, Univerzita Palackého, 2002, s. 93-110: 99-100.

107. Dudík, *Olmützer Sammel-Chronik*, p. 34.

108. ZAO-O, AO, Kopiář 1571, inv. no. 68, sign. 11, fol. 221r; Kopiář 1572, inv. no. 69, sign. 12, fol. 133v-134r, 135v; MZA, G 83, Kopiář XXI, 1584, cart. no. 47, inv. no. 174, 28. 12.

109. MZA, G 83, Kopiář XXIV, 1586, cart. no. 50, inv. no. 177, fol. 269, 698-699; Kopiář XXVI., 1588, cart. no. 52, inv. no. 179, fol. 375.

110. MZA, G 83, Kopiář XXVI., 1588, cart. no. 52, inv. no. 179, fol. 520.

faithful in unique forms that satisfied their spiritual needs. The Jesuits also organised celebrations, including pilgrimages to the church of St Anne in Libavá outside Olomouc. And they played an essential role in Corpus Christi processions in Olomouc. The Jesuits likewise organised a wide range of religious theatre performances and built mangers and the Holy Sepulchre.

The Jesuits were also known for organising religious confraternities. Their attractive offer of community devotion was a suitable form of "missionary" activities through which they were able to attract the faithful through membership and public presentations. These groups, as prominent centres of lay piety, were attractive because they offered "alternative liturgy", characterized by popular baroque devotion and grand public celebrations. As many as five sodalities (some sources mention only three) were formed at the Olomouc academy in the pre-White Mountain period: The Visitation of the Virgin Mary (1575), The Assumption of the Virgin Mary (1580), Mary the Queen of Angels (1591), The Annunciation of the Virgin Mary (1607) and The Queen of the Angels (1607). Three others were formed in the post-White Mountain period: Dedication to the Virgin Mary, The Immaculate Conception of the Virgin Mary and St Isidore, and The Virgin Mary at the Manger (1630, 1635). With their active presence and expressions of piety (self-discipline, asceticism, self-flagellation), members of the urban religious confraternities were a type of "pious militia" manifesting their "confessional monopoly" of salvation in a manner characteristic of the period.[111] At the same time, their pronounced Marian devotion had a deep confessional subtext in the post-Tridentine period that set them apart from non-Catholic faiths and their followers. In predominantly non-Catholic Olomouc these extreme expressions of Catholic piety created tension, and the Jesuits and confraternity members often faced attacks from non-Catholics. Testifying to their perception of these festivities is an entry in the Lutheran Kranich Chronicles that in 1580 makes derisive reference to the first Mass of the Olomouc Brotherhood of St Anne at which "everyone took only bread at Communion and served an oath while holding a green candle. Many lunatics gathered for this spectacle".[112]

Ceremonies and rituals were important aspects of the material presentation of Catholicism. Therefore – although church authorities took a sharp stand against the lack of discipline, disobedience and participation of non-Catholics at these rituals – efforts were made to organise and present them as best as possible. The gatherings of elite members of the Catholic community through Catholic rituals, often organised by the Olomouc bishops beginning in the 1570s, changed into manifestations of confessional conviction and served as both indoctrination and expression of confessional loyalty and allegiance. Against the background of bi-confessional Olomouc and its Lutheran population, these activities also served as clear manifestations of Catholic culture. The activities often included sermons by interesting Catholic priests, Jesuit plays, fairs, Corpus Christi processions and,

111. Zdeněk Orlita, "Olomoučtí jezuité a náboženská bratrstva v 16.-18. století", *Střední Morava*, no. 20 (2005), pp. 43-54.

112. Dudík, *Olmützer Sammel-Chronik*, p. 38.

perhaps most interesting, public conversions. It was these conversions that documented the deepening polarisation of the denominational camps.[113]

It would be impossible to claim that the bishops were unsuccessful. One prominent conversion involved Nicolas of Hrádek, vice-chamberlain and an important ally of Bishop Pavlovský. The bishops used both Jesuit missions and special clerics certified to perform conversions.[114] Pavlovský also oversaw the work of the parish clergy and requested lists of converts.[115] A Jew was baptised at the church of St Maurice in Olomouc before 1570, an event viewed as a ceremony manifesting the confessional solidarity of the minority Catholic community.[116] As such, the Olomouc bishops controlled a broad range of customary confessionalisation instruments as forms of indoctrination both inside and outside the city: preaching, education, fine art, music, theatre and literature and print were all used as a propaganda tool *par excellence*.[117] Confessionalisation practices were also closely linked to ceremonies, either of a purely personal nature that took place in narrow social circles (baptisms, weddings, funerals) and those that were more ritualised (the consecration of churches, public conversions and mass confirmation, pilgrimages, processions). From the perspective of the bishops these ritualised gatherings often aimed at strengthening confessional-political alliances and improving the confessional confidence of the participants. Moreover, while these ceremonies were mostly organised from above by the Olomouc bishops, the forms of devotional practices, religious behaviour and rituals were based on the broader Catholic layers between which a certain process of self-confessionalisation took place. Therefore, confessionalisation in pre-White Mountain Moravia was manifested both as pressure from above and as a conscious choice.[118] In fact, even among Olomouc burghers there was a group of prominent Catholics such as Wenzel Edelmann who systematically worked to strengthen ties with the Olomouc church authorities. Edelmann also worked well with the Olomouc community, as evidenced by his high posts in the city government.

The studied communication and confrontational axis between the bishop and the city is documented well in available sources. But perhaps they overly ac-

113. Hrubý, "Moravská šlechta", p. 124; Jörg Deventer, "Grenzen überschreiten. Konversionen zum Katholizismus in Böhmen und Schlesien im späten 16. und im 17. Jahrhundert", in *Náboženský život a církevní poměry v zemích Koruny české ve 14.-17. století*, ed. by Lenka Bobková and Jana Konvičná, Prague, Filozofická fakulta Univerzity Karlovy v Praze, Casablanca, 2009, pp. 670-682.

114. Jakubec, *Kulturní prostředí a mecenát*, pp. 72-75, 85-91, 126

115. MZA, G 83, Kopiář XXVIII, 1590, fol. 100.

116. VKOL, sign. II 32. 070, Tomáš Bavorovský, *Postylla Česká aneb Kázání a vejklady na Evangelia*, Olomouc, 1557, note in pen on the inside of the back cover. The *terminus ante quem* is the year 1570.

117. Wolfgang Reinhard, "Was ist katholische Konfessionalisierung?" in *Die katholische Konfessionalisierung*, ed. by Wolfgang Reinhard and Heinz Schilling, Gütersloh, Verein für Reformationsgeschichte, 1995, pp. 419-452: 429.

118. Marc Forster, *The Counter-Reformation in the Villages. Religion and Reform in the Bishopric of Speyer, 1560-1720*, Ithaca and London, Cornell University Press, 1992, p. 5; Ondřej Jakubec, "'Sebekonfesionalizace' a manifestace katolicismu jako projev utváření konfesní uniformity na předbělohorské Moravě", *Acta Universitatis Palackianae Olomucensis. Historica*, 31 (2003), pp. 101-119.

centuate conflict and suggest that Olomouc was merely a passive target for the bishops' complaints and the object of their manipulative confessional and blatantly re-Catholicisation policies. The city and its non-Catholic community and elite were naturally active agents of their own interests, including a confessional policy. The city was not just interested in satisfying the liturgical needs of the non-Catholic community (preachers, church, burials); it also provided schools. These city schools served as the primary locus of Lutheran confessionalisation or self-confessionalisation (internal confessionalisation of the Lutheran community may also have taken place as part of city charity institutions or within guilds).

Pressure from the bishops definitely did not render Olomouc a confessionally uniform city. Their systematic pressure led to the "Catholicisation" of certain city institutions, especially the city council. As was the case elsewhere,[119] a large part of the Olomouc population remained non-Catholic and found for its religious life (worship, burials, etc.) a certain *modus vivendi* realised privately or beyond the borders of the city. This part of the population hoped for the legalisation and institutionalisation of its confession and perhaps worked toward the creation of a "communal church". Likewise, the temporary departure of Lutherans from the city council and other positions within city administration and government did not mean that their influence disappeared. Relationships between members of the Lutheran community and the ruling elite, their influence on conditions in the city thanks to their "networking", and their views toward changing the conditions definitely persisted. In this situation the pressure of the bishops' confessional policies must have been quite ineffective, as is suggested also by the results of unsuccessful disciplinary campaigns in bi-confessional environments.[120]

As in other royal cities,[121] religious tension in the pre-White Mountain period latently persisted in Olomouc. It appeared with renewed intensity in 1610 when the city's non-Catholic community united under a collective strategy and prepared complaints and demands concerning religious matters for the assembly in Olomouc. They again demanded their own church and minister, equal representation on the council and an exemption from unacceptable pledges to the Virgin Mary and All Saints. The situation escalated again when Bishop Dietrichstein instigated the investigation and imprisonment of a number of active non-Catholic burghers whom he then tried to have expelled from city. This approach radicalised the Lutheran community and raised the threat of an open rebellion again after half a century.[122]

119. Miller, *Urban Societies*, p. 200.

120. Thomas Winkelbauer, *Gundaker von Liechtenstein als Grundherr in Niederösterreich und Mähren. Normative Quellen zur Verwaltung und Bewirtschaftung eines Herrschaftskomplexes und zur Reglementierung des Lebens der Untertanen durch einen adeligen Grundherrn sowie zur Organisation des Hofstaats und der Kanzlei eines „Neufürsten" in der ersten Hälfte des 17. Jahrhunderts*, Vienna, Böhlau, 2008, pp. 92-95.

121. Petr Vorel, "Nacionalita a konfese v politickém životě jagellonských Čech (Utváření nového modelu společenské normy prostřednictvím Viléma z Pernštejna)", *Theatrum historiae*, 2 (2007), pp. 71-79: 78.

122. Nešpor, *Dějiny Olomouce*, pp. 130-132.

Figure 19: St Wenceslas as an intercessor of Moravian Catholic church accompanied by Bishop Stanislaus Pavlovský, 1585.

Conclusion

The advance of the German Reformation was clearly visible in the Bohemian lands including Moravia. Even though at its start Olomouc burghers always stressed their Catholic orthodoxy, the majority of the city's population turned to the new trends and tendencies of urban spirituality. Conflicts occurred more frequently among the city dwellers, their representatives, the bishop and secular land authorities. There was a changing power equilibrium that could not yet be stabilised. The Olomouc bishops achieved certain victories in Moravia around the year 1600, and although they were short-lived they provided a sense of satisfaction. As a result, Bishop Pavlovský at the end of his episcopate could proudly declare: "By the gift of God … the number of churches and presbyteries has increased at many places in this diocese, and not even my seminary in Olomouc has enough priests to staff them … holy religion is being renewed in this region and churches are being built again".[123] However, this turnaround mostly concerned the bishop's Catholic domains. For non-Catholic and denominationally mixed areas, including Olomouc, little had changed. Non-Catholic burghers proved to be resistant to pressure from the Catholic authorities and continued to hope for their religious emancipation.

123. MZA, G 83, Kopiář nesign., cart. no. 42, inv. no. 168, fol. 279, 287.

4. The Stormy Path to a Single Religion, 1600-1650

Tomáš Parma

Difficult Continuity: Olomouc in the pre-White Mountain Period

"On the Tuesday after the feast of the Holy Trinity Francis of Dietrichstein arrived in Olomouc, as the newly elected bishop of Olomouc, and was received by the clergy and city council with great fanfare, under a canopy, which was carried by six priests, and was taken into the cathedral church."[1] The arrival of a new bishop in Olomouc was accompanied with church celebrations where the bishop personally carried the Eucharist during the procession of Corpus Christi and preached in the town's main church at vespers. Dietrichstein, however, even during this stay in Olomouc fell afoul of land community representatives who were assembled there in the land court.[2] The bishop was according to established tradition the leading member of this important assembly. The non-Catholic nobility, led by a member of Bohemian Brethren Karel the Elder of Žerotín, emphasised another tradition: meetings taking place exclusively in the Czech language, which Dietrichstein, born in Madrid and raised mostly in a German-speaking environment, managed rather passively. Naturally, Dietrichstein did not allow himself to be outdone by the Moravian non-Catholics in this process; he opposed the acceptance of oaths from the non-Catholic court officials that omitted any mention of the Virgin Mary and all the saints. This Olomouc dispute symbolically opened a period of deepening and intensifying confessional conflicts. In Moravia, traditionally favouring peace and order in the face of religious conflict in the region, this meant the end of the delicate balance described by some historians as "supraconfessional Christianity" (J. Válka).

As one of the two capitals of Moravia, Olomouc (like Brno) was a royal city where clashes between confessions were strongest and relatively well documented. Olomouc was the most populous and probably most economically developed city in Moravia. Although it is difficult to estimate the number of inhabitants (possibly 10-12,000) we know there were 581 houses and 1,562 homes outside the

1. Beda Dudik, ed., *Olmützer Sammel-Chronik vom Jahre 1432 bis 1656*, Brünn, Rohrer, 1858, p. 45.

2. *Spisy Karla staršího ze Žerotína, Oddělení I, Žerotínovi zápisové o soudě panském*, ed. by Vincenc Brandl, Brno, 1866, pp. 236-237.

city walls.[3] Clashes unfolded on several levels. In the urban community there was a traditional level of antagonism among the city council, city municipalities and townspeople. The bishop was obviously a crucial protagonist, but also the sovereign who managed the royal city through the Moravian vice-chamberlain. The estates community and its individual representatives, especially the land captain (*zemský hejtman, capitaneus terrae*), also came into play and used confessional disputes to strengthen their political power. One cannot forget the Catholic institutions in the city. In addition to the cathedral and eleven monasteries there were five other large churches, several hospitals with chapels and at least three smaller detached chapels and churches in the suburbs. The Jesuit college, having the right to confer academic degrees, was probably the most powerful Catholic element in the city, due to the large number both of the Jesuits themselves (about eighty) and their pupils (about a thousand).[4] The latter were brought up in the Catholic faith and organised in their respective elite sodalities.

The new bishop Dietrichstein, who was created cardinal just two months before he became bishop of Olomouc, continued in the line of his predecessors and tried to use his contacts to strengthen Catholic positions in the city. Even before his arrival in Moravia in 1599 his brother Sigismund Dietrichstein, then Moravian vice-chamberlain, ordered the city council and guilds to participate in what was probably the most spectacular expression of Catholic religious life: the Eucharistic procession on the feast of Corpus Christi. Already in 1601 the Cardinal prevented non-Catholics from being buried in churches and consecrated cemeteries; so they were buried in the garden of the Observant Franciscan friary, or in the nearby towns of Šternberk and Litovel.

At the beginning of 1602 Emperor Rudolf II expelled non-Catholic clergy from royal cities and forbade the burghers to follow them.[5] The city council responded to the emperor's command and even named specific persons. This led the emperor to the decree of April 1602 under which people attending non-Catholic worship outside the city had two months to sell their homes and move out of the city.[6] The cardinal also tried to ban the sale of non-Catholic books and even eliminate non-Catholic printers. He achieved, however, only the right to monitor book production.[7] Another blow to Olomouc non-Catholics, almost exclusively Lutherans, occurred during the restoring of the city council in August 1602 when the Supreme Chamberlain Ladislav Berka of Dubá got the order to appoint exclusively Catholics to the council. The council's becoming exclusively Catholic cre-

3. For data for 1619, see František Hrubý, "Moravská šlechta r. 1619, její jmění a náboženské vyznání", *Časopis Matice moravské*, 46 (1922), pp. 107-169: 155.

4. Jiří Fiala, "Jezuitská akademie a univerzita v Olomouci (1573-1773)", in *Univerzita v Olomouci (1573-2009)*, Olomouc, Univerzita Palackého, 2009, p. 33.

5. See Jan Tenora and Josef Foltynovský, *Bl. Jan Sarkander. Jeho doba, život a blahoslavení*, Olomouc, Matice cyrilometodějská, 1920, p. 86. However, the instruction is preserved only for Brno (28 January 1602). For an edition, see Vladimír Burian, *Vývoj náboženských poměrů v Brně*, Brno, ÚNV, 1948, p. 90.

6. SOkA Olomouc, AMO, Sbírka listin, inv. no. 1203. The deadline was extended on 9 August 1602 for an additional four weeks: see *ibid.*, inv. no. 1209.

7. Tenora and Foltynovský, *Bl. Jan Sarkander*, p. 87.

ated another source of tension between the council and the residents of the city.[8] This is understandable since most of the urban community at the time was apparently non-Catholic, predominantly of the Augsburg Confession. A list of Catholic burghers from 1602 counted a total of 172 people as Catholics.[9] Interventions against the non-Catholics of Olomouc can be put into the broader context of the political struggle against non-Catholics in Moravia: in 1602 the leader of the non-Catholic party, Karel the Elder of Žerotín, was relieved of his magistracy as the land judge and with it the possibility of influencing official policy of the estates. The highest provincial officials were exclusively Catholic.

After Easter 1603 the bishop abolished permission to receive communion under both kinds in the whole diocese. For non-Catholic Moravians this meant new limits on the ability to participate covertly in their religion. The strict regulation of the time of Rudolf II allowed Olomouc burghers at least some non-Catholic worship in one case: when the land court, diet or congress was in session in Olomouc (theoretically twice a year). Non-Catholic nobility were allowed to have preachers conduct private worship in their city houses,[10] and this situation could be used by the burghers to their advantage.

The year 1608 marked the culmination of a dispute between the Habsburg brothers Rudolf and Matthias, known as *Bruderzwist.* Rudolf, in an attempt to win over Dietrichstein among others, restored the Olomouc bishop's right to mint his own coins. This was a great economic advantage.[11] Under the peace treaties in Libeň on 25 June 1608 Matthias became successor of Rudolf to the Czech throne – recognised even by the Czech estates and endowed with the administration of Moravia, which was temporarily legally separated from the Bohemian state – and received the Kingdom of Hungary and archduchies of Austria.

Matthias' victory was also a victory for the estates communities in his region. The estates signed a secret memorandum on 29 June stipulating that worship of the new sovereign was contingent on the estates' freedom, especially freedom of confession and religion. In Moravia the next land diet in Olomouc on 15 July 1608 clearly showed how these freedoms were manifested. The diet was convened by the estates themselves. They alone elected Žerotín as the land captain and resolved to eliminate any mention of the Mother of God and all the saints in the oaths of land officials. They even discussed the expulsion of the Jesuits, who in Olomouc held special religious services to avert this danger.[12] Also, the non-

8. For the conflicts between the city council and the inhabitants of the city, see *Dějiny Olomouce*, vol. I, ed. by Jindřich Schulz, Olomouc, Univerzita Palackého, 2009, pp. 279-284 (Jaroslav Miller).

9. SOkA Olomouc, AMO, Zlomky registratur, kart. 20, inv. no. 531.

10. On city houses of the nobility, see *Dějiny Olomouce*, vol. I, pp. 278-279 (Radmila Pavlíčková).

11. Rudolf's privilege on 25 January 1608, cf. Jan Videman and Dan Suchomel, *Mincovnictví olomouckých biskupů a arcibiskupů (1608-1820)*, Kroměříž, ČNS Kroměříž, 1997, esp. pp. 19-22 and 330-331.

12. Joannes Schmidl, *Historiae Societatis Iesu Provincie Bohemiae Pars II.*, Pragae, Typis universitatis Carolo Ferdinandeae in Collegio S. J. Ad S. Clementem, per Jacobum Schweiger Factorem, 1749, p. 516.

Catholics of the Augsburg Confession in the royal cities filed a request to the estates for certain religious liberties: free conduct of Lutheran religion, free building of churches and the possibility of appointing non-Catholics to local city councils.

St Bartholomew's diet of Brno in 1608, which led to the acceptance of Matthias as the margrave, marked the success of the estates in the political sphere. In the religious sphere Matthias promised rather vaguely to preserve everything as his predecessors had done, thus actually maintaining the status quo. The new freedoms for non-Catholics extended only to permitting their presence in city councils and the opportunity to conduct their trades, buy houses and settle in cities. Public expression of Lutheran religion in the royal cities was not allowed.

King Matthias attended another of the land diets, that in Olomouc at the Feast of the Holy Trinity in June 1609. The Catholic party feared further pressure on religious freedoms. The pope even sent Matthias and Cardinal Dietrichstein a special breve on this issue and the diet was attended by the papal nuncio. Matthias stayed in the bishop's palace of Olomouc, attended the Corpus Christi procession and even let it be repeated again. He evasively responded to the requests to permit non-Catholic churches in cities. The estates sought authorisation from the cardinal to hold funeral services for non-Catholics in churches and ring the bells during funerals. When he protested that this required permission of the pope, they asked him to obtain it.[13]

It was Rudolf's Letter of Majesty on religious freedom issued on 9 July 1609 (the effects of which naturally did not apply to Moravia) that triggered Olomouc's non-Catholics to forcefully demand and effectively promote religious freedoms. In the Olomouc diet of January 1610 they asked for approval of a non-Catholic church, a German school, the elimination of the Virgin Mary from oaths, the freedom of non-Catholic funerals, parity representation in the city council and other primarily political freedoms.[14] King Matthias decided to set up a commission to meet in May 1610 to investigate everything. On 16 March 1610 the Olomouc non-Catholics assembled without the express permission of the city council. They voted for twenty-four representatives and entrusted them with the task of negotiating with the royal commission of 15 May 1610. The burghers even released a power of attorney. It was signed and sealed by 519 of them, a majority of the urban population's non-Catholics.[15]

Despite their intensive preparation for the hearing before the royal commission, the discussion did not happen. A few years later this meeting and publication of authorising documents was interpreted by the monarch as an attempted revolt.

13. In the supplication to the pope (sent on 3 November 1609) the cardinal requested permission for communion in both kinds and bell-ringing during the funerals of non-Catholics (BAV, Fondo Boncompagni-Ludovisi, E 12, fol. 38r-39v). It was forwarded to the Holy Office, which rejected both requests but suggested not to issue an official document. It only sent the information to Dietrichstein through the nuncio Marra. This procedure, however, did not appease the estates.

14. SOkA Olomouc, AMO, Knihy, sign. 1562, fol. 347-351.

15. NA Prague, sign. SM R 109/14; ed. by Libuše Spáčilová in Jiří Libor Bílý and Zdeněk Kašpar, *Staromoravští rodové I. Olomoučtí protestanté ve zmocňovací listině z roku 1610 I.*, Ostrava, Key Publishing, 2013, pp. 133-139.

The Olomouc Protestants ascribed their unwillingness to negotiate to the fact that they tried to impose their religious requirements *via facti*. A subsequent revote of representatives along the lines of Rudolf's Imperial Charter elected directors (their number decreased to twelve and then to five) showing that Olomouc non-Catholics had created unofficial administrative structure that in many ways duplicated the function of the Catholic city council.[16]

The next step was to build a Lutheran chapel in the city.[17] In their efforts they were not loudly, but quite emphatically, supported by the land captain Karel the Elder of Žerotín. Since March 1610 Olomouc housed the soldiers of the regiment of Friedrich Tiefenbach. Tiefenbach was a zealous Lutheran who even brought with him a Lutheran preacher to Olomouc. On 1 August 1610 the city council was renewed (new members named), and after a long time non-Catholic members were included. For non-Catholics, however, it represented a disappointment because it was not proportional; in both the retiring and acceding councils there were twenty-two Catholics but only three non-Catholics.

Since the presence of the Tiefenbach regiment was only temporary the non-Catholics wished to ensure their worship permanently. They chose the house of Victorin of Žerotín in Česká Street, near the town's main church of St Maurice and within sight of the town hall on the main square. Here they placed an altar. The house was originally built by Jan Filipec, administrator of the bishopric in the late fifteenth century. On 20 November 1610 they inaugurated the preacher Adam Windörfer, who was originally in the services of Tiefenbach. The procession passed through the square and streets of the town. The preacher (already called the pastor of Olomouc) was accompanied by non-Catholic councillors, burghers and soldiers to the house where on Sunday he preached, celebrated marriages and conducted baptisms. The following Monday the yard was cleared, the trees cut down, the stables demolished and courtyard balconies constructed for the worshippers. The burghers themselves were involved in the construction, supplying materials for free and payment for workers. Already on 9 December the house had a gallery for worshippers, choir, altar and pulpit with canopy. Friedrich of Tiefenbach formally purchased the property from Victorin of Žerotín, but it was clear that it was bought on behalf of Olomouc's Lutheran community. The non-Catholics were supported by Karel the Elder of Žerotín. The land captain, tolerantly ignoring reality, responded evasively to repeated complaints from the cardinal (who was kept informed by the city council) and to requests from the city council itself to keep legal order. The cardinal tried to dismiss the Tiefenbach regiment from Olomouc, which would have enabled a thorough termination of non-Catholic worship. He even offered his silver tableware as payment. The regiment was disbanded before Christmas 1610. The oratory remained

16. Cf. Václav Nešpor, *Dějiny města Olomouce*, Brno, 1936 (repr. Olomouc, Votobia, 1998), p. 131.

17. This event is well documented in the city sources, the *Acta quotidiana* and copybooks sent by the city council to Cardinal Dietrichstein. For excerpts, see Paul Dedic, "Die Geschichte des Protestantismus in Olmütz IV.", *Jahrbuch der Gesellschaft für die Geschichte des Protestantismus im ehemaligen und neuen Österreich*, 55 (1934), pp. 69-112 and Tenora and Foltynovský, *Bl. Jan Sarkander*, pp. 244-271.

without a preacher but non-Catholics continued to assemble. They were being baptised and held services outside the city. The city council had difficulty keeping control. Some undisciplined residents even abused the situation by decrying as religious oppression any disciplinary interference by the council. The cardinal complained to King Matthias and asked him to take decisive action.[18] Matthias, however, concerned with the tense political situation in the region asked the cardinal for patience.

At the beginning of 1613 there was an attempt to establish a permanent Lutheran preacher in the chapel. One was moved to the chapel with his wife and children after the land court when non-Catholics in the city could worship legally. He preached, baptised and celebrated marriages and funeral services. Non-Catholics supplied food, collected alms and remembered the house in their wills. This time the monarch took the cardinal's report seriously, and in February 1613 ordered the city council to send three non-Catholic councillors and five leading Olomouc Lutherans to his court. The Viennese court interpreted the activities as sedition and rebellion. The five directors were arrested and the city was searched for their writings. This caused great unease in the city. Caricatures circulated of the cardinal with mocking verses, and in nearby Šumperk a picture of him was nailed to the gallows.[19] Žerotín began to personally take a stand for the directors arrested at court. His intercession was successful. By the emperor's wishes, however, the chapel was closed and the preacher left the city. The directors were released at the beginning of June 1613. The failure of efforts to establish a chapel and the punishment of the directors meant an end to the presence of non-Catholics in the city council and their official influence on events in the community.

In July 1614 the land diet took place in Olomouc. It was attended by Archduke Ferdinand of Styria. Despite his pleas, non-Catholic preaching was organised in the Tiefenbach house again during the land diet; otherwise it was closed. In the presence of Archduke Ferdinand another event took place: on 20 July 1614, in front of the *Střední* (Middle) gate on the land purchased two days earlier, Cardinal Dietrichstein said mass and erected and blessed a cross. This led to the foundation of Olomouc's Capuchin friary. Construction was carried out until 1619 when the friary was for the first time destroyed during the estates revolt.

Sources in this period leave somewhat aside the Catholics and their institutions. However, a view of the Catholics as standing only on the defensive against non-Catholics would be one-sided. In the city there were many Catholic churches that regularly held services. The centre of liturgical life was the cathedral, which was renovated in 1617. In this period the demolition of the old cathedral choir began, being replaced gradually with a building that could be considered the first proto-baroque building in Olomouc, and possibly Moravia. Liturgical ceremonies, processions and songs were part of the everyday life of the city. And this was certainly not confined to the procession of Corpus Christi; weekly processions were held at every parish church. The height of the liturgical year of course consisted of Easter ceremonies with their elaborate liturgy. Catholic clergy and members of religious orders paced the streets of the city in various forms of church and monastic clothing, from

18. SOkA Olomouc, AMO, Zlomky registratur, kart. 162, inv. no. 4587, sign. 1374.
19. Dedic, "Die Geschichte des Protestantismus in Olmütz IV", p. 86.

the canons' opulent leather almuces to the Dominicans' snow-white robes, from the Franciscans' dark brown, coarse habits to the Jesuits' austere black cassocks.

In 1617 Cardinal Francis of Dietrichstein began rebuilding the cathedral's above-mentioned presbytery in a proto-baroque mannerist style. Its construction was supposed to demonstrate the power and greatness of restored Catholicism. And the internal composition, according to the cardinal's intentions, was supposed to lead to its internal stability. Below the great liturgical space of the presbytery a crypt was constructed, evidently inspired by those of Roman basilicas, especially the *grotte vaticane* under the Basilica of St Peter in the Vatican. It was supposed to be a place to inter the remains of Saints Cyril and Methodius, the Apostles of Moravia in the ninth century. Since St Cyril was buried in Rome and in the seventeenth century it was believed that his brother Methodius was buried there too, the cardinal repeatedly asked the pope for their relics, though always unsuccessfully. The cardinal himself was buried in the crypt along with several of his successors.

The Jesuits, whose subsidy from the Olomouc bishopric the cardinal had already increased in 1614, devoted themselves to their activities in the Olomouc grammar school and academy. About a thousand students studied there. They included nobles (many of them non-Catholics) and students sponsored by the bishop or papal curia studying at the episcopal and papal seminary. About the city the students wore uniforms, which sometimes replaced the uniforms of five different Marian sodalities. Sodality members would cause a spectacle in the city with public flagellation, for example, a typical contemporary expression of Catholicism.[20] On 17 December 1617, by request of the cardinal, Matthias confirmed to the Jesuit college all the privileges granted by his predecessors and reiterated that the college should enjoy the same rights and privileges as any other European university.[21]

The outbreak of the Bohemian estates' revolt, whose origins are associated with the well-known defenestration of imperial governors on 23 May 1618, initially did not extend to Moravia. The leadership of the estates, headed by Karel the Elder of Žerotín, did not support the rebellion. Žerotín emphasised loyalty to the ruling house of Habsburg, which for him was a guarantee of political and religious freedoms. Probably he held little hope of the revolt's success, as in his view there could be a disturbance in the balance of power to the detriment of the estates.[22]

At the end of November 1618 in the newly built Olomouc Capuchin friary there was a meeting of three nobles from different parts of Europe. Duke Charles Gonzaga-Nevers, Count Michael Adolf of Althann and Giovanni Battista Petrignani met here after the mass celebrated by the Capuchin Valerian Magni. They

20. Cf. Jiří Fiala, "Dějiny jezuitského konviktu v Olomouci", in Jiří Fiala, Leoš Mlčák and Karel Žurek, *Jezuitský konvikt – sídlo uměleckého centra Univerzity Palackého v Olomouci. Dějiny, stavební a umělecké dějiny*, Olomouc, Univerzita Palackého, 2002, pp. 33-158: 45.

21. *Listář olomoucké univerzity 1566-1946*, ed. by Olga Uhrová-Vávrová, Olomouc, 1946, pp. 75-79.

22. Cf. Josef Válka, "Karel starší ze Žerotína a problém jeho zrady", in *Morava v době renesance a reformace*, ed. by Tomáš Knoz, Brno, Moravské zemské muzeum, 2001, pp. 8-16; Tomáš Knoz, *Karel starší ze Žerotína. Don Quijote v labyrintu světa*, Prague, Vyšehrad, 2008, pp. 217-230.

Figure 20: Olomouc, St Wenceslas cathedral, presbytery, after 1617.

founded a new military order – the Order of Christian Knights of the Immaculate Conception of the Virgin Mary and St Michael – whose aim was to unite Christendom in the fight against the Turks. Members of the Catholic order, however, were to play an important role especially in the events of Central Europe.[23]

Revolt of the Estates: The Temporary Hegemony of non-Catholics[24]

The death of Emperor Matthias in March 1619 and the ascension of Ferdinand II were singularly important stimuli for the escalation of the situation with radical non-Catholics, whose head was a cousin of Karel the Elder, Ladislav Velen of Žerotín. The arrival of Bohemian troops in Moravia in April 1618 led to a further increase in tensions. In this situation, the pro-Habsburg party planned to make Olomouc the centre of resistance against the insurgents. This plan, however, was thwarted by the departure of the Wallenstein regiment in April 1619. Wallenstein also took with him to Vienna the land treasury with the total of ninety-six thousand florins that had been stored in Olomouc.

The coup in Moravia took place at the Brno land diet in May 1619. The leaders of the pro-Habsburg side, Karel the Elder of Žerotín and Cardinal Dietrichstein, were interned in their homes. The diet elected a twenty-nine-member directorate that incorporated one representative of the city of Olomouc and established a non-Catholic consistory and defenders of the faith. The Jesuits were expelled from the land and their property secularised. The diet also dissolved the municipal councils in the royal cities and named their new members, regardless of religious orientation.

The diet sent Albrecht Sedlnický of Choltice and Václav Bítovský of Bítov as commissioners to Olomouc, armed with appropriate instructions and the letter for the non-Catholic Olomouc burghers.[25] On 10 May the Catholic city council convoked the community of the city (the wealthy burghers) and called for a renewed oath of allegiance to Ferdinand II. The community, apparently still doubting the support of the estates, composed the oath. Almost immediately at the city gates, which had been closed since the morning by command of the city council, the estates commissioners appeared with two cornets of cavalry. The commissioners had to spend the night outside the city. They entered only the next morning and handed over the letter of the Moravian estates to the council and community. After

23. Charles Göllner, "La Milice Chrétienne, un instrument de croisade au XVIIe siècle", *Mélanges de l'École roumaine en France*, 12 (1936), pp. 59-118; Tomáš Parma, "Řád Křesťanského rytířstva: mezi řeholní společností a konfraternitou", *Folia historica Bohemica*, 26, no. 1 (2011), pp. 247-265.

24. The most relevant source for the period of the estates revolt in Olomouc is *Chronik der Stadt Olmütz über die Jahre 1619 und 1620*, ed. by Beda Dudík, Brünn, Rohrer, 1851. See also *Relacio*, written after the revolt for the new city council (*Gründliche und warhafftige Relation ...*), ed. by Christian d'Elvert, *Mährische und schlesische Chroniken I*, Brünn, 1861, pp. 395-412. Cf. *Dějiny Olomouce*, vol. I, pp. 333-367 (Miroslav Koudela).

25. Both from 6 May 1619. See Libuše Urbánková-Hrubá, *Povstání na Moravě v roce 1619. Z korespondence moravských direktorů*, Prague, Archivní správa, 1979, pp. 41-42.

a formal protest the council was finally dismissed and the non-Catholic members of the community, led by Karl Hirsch and others, ventured into a radical and unusual step. They called together the entire population of the city: the burghers, those from outside the city walls and the tenants. The letter of the Moravian estates was read to them on the steps of city hall. Most members of this assembly showed boisterous agreement when they were asked whether they wanted to help the commissioners in the execution of their tasks.

The commissioners began to act according to their instructions. Apart from taking the keys to the city and city hall, they read to the rector of the Olomouc college a decree to dissolve his order and requested the Jesuits to leave the city the next day. Then they took the keys of St Maurice Church from the Catholic priest and handed them over to the non-Catholics' representatives. They immediately sent for the local Lutheran pastor to take over the church so that the next day he could lead non-Catholic worship. The whole Olomouc coup was completed on 14 May 1619 when the new city council was established. The office of mayor alternated between four councillors – two Catholics (Bartholomäus Heilig and David Heinz) and two non-Catholics (Karl Hirsch and Johann Obersdorfer). Among the sworn members of the council were two Catholics and five non-Catholics. Catholics also continued to keep the post of the reeve, the municipal judge (Jan Scintilla remained in the post). By this change of municipal leadership, which meant a serious inroad into the traditional leadership structures of the city, Olomouc became a party to the estates revolt within a few days.

Along with the other royal cities Olomouc was asked for a loan by the estates. The city had no intention to grant it. But from the end of May 1619 Olomouc became a rallying point for estates, troops, at a considerable burden for individual burghers, especially after the estates' army expanded by another 1,000 musketeers. After equipping units, however, the soldiers were assigned to different places in Moravia. Only a permanent military garrison was left in Olomouc, under the command of captain Hartmann of Buchheim. The commander acted radically; at the end of July, along with 500 farmers, he occupied the monastery of Hradisko near the city. Abbot Leodegarius preferred not to resist. The monastery was secularised and monks were meted out daily provisions of food and drink. The farmers occupied the monastery and their captain oversaw the proper management of the estate.[26]

In July 1619 the Bohemian Confederation, the new state constitution that greatly favoured non-Catholics, was adopted in Prague. The Moravian land diet ratified the Confederation treaty in Brno in August 1619. This land diet also confiscated the ancestral estates of Cardinal Francis of Dietrichstein and exiled him from the country. It confiscated the Olomouc bishopric's property and Moravian chapters and monasteries. It also cancelled the Olomouc bishopric's feudal system that had been in place since the Middle Ages. Thus it virtually destroyed all the important Catholic institutions in the country and secularised their property. In royal cities Catholics were forced to resign from city councils, their houses were searched on suspicion of conspiracy, and their arms and ammunition seized.

26. Dudík, *Olmützer Sammel-Chronik*, p. 23.

Another Catholic institution on which Buchheim focused was Olomouc's cathedral chapter. On 15 August 1619 he invited for lunch eight Olomouc canons who were still in the city. After lunch they were arrested and quite symbolically imprisoned in the house, which in the years 1610-13 served as a Lutheran chapel.[27] There the canons remained, living on bread and water, until 19 January 1620. The chapter deanery, provostry and other canon houses were cleaned out of all valuables and subsequently looted. The Catholic priest from St Maurice was expelled from the city, along with two vicars, and in September the Capuchins and Observant Franciscans were expelled. After the intervention of the directorate the Observants and Capuchins were allowed to return, but the Capuchins found they had nowhere to return to; the friary was uninhabitable. At the same time a mint for the Moravian estates was established at the Jesuit college where the confiscated ecclesiastical silver was rapidly converted to coins. On 16 August, immediately after the August land diet and the internment of the canons the Olomouc Catholic burghers were also disarmed.[28]

After the deposition of Ferdinand II, Frederick the Elector Palatine was elected as king of Bohemia. According to the directorate's regulation, all clerics had to announce his election from the pulpit and pray prescribed prayers for Frederick on certain days. Catholic clergy refused on the grounds of freedom of conscience, leading to their internment. Additionally, from October 1619 the Catholics of Olomouc found themselves without priests. This engendered great unrest and at least some monks were released to "house arrest" in their monasteries from where they could administer pastoral care. October 1619 also meant the realisation of an oath to the Confederation by Catholic burghers. The burghers decisively rejected it and their resistance was broken by the threat of muskets aimed by Buchheim's soldiers.

In January 1620 King Frederick came to Moravia and was admitted as lord of the land. The land diet in Brno gave him Mikulov, the confiscated domain of Cardinal Dietrichstein, and Kroměříž, originally the estate of the Olomouc bishop. His wife, Queen Elizabeth, was given the bishop's domain in Chropyně. On 15 February 1620 King Frederick arrived in Olomouc. The next day, Sunday, the court preacher Abraham Scultetus led a festive Calvinist church service in the Jesuit church, opened for the first time since the beginning of the revolt. A Catholic chronicler sarcastically commented on the Olomouc burghers that at the sermon "many Lutheran bootlickers dressed in Calvinist skin" participated in it. After the service Olomouc burghers paid tribute to the king on the square. This was followed by a festive lunch after which the monarch continued his journey to Wrocław to take hold of the Silesian estates.

Even before the arrival of the king, however, the Moravian territory was invaded by the *lisowczycy*, Polish Cossacks who received no salary but had permission to plunder any territory in which they found themselves. They marched to the endangered Vienna, which requested them for assistance against Gábor Bethlen. During

27. *Ibid.*, pp. 23-24.

28. *Ibid.*, pp. 26-28. Buchheim ordered the disarming of all the townspeople. The arms were returned to the non-Catholics. Those of the Catholics were confiscated and taken to Brno.

their Moravian expedition an incident occurred involving the priest Jan Sarkander. Sarkander worked as a parish priest in Holešov, the domain centre of the Catholic leader Ladislav Popel of Lobkovice. In the early days of the revolt in Moravia, in the spring of 1619, the priest lived temporarily in Poland. His stay coincided with the residence of the Habsburg delegation, which was in Cracow negotiating Polish support. When these *lisowczycy* approached Holešov on 6 February 1620, Jan Sarkander, as the parish priest, came out to meet them at the head of a Eucharistic procession. He thus saved the city from their looting. Non-Catholics concluded, however, that the whole event was prearranged during Sarkander's Polish stay and the Eucharistic procession was only a sign. Sarkander fled and hid but was eventually captured and brought to Olomouc where a nine-member commission was created for his interrogation. Because the charge was treason, hearings were conducted with the use of torture. Besides the members of the commission, the municipal reeve Jan Scintilla was also present.[29] Four hearings were held from 13 to 18 February 1620 when the last torture mandated by the not very sober commissioners overstepped the law, as Scintilla pointed out on the spot. He reported that during the torture Sarkander was interrogated about things he learned in the confession of Ladislav Popel of Lobkovice, and therefore refused to speak. Sarkander died a month later (17 March 1620) in prison from his injuries and burns. He very quickly became revered as a martyr.

Already in April 1620, shortly after the death of Sarkander, cardinal and bishop of Olomouc Francis of Dietrichstein had a pamphlet printed in Vienna that showed Sarkander's torture in its upper section. The author was a Viennese coppersmith Tobias Bidenharter. The pamphlet served to promote respect for the priest, identified in the accompanying text as a martyr. The cardinal distributed it throughout Europe. It became the model for official views of the saint's martyrdom, such as we know it from the surviving gravestone Sarkander's brothers made for him in 1621. Still in 1620, a book about his death was published in Paris, followed by others in various European countries. Sarkander's official beatification, however, did not occur until 1859. He was canonised in 1995.

Autumn 1620 was marked by the progress of the emperor's troops and the Catholic League of South Bohemia toward Prague. In Moravia this was the time of growing influence of the conservative part of the land community, headed by Karel the Elder of Žerotín and his son-in-law Jiří of Náchod. The defeat of the Czech army in the battle of White Mountain on 8 November 1620 did not mean an immediate end to the rebellion in Moravia. However, the December land diet in Brno was already fully directed by moderate parties. And representatives of the Palatine party preferred to quickly leave the city after the outcome of the vote on 14 December. This led also the city of Olomouc to surrender and on 16 December to ask the estates to include the city in peace negotiations.[30]

29. A concept of the report of Scintilla for Cardinal Dietrichstein, SOkA Olomouc, AMO, Zlomky registratur, sign. 1877/1, ed. by Tenora and Foltynovský, *Bl. Jan Sarkander*, pp. 677-688; cf. also Dudík, *Olmützer Sammel-Chronik*, pp. 45-50.

30. *Dějiny Olomouce*, vol. I, p. 349 (Miroslav Koudela).

REVERENDVS DOMINVS IOANNES SARCANDER DE SKOCZOVIA PAROCHVS HOLOSCHOVENSIS DIOECESIS OLOMVCENSIS MENSE FEBRVARIO Aº MDCXX MARTYRIO AFFECTVS

Fvit vir hic ut semper in omni vita ab innocentia vitæ notissimus, sic in morte à virtutis constantia extitit clarissimus. Hoc ille anno ab Hæreticis rebellibus in Moravia, in odium Religionis Catholicæ Olomucij in carcerem cōjectus, crudelibusq; subjectus quæstionibus, admotis etiam facibus, pice sulphureq; excarnificatus, malitiæ non cessit; Sed DEO & Religioni fidus constantiam immotus retinuit, non aliud inter acerbissimos cruciatus, quam Ss.ª IESV, MARIÆ & ANNÆ nomina ingeminans, nec multo post in eodē carcere gravissimis obrutus doloribus, sine querela, sine gemitu, plenus spei & DEI expiravit. Corpus ejus septimo ab obitu die incorruptū viuidumq; in ore præsertim honorifice à Catholicis in Divæ Virginis æde conditum jam miraculis celebrari fama est.

HErr Johannes Sarcander von Skotzau Pfarrherr zu Holeschau in Mähren / wie er allzeit durch sein gantzes leben / wegen seiner Unschult bekant / also ist er auch im Todt / wegen seiner / in den Tugenden Beständigkeit / beruhmet vnd herrlich worden. Er ist dises Jahr 1620. in Monat Februarij von den Rebellischen Ketzern in Mähren / auß haß der Catholischen Religion zu Olmutz in die Gefängnüß gezogē vñ graussamen Peinen vnterworffen / mit Fackeln / heissē Pech vñ Schwefel gemartert worden / wiche aber nicht der Boßheit / sonder bliebe GOTT vnd der Religion getrew / vñ erhielte vnveruckt die Beständigkeit / in seinen schmertzlichsten Peinen / wurde nichts anders von jhm gehöret / dann die zum öfftern widerholten heilige Nahmen / JESVS / MARIA vnd ANNA: Hat auch nicht lang darauff / mit höchsten Schmertzē bedrengt / sein heiligen Geist / ohn klag vñ seüfftzen / voll der Hoffnung Gottes / auffgeben. Sein Heiliger Leib ist den sibendē Tag / von seinem abschied vnverwesen / vnd im Mund fürnemblich gantz liebhafft / ehrlich von den Catholischen in vnser lieben Frawen Kirchen begraben worden / wirdt / wie man sagt / klar vñ herrlich mit Wunder vnd Zeichen gesehen.

Tobias Biden: Sculp: Vien:

Figure 21: Cardinal's pamphlet of Jan Sarkander, Tobias Bidenharter, April 1620.

Some non-Catholic leaders left the city, including Captain Hartmann of Buchheim.[31] The Olomouc city council vainly tried to resist just before the occupation of the city by the imperial army, apparently under pressure from the non-Catholic majority. On 11 January 1621 by eight o'clock in the morning the imperial army entered Olomouc. Two days later, Olomouc burghers renounced the Confederation and King Frederick and passed allegiance to Emperor Ferdinand into the hands of the imperial commissioner Johann Christoph Thonradel.[32] Moravia was subsequently occupied by imperial troops, as the emperor won Moravia without having to swing a sword and without losing a single man.[33]

State Enforced re-Catholicisation and Decline of the City

Immediately after the occupation the emperor forcibly ordered the city to provide a loan of 100,000 Rhenish florins.[34] After the imperial army gained the city Catholic institutions began to revive. As early as 18 January 1621 two carriages of thirty-four Jesuits came to Olomouc. They quickly restored teaching operations of the university, which began on 10 March.[35] Shortly afterwards on 28 March 1621 Cardinal Dietrichstein issued a decree from the emperor that enabled the restitution and reintroduction of the Jesuits in Moravia. The Jesuits, however, already on 22 January took over Catholic worship in the Olomouc church of St Maurice, taken from the non-Catholics by imperial commissioners. Two days later the cathedral was opened and a Mass was celebrated with preaching and a *Te Deum.* At the end of January bells began ringing and the evening *Ave Maria* prayers were recited. Already on 1 February all non-Catholic clergy were brought from the city under military escort and interned in the village of Ruda, about forty kilometres from Olomouc.

The current non-Catholic city council was in office until 2 April, when the council was renewed and recomposed entirely of Catholics. The next day all Olomouc burghers were disarmed and six non-Catholic leaders arrested.[36] From the beginning of May an imperial rescript set up the office of the royal reeve, the representative of the sovereign, and reviewed the activities of the city council, which meant significant limitation of the city's internal autonomy.

In June 1622 more offenders from the period of the rebellion were incarcerated. Even some noble rebels from Olomouc and the surrounding area were interned at the city hall. The incarceration of the offenders coincided with the first major festivals and manifestations, organized by the Jesuits, celebrating Catholicism's triumph in the post-White Mountain period. These included a celebration of the canonisation of their order's founding figures Ignatius Loyola and Francis

31. D'Elvert, *Mährische und schlesische Chroniken*, p. 409.
32. *Ibid.*, pp. 409-412.
33. František Hrubý, "Pád českého povstání na Moravě 1620", *Český časopis historický*, 29 (1923), pp. 71-120, 358-388: 388.
34. *Dějiny Olomouce*, vol. I, p. 350 (Miroslav Koudela).
35. Dudík, *Olmützer Sammel-Chronik*, p. 47; Fiala, "Jezuitská akademie", p. 33.
36. Dudík, *Olmützer Sammel-Chronik*, p. 47.

Xavier. The celebrations lasted eight days and were attended not only by the Jesuits, but also the Olomouc chapter, all present clergy, guilds, confraternities, the city council and the townsfolk.[37]

In July 1622 an inquiry was launched that initially judged the rebellion's directors and those who actively participated in the closure of the Confederation in Prague. On 3 November 1622 judgments were read to the insurgents at the Brno city hall. Two Olomouc burghers, Jan Adam and Vit Oesterreicher, were sentenced to death. But, as in all other death sentences, their punishment was reduced to a property sanction. Jan Adam and four other Olomouc burghers had to suffer their ignominious punishment of forced labour in chains. The punishment of the rebels was concluded in November 1622 by the emperor's general pardon for those who stayed in the country or were about to return. Those who returned included Adam Schäffer, an active participant in the rebellion who even subsequently won a confiscated nobleman's house in Olomouc and became an imperial master of the mint.[38]

In the years 1623-24 property punishments were introduced and organised by the confiscation commission which, like the commission of inquiry and tribunal over the insurgents, was presided over by Bishop and Cardinal Francis of Dietrichstein, officially appointed governor (*Gubernator*) of Moravia and imperial governor. In Olomouc the commission confiscated seventeen aristocratic and thirteen burgher houses, along with movables, ready money and standing promissory notes. It sentenced ten burghers to the loss of all property, others to the loss of one to three quarters of their assets. About forty burghers who participated in the revolt were sentenced to forced donations in cash and bonds surpassing a total of 120,000 Moravian florins. The worst affected was non-Catholic leader Karl Hirsch (44,250 fl.) and a Catholic member of the city council during the revolt David Heinz (about 30,000 fl.). On 28 August 1624 the confiscation commission ordered the sale of the confiscated houses of rebels and their other property. And thus in Olomouc its activities ended.

Compared to what occurred in the rest of the country, the redistribution (or restitution) of the confiscated property in Olomouc took more fully into account the Catholic Church, or rather some of its institutions. Legal acts from the time of rebellion had been declared null, so the church got back all the property from the time before the rebellion. The Olomouc chapter, whose members had proven loyalty to the emperor and had been persecuted for it during the revolt, was redressed for its suffering and injustice. In the great privilege of August 1623[39] Ferdinand II granted them the honorary epithet "always faithful" and augmented their coat

37. Maria Pötzl-Malikova, "Die Feiern anlässlich der Heiligsprechung des Ignatius von Loyola und Franz Xaver im Jahre 1622 in Rom, Prag und Olmütz", in *Bohemia Jesuitica 1556-2006*, 2 vols., ed. by Petronilla Čemus, Prague, Karolinum, 2010, vol. II, pp. 1239-1254: 1250-1254.

38. Miroslav Hradil, "Adam Schäffer – poslední olomoucký mincmistr", in *Ročenka Státního okresního archivu v Olomouci 1990*, Olomouc, Státní okresní archiv, 1991, pp. 80-84.

39. Ferdinand II's privilege for the Olomouc chapter, 28 August 1623, ZAO-O, MCO, sign. E I 4, ed. by Anton Kobliha, *Urkunden-Sammlung betreffend die Privilegien und Rechte des Hochwürdigst-getreuen Metropolitankapitels zu Olmütz*, Olmütz, Verlag des Metropolitankapitels, 1890, no. 11, pp. 18-23.

of arms. He moreover gave them special privileges in the treatment of property, donating the confiscated farm in Haňovice and the Olomouc house where canons were imprisoned as compensation for wrongs suffered. Even in the period after 1650 the property provoked disputes; the chapter served beer and wine in it without proper privileges, much to the city council's dismay and protests. An 1860 photograph shows the house after its reconstruction in 1748, of which only a sopraporta with the coats of arms of the Olomouc chapter was preserved. Shortly after the picture was taken the house was demolished and in its place and that of four other houses the Czech National House was built.

Compensation was also given to the Jesuits. Ferdinand II donated to them in 1622 as compensation for war damages a profitable confiscated farm in Čejkovice and two years later the domain and town of Nový Jičín. The second donation was intended to support the operation of the extended ("Ferdinand's") convent, and thus the university's activities. In 1625 there were as many as forty-eight Jesuits in the college.[40] Another monastic community, the Capuchins, whose monastery was razed to the ground during the revolt, returned to Olomouc in June 1622 and immediately started rebuilding the convent. Simultaneously, Cardinal Dietrichstein ordered the city council to re-build the Capuchin monastery, using the money raised from the insurgents' property.[41] The flow of money from confiscations and "voluntary donations" meant that the Capuchins could move into the monastery as early as 1623. Other Catholic institutions, however, in their compensation claims for mostly chattels rather than property (furniture and household goods, cattle, ravaged farms) were less successful.

In the years 1623-24 the city suffered a great plague (apparently exaggerated by chronicle reports that recorded that 14,236 people succumbed).[42] The city council issued a number of anti-plague articles in June 1623 with rational precautions. The plague epidemic also exacerbated the religious feelings of the people and encouraged extraordinary manifestations of piety. On 8 October 1623 the Olomouc Jesuits led a procession with the relics of St Pauline, recently brought to Olomouc.[43] After the procession the epidemic subsided and then stopped. Nevertheless, it erupted again in Olomouc Předhradí a year later. On the recommendation of the canon Julius Caesar Ginanni, the city council organised an eight-day series of services accompanied by private prayer and fasting by burghers and clergy. After the eight days

40. Fiala, "Jezuitská akademie", p. 33.

41. SOkA Olomouc, AMO, Zl reg., inv. no. 4631, sign. 1527, cart. no. 162.

42. Dudík, *Olmützer Sammel-Chronik*, p. 48.

43. The relics of the early fourth-century Christian woman were discovered in the Roman catacombs on 29 January 1622 and given by Pope Gregory XV to the Jesuits together with a clay lamp from her grave. On the plague in Olomouc, see Eduard Wondrák, "Mor a některé moravské protimorové spisy v 17. století", in *Ročenka Státního okresního archivu v Olomouci 1982*, Olomouc, Státní okresní archiv, 1983, pp. 73-86; on St Pauline's cult Ondřej Jakubec, "Protimorové procesí s ostatky sv. Pavlíny v Olomouci roku 1623", in *Olomoucké baroko*, 3 vols., *Výtvarná kultura let 1620-1780*, vol. II, *Katalog*, ed. by Ondřej Jakubec and Marek Perůtka, Olomouc, Muzeum umění Olomouc, 2010, p. 295; Leoš Mlčák, "Mor, hlad, války a živelné pohromy v Olomouci", in *Olomoucké baroko*, vol. I, pp. 125-135.

Figure 22: Olomouc, house no. 514: a) sopraporta with coats of arms of Olomouc chapter, 1720s; b) photo from 1860.

of prayer the plague retreated. The city council therefore opted for St Pauline as the patron of the city and her feast was celebrated with an annual procession.[44]

After the plague ceased, re-Catholicisation efforts were undertaken. On 20 January 1625 Cardinal Dietrichstein issued a decree that homeowners in Olomouc who did not want to become Catholics had to sell their property and move out of the country. They were given until Easter 1625 to do so, later extended until Pentecost. The decree also prohibited the acceptance of non-Catholics as Olomouc burghers and inhabitants of the suburbs.[45] The city council reported to the cardinal in July 1625[46] about this re-Catholicisation of the city. Even better sources on the subject are lists of townhouses marked for denominational affiliation of their respective owners.[47] According to the first list, which must have been made in the first half of 1625, 396 non-Catholic houses were still in the city, suburbs and Předhradí.

In June 1625 there was a stormy meeting at the city hall to which the new city council invited both Catholics and stubborn Lutherans. In all, 117 non-Catholics were admonished, invited to convert and threatened. Sixty-four of them promised to convert by the end of June. Fifty-three stubbornly persevered in their faith, leaning on the example of their leader Karl Hirsch. After further interventions there were only twelve non-Catholics left led by Karl Hirsch. They were given to the priests to be lectured and instructed to confess by the deadline of the feast of St Michael. According to the list of non-Catholics, made around 1626, very few non-Catholics remained in Olomouc. Only 306 non-Catholics lived in a total of 1,336 houses in the city and the suburbs. About half were women. In the case of 150 married couples the husband became a Catholic in order to save the house and property, and the woman remained non-Catholic. Among the Olomouc burghers only three remained non-Catholics and eventually even Karl Hirsch converted, who would otherwise have lost considerable property and his network of business contacts through eviction. Those who longest withstood the pressure to re-Catholicise were widows and wives of the already Catholic burghers. Still at the beginning of 1626 Cardinal Dietrichstein called them to the bishop's court and appealed to them to convert within six weeks.[48]

This massive conversion of many of the city's inhabitants began to create in the urban community a rift between "old Catholics" and "new Catholics", who were suspected of insincere and expedient conversion (which in many cases seemed to be the reality). At a meeting on 1 July 1625 the "old Catholics" expressed concerns that the "new Catholics" would force them out of their positions within the com-

44. The feast was originally on 6 June. From 1678 it was on the fourth Sunday after the Feast of the Holy Spirit. From the mid-eighteenth century it was on the fifth Sunday. The procession was cancelled by Joseph II in 1783.

45. František Snopek, "Akta kardinála Ditrichštejna z let 1619-1635", *Časopis Matice moravské*, 39 (1915), pp. 98-194: 133-134.

46. *Ibid.*, pp. 143-145.

47. The first list is undated; it is clearly from the period before the re-Catholicisation measures. The other is from the period after the re-Catholicisation measures, SOkA Olomouc, AMO, Zlomky registratur, sign. 1590. Cf. Václav Nešpor, "Kdy a jak byla provedena protireformace v Olomouci", *Časopis Vlastivědného spolku muzejního v Olomouci*, 57 (1948), pp. 45-47.

48. Dudík, *Olmützer Sammel-Chronik*, p. 48.

munity.[49] In 1625/1626 one of the Olomouc burghers who converted was Valentin Ecker, a locksmith master and author of one of the Olomouc chronicles. His conversion is evidenced in his work. In 1625 he still speaks of "*wir evangelische*", while in 1626 the same group is designated as "*Unkatholische*". And from mid-1626 any mention of religious issues disappeared from his work. Until the beginning of the Swedish occupation he talks exclusively about politics, wars, soldiers, prices, markets, crimes and punishing criminals. It is obvious that for him the world of religion had become something of which it was better not to speak. Many of the "new Catholics" probably continued to feel rather like Lutherans, although apparently unable to share their feelings with others. The question of religious practice was also out of discussion. "New Catholics" were required to attend Catholic worship and provide the appropriate certification of Easter confession and communion.[50]

Catholic institutions produced not just administrative measures; they were also building or altering sacred spaces or monasteries.[51] Perhaps the most significant example is the construction of the pilgrimage chapel on a hill near the town, later called Svatý Kopeček (literally Holy Hill). The founder was Jan Andrýsek, a wealthy Olomouc merchant and purchaser of some confiscated properties. He was a resolute Catholic even before the revolt and fulfilled his promise to the Virgin Mary.[52] In the years 1629-33 he erected a chapel on the property of the Premonstratensian monastery of Hradisko and placed there a shallow stone relief of the Madonna with Child.[53] The chapel was consecrated in 1633, and despite being burned down in 1645, a church building arose in its place under the direction of the Premonstratensians of Hradisko after the Thirty Years' War. Olomouc and its surroundings gained a monumental landmark (the basilica with adjacent residences and access roads forming the sign of the cross was visible from afar) and a place of pilgrimage that would attract thousands of pilgrims.

The year 1636 was marked by the confirmation of all the city's privileges by Emperor Ferdinand II.[54] It was also, and especially, marked by the death of

49. *Ibid.*

50. By the cardinal's order to the royal cities on 10 May 1629. New Catholics had to submit their confession confirmation (*Beichtzettel*) by Easter or Pentecost. Snopek, "Akta kardinála Ditrichštejna", pp. 182-183.

51. In 1640 the "wealthy" Jesuits bought more houses from the city to enlarge the schools and build a poorhouse. SOkA Olomouc, AMO, Listiny, inv. no. 1381.

52. For details, see the next chapter. For the pilgrimage site cf. e.g. [Bernard Wancke], *Mons Praemonstratus, Das ist: Außführliche Beschreibung* ..., Olmütz, 1679; Bohumír Smejkal, *Svatý Kopeček. Poutní chrám Navštívení Panny Marie*, Velehrad, 1994.

53. It is a historicising mannerist image from the early seventeenth century, influenced by a quattrocento painting. According to Ivo Hlobil the image originated in Italy. See Ivo Hlobil, "Pochází Madona svatokopecká z Itálie?", in *Město v baroku, baroko ve městě*, ed. by Ladislav Daniel and Filip Hradil, Olomouc, Vlastivědné muzeum v Olomouci and Univerzita Palackého, 2012, pp. 130-135; Leoš Mlčák, "Manýristická poutní kaple na sv. Kopečku u Olomouce", in *Ročenka Státního okresního archivu v Olomouci 2000*, Olomouc, Státní okresní archiv, 2001, pp. 88-109; Martin Pavlíček, "Kostel navštívení Panny Marie s premonstrátskou rezidencí", in *Olomoucké baroko*, vol. II, pp. 88-91.

54. SOkA Olomouc, AMO, Listiny, inv. no. 1378 (26 April 1636). For a similar confirmation by Ferdinand III on 16 September 1639, see *ibid.*, inv. no. 1380.

Olomouc Bishop Francis Cardinal of Dietrichstein on 19 September 1636. In Bishop Dietrichstein's person died both a religious dignitary and the long-reigning de facto ruler of Moravia. His death allowed a long-planned change in the administrative structure of the country. The Moravian royal tribunal started to operate as a modern central bureaucratic office with judicial, political and financial competencies. It was seated permanently in Brno from 1641, which meant a decline in Olomouc's political prestige. At that time the emperor decided that the provincial courts would be held only in Brno, and the land records from Olomouc would be transported there. Olomouc, in the words of the chronicler, "was robbed of a gem it had cherished for several hundred years",[55] and thus it de facto lost its position as the capital of the province. Nevertheless, it remained a royal city, the seat of the bishop and the only Moravian university, and an important military centre. Olomouc retained only the empty title of the royal capital, and jealously guarded it, regardless of how little it corresponded to the actual situation.[56]

Other events after Bishop Dietrichstein's death were a clear demonstration of the church's position in society. After the victory over the non-Catholic rebellion the church and many of its leading representatives expected that besides the returned property it would acquire the accompanying political influence afforded by ecclesiastical immunity and independence. Already during the twenties, however, it was becoming increasingly clear that the church would remain subordinate to secular political power in all major issues. The Olomouc chapter had the privilege of free election of the bishop, guaranteed since the thirteenth century both by the kings of Bohemia and popes. After the cardinal's death the chapter exercised this privilege by appointing the provost of the chapter, John Ernest Plateis of Plattenstein. Plateis was a zealous executor of the reconversion policy of papal nuncio Carlo Caraffa and Cardinal Dietrichstein himself. The problem was that Emperor Ferdinand II strongly suggested to the canons that they choose his younger son, Archduke Leopold Wilhelm, a twenty-two-year old youth who was at that time bishop in four other dioceses but lacking any major holy orders. The choice of Plateis shocked and offended the sovereign. The emperor, through his representatives and agents at the papal court, tried to ensure the revocation of the nomination. He managed only to delay the papal confirmation of Plateis' selection until 1637. News of this arrived in Olomouc a few days after Plateis' death. The subsequent vote dutifully elected Archduke Leopold Wilhelm bishop of Olomouc for the next twenty-four years. Wilhelm apparently arrived in Olomouc only twice during this time. But he managed to use the administration of the bishopric, which was already entrusted to experts among the Olomouc canons, to redirect profits into his personal coffers. This funded primarily works of art, the transport of court musical ensembles and war

55. Dudík, *Olmützer Sammel-Chronik*, p. 51.

56. On administrative changes and the decline of Olomouc and rise of Brno, see Pavel Balcárek, *Brno versus Olomouc. O primát hlavního města Moravy. Pod Špilberkem proti Švédům*, Brno, Jota, 1993; Josef Válka, *Dějiny Moravy*, vol. II, *Morava reformace, renesance a baroka*, Brno, Muzejní a vlastivědná společnost, 1995, p. 108.

campaigns, particularly during his seven years in Brussels as vice-regent to the Spanish king.[57]

Cardinal Dietrichstein sent a report on the state of the diocese to the pope shortly before his death. He could boast that of the 150,000 Moravian non-Catholics, already 110,000 had converted;[58] the situation in Olomouc, however, allows us to look at the issue in a nuanced way. Certainly, conversions forced by political power could have been sincere, provided that the person in question had a particular religious belief at all, or could easily get used to a different denomination and adopt it as his or her own. This is actually one of the limits of the broadly applied concept of confessionalisation as such: it assumes that everyone participates in a profound and intimate self-identification with a particular confession and its specifics. In any case, for individuals with a less profound attitude of religious self-identification, the change of confession did not pose too fundamental a problem. In Olomouc, however, there was apparently a relatively large number of new Catholics who remained inwardly inclined to their original confession, as evidenced by the fact that after the Swedish occupation of the city in 1642 only 176 Olomouc burghers registered as Catholic.[59]

Swedish Occupation[60]

At the beginning of June 1642 the Swedes appeared in the vicinity of Olomouc. After a relatively short siege of the city, which was caught completely unprepared, an accord was signed by makeshift city commander Colonel An-

57. On Leopold Wilhelm, see Renate Schreiber, *"ein Galeria nach meinem Humor", Erzherzog Leopold Wilhelm*, Wien and Milano, Kunsthistorisches Museum and Skira, 2004.

58. See a modern edition in Tomáš Parma, "Modernus Olomucensis dioecesis meae status. Le visite ad limina del Francesco cardinale Dietrichstein, vescovo di Olomouc (1570-1636) e le sue relazioni sullo stato della diocesi", *Römische Historische Mitteilungen*, 50 (2008), pp. 335-382: 367.

59. *Specifikation der Burger so Catholisch verbleiben wollen* ..., SOkA Olomouc, AMO, Zlomky registratur, inv. no. 531, cart. 20. Some Catholics, however, might have left the city before it was taken by the Swedes and the accord handing over the city allowed that too. Cf. Dudík, *Olmützer Sammel-Chronik*, p. 51.

60. A number of narrative sources on the Swedish occupation were preserved. Apart from the afore-mentioned Olomouc chronicle (Dudík, *Olmützer Sammel-Chronik*), cf. a well-documented diary of the city scribe Friedrich Flade, who, however, left the city in 1644 (Beda Dudík, ed., "Tagebuch des feindlichen Einfalls der Schweden in das Markgrafthum Mähren während ihres Aufenthaltes in der Stadt Olmütz 1642-1650 geführt von dem Olmützer Stadtschreiber und Notar Magister Friedrich Flade", *Archiv für österreichische Geschichte*, 65 (1884), pp. 307-485); a chronicle of the Franciscan superior (*guardianus*) Paulinus Zaczkowicz (Beda Dudik, ed., "Chronik des Minoriten-Guardians des St. Jakobs-Kloster in Olmütz, P. Paulinus Zackowic über die Schwedenherrschaft in Olmütz vom 1642 bis 1650", *Archiv für österreichische Geschichte*, 62 (1881), pp. 451-611); a diary of Georg Schönberger, a Jesuit rector (Beda Dudík, ed., "Ex Diario r.mi Patris Schönberger, rectoris Collegii Societatis Iesu Olomucii", *Archiv für österreichische Geschichte*, 62 (1881), pp. 612-624); an unpublished *Archivum* of the Olomouc Franciscan friary (MZA, E21, Františkáni Dačice, book no. 9); and a report of

tonio Miniati with Generalissimo Lennart Torstensson on the release of the city.[61] In these circumstances the accord was relatively favourable for the city. And owing to the fact that it was formulated in part by the administrator of the bishopric Jan Kašpar Stredele of Montani, it contained many positive elements for the Catholic Church. All rights of the Church would be preserved and existing rites maintained, in addition to the presence and property of all Catholic institutions, including the Jesuit academy and the Hradisko monastery outside the city walls.

The Swedes entered the city early in the morning on 15 June 1642 and stayed eight years. This relatively long stay was crucial for the coexistence of confessions. The Swedish period can be divided into two parts. In the first, the imperial army attempted to reconquer the city and its surroundings. The city's siege and bombardment further decreased the population, and tensions grew between the Swedish military administration and city residents suffering from the resident troops, sieges and considerable war contributions. During the second part, from late 1645 until the withdrawal of Swedish troops in summer 1650, Moravia was divided into two spheres of influence: that of the imperial and that of the Swedish troops. Swedes at this time ruled not only Olomouc, but also a large part of northern Moravia and the Bohemian-Moravian border, collecting war contributions and managing the land in place of the imperial administration.

Although the Swedish military government tried to maintain a balance between the confessions and essential elements of the accord from 1642, this was not always successful. Already at the beginning of the Swedish occupation, houses were demolished on the outskirts of Olomouc in order to better defend the city. The monastery of Hradisko and the Capuchin monastery before the *Střední* (Middle) gate, the two large monastic buildings, could not escape demolition.

Shortly after their arrival the Swedes asked for the church of St Blaise to conduct their worship. The parish church, however, quickly proved inadequate. Swedish commander Georg Paykul already in December 1642 suggested to the community assembled at city hall that Catholic and Lutheran services could alternate at the city's largest church of St Maurice. The burghers opposed, including Olomouc native and Jesuit Father Georg Pelinka, who was at that time the church's parish priest. On Sunday morning of 14 December the church was found locked, with no priest. Pelinka had sent word to the soldiers that the keys to the church were on the main altar. So the soldiers had to enter the church through a broken window to retrieve them. The non-Catholics were thus manipulated into the biblical image of the thief and robber, who climbs the fence to the sheepfold rather than entering through the door like the shepherd.[62]

an unknown Jesuit, possibly Georg Pelinka (ed. by Tomáš Parma, "Neznámý jezuitský pramen o švédské okupaci Olomouce", in *Město v baroku, baroko ve městě*, pp. 13-22).

61. Dudík, "Tagebuch des feindlichen Einfalls", pp. 9-12 (4/14 June 1642).

62. John 10: 1-2. See Martin Elbel, "Dva světy? Konfesijní hranice za švédské okupace Olomouce 1642-1650", in *Historická Olomouc XIII, Konec švédské okupace a poválečná obnova ve 2. polovině 17. století*, ed. by Martin Elbel and Milan Togner, Olomouc, Univerzita Palackého, 2002, pp. 99-105.

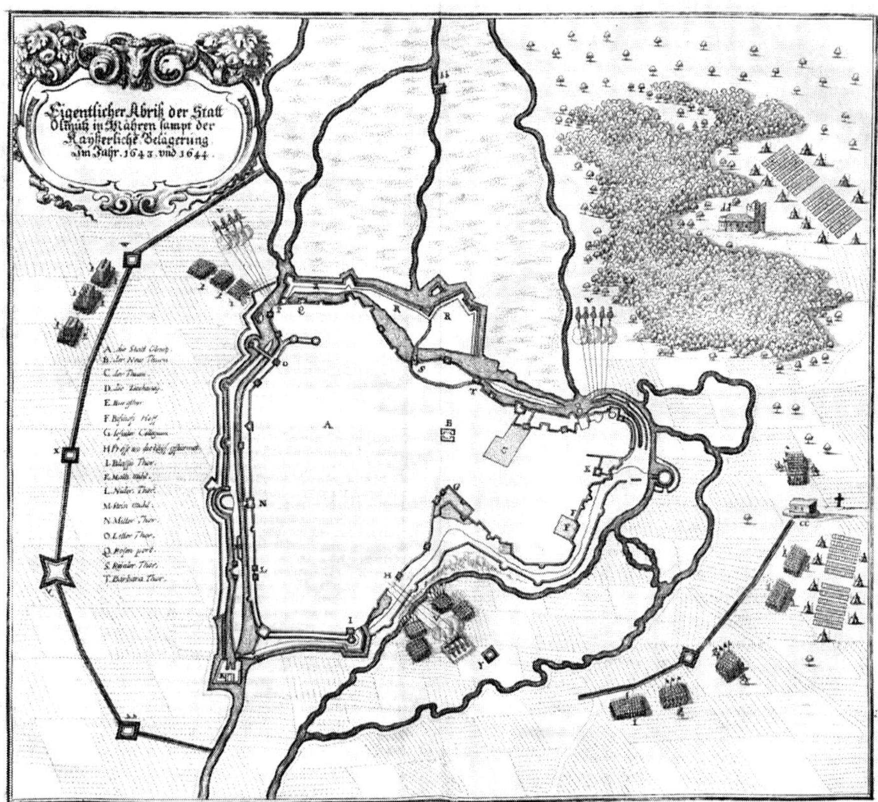

Figure 23: Siege of Olomouc by imperial troops (1643-44), 1650.

The Swedes violated the terms of the accord and began to collect war contributions from the clergy. A few days after the events at St Maurice they brutally exorted contributions from the administrator of the bishopric and the auxiliary bishop Stredele, who in reference to the initial settlement refused to pay. Twenty-four soldiers raided the bishop's residence and locked up the sixty-year-old administrator together with the other auxiliary bishop, Sigismund Miutini of Spillimberg. In a room with closed windows, tobacco smoke was blown at them all day and night. Stredele caught a strong cold and died ten days later, on 28 December 1642.[63] His funeral was celebrated at the beginning of January 1643, with all possible pomp and the participation of the entire Swedish regiment that deeply impressed with its solemnity. The bishop was accompanied to his final resting place by all the senior Swedish officers, apparently haunted by remorse and even fearing unrest in the city. "Lamentation and weeping women, particularly Swed-

63. As reported by Flade's diary. Dudík, "Tagebuch des feindlichen Einfalls", p. 368. The other sources refer to it as well; Flade seems to be the most accurate.

ish, filled the streets and squares," says Franciscan superior Paulinus Zaczkowicz, who attended the funeral as one of the main actors.[64]

Catholic clergy were seen as potential allies of the enemy, especially during the imperial siege. In October 1643 the Jesuits were expelled from the city (only Pelinka remained as the parish priest of St Maurice), then the remaining chapter canons and finally even the Augustinians were also expelled. Only some parish clergy and members of the mendicant orders remained at the site. Among these was privileged Franciscan lecturer Michael Jahn, who understood the Swedish officers and the commander of the fortress well, since they were both originally from Pomerania. They had even entrusted him to hide and guard their personal treasures. He took care of the cathedral and lived in the chapter deanery. And because he was collecting alms he could even come and go from the city. The Swedes also had him spy in the imperial camp besieging the city. The Swedes did not notice, however, that Jahn was acting as a double agent. In late September he organised a fake attack on a remote part of the city. Sending the Swedes in that direction, he then smuggled 1,100 imperial soldiers to the unprotected Předhradí. Only through the indecision of the imperial commanders and their lack of coordination did the Swedes manage to defend the city. Jahn escaped to the imperial camp, but under threat of the demolition of his friary he had to disclose to a friar sent by the Swedes where he had hidden their personal valuables.[65]

During this attempt to conquer the city a large number of troops on both sides fell and had to be buried. Officers could mostly be identified, but there was a problem with the sorting of the bodies of soldiers. It was necessary to determine whether they would be buried in a Catholic cemetery at the church of St Peter or the non-Catholic church at St Blaise. The Conventual Franciscan superior Zaczkowicz established a method for resolving the soldiers' denominational affiliation: the ones with small devotional objects (medals, Agnus Dei, rosaries etc.) were declared Catholics; the others as members of the Swedish army. The procedure was approved by the Swedish commander. The commander, who along with the superior was aware of the system's inconclusiveness, forbade the presence of Swedish women at Catholic funerals. According to the superior many of them came anyway because they were aware that the Catholic priest was burying their husbands. He himself stated that imperial soldiers were not even half of the 174 buried.[66] This incident illustrates well the blurring of confessional boundaries in the city. It is possible that the Swedish army contained a certain percentage of secret Catholics, and that non-Catholics were clearly convinced of the protective magic powers of the consecrated Catholic devotional objects that they carried into battle on themeselves.

The Swedish officers were interested in more solemn Catholic rites, perhaps out of curiosity or in their efforts to contribute to the peaceful coexistence of various denominations in the city. In 1643, for example, the soldiers participated in the Jesuit celebrations of the feast of St Ignatius. The Jesuits hosted them

64. Dudik, "Chronik des Minoriten-Guardians", pp. 491-492.
65. See Elbel, "Dva světy?", pp. 101-102.
66. Dudik, "Chronik des Minoriten-Guardians", pp. 500-501.

afterwards and showed them apparently some interesting physical experiments, so that the officers were very satisfied.[67] They watched the procession of Corpus Christi in 1644 with interest, even though the procession was allowed only around Předhradí. After the departure of the majority of cantors and bell ringers in October 1644, however, it was not possible to celebrate Catholic worship with the usual musical accompaniment.[68] It became markedly less attractive and more similar to austere non-Catholic worship.

Catholics sought privileges from the military administration that would facilitate their pastoral care. For example, the Jesuits acquired the right of free movement at night so that they could administer the last sacrament.[69] A Franciscan confraternity was allowed to be established in the city, which attracted fifty-six burghers.[70] And there was a Catholic school in addition to the Lutheran one. The teachers of both schools were named Michael and thus nicknamed the Catholic Michael and the Lutheran Michael.[71] Catholic Michael Sartorius had the authorisation of the Jesuits to oversee their college and when in 1647 books of the chapter and various religious houses (Capuchins, Dominicans, Franciscans and Jesuits) were requisitioned, he rescued some valuable manuscripts from the Jesuit library, including the registers of the Olomouc University.[72] The situation for Catholics changed dramatically in October 1645 when their clergy were unable to pay tribute and were expelled from the city. But plague ravaged the town and so some were called back. After this incident very few Catholic priests remained in the city, in total four or five.

The Peace of Westphalia in September 1648 was announced from the pulpit on Sunday, 22 November. After the ratification of peace, all Catholic and Lutheran churches celebrated a *Te Deum* on 11 January 1649. Peals of gunshot sounded and bells rang through most of the day, which was prohibited during the Swedish occupation. The celebration ended in the evening with popular festivities. Soldiers and their women, however, were terrified of the sudden peace. Almost an entire generation had only known conflict. They had no idea how they would live in peace. Some even begged Olomouc burghers to adopt their sons and daughters, for they did not know what to do with them.[73]

67. Parma, "Neznámý jezuitský pramen", p. 21.
68. Flade, Dudík, ed., "Tagebuch des feindlichen Einfalls", p. 477.
69. Parma, "Neznámý jezuitský pramen", p. 21.
70. Dudik, "Chronik des Minoriten-Guardians", pp. 569-570.
71. *Ibid.*, pp. 545-546.
72. Zaczkowicz claims that a Jesuit Georg Pelinka was responsible for the requisition of books because he told the Swedes about their value (*ibid.*, pp. 575-577). It was, however, planned before and there was a trained officer in the Swedish army with special instructions of the chancellor Oxenstierna. See Václav Pumprla, "Odvoz knih z Olomouce do Švédska na konci třicetileté války", in *Ročenka Státního okresního archivu v Olomouci 1997*, Olomouc, Státní okresní archiv, 1998, pp. 63-76; Emil Schieche, "Umfang und Schicksal der von den Schweden 1645 in Nikolsburg und 1648 in Prag erbeuteten Archivalien", *Bohemia*, 8 (1967), pp. 111-133.
73. Dudík, *Olmützer Sammel-Chronik*, pp. 60-61; Dudik, "Chronik des Minoriten-Guardians", pp. 579-600.

Even after concluding the peace treaty the Swedish troops remained in the city; they waited until the imperial party paid them a high compensation. On their leader's command the soldiers significantly changed their attitude towards the population. "They changed their wolfskin for a sheepskin robe and former enemies became good friends," as it was characterised by Zaczkowicz.[74] Members of Catholic religious orders gradually began to come back to the city. The return of objects of devotion was negotiated. The members of the Olomouc chapter arrived. On the morning of 8 July 1650 the Swedish garrison commander Winter passed the keys of the city to the imperial commissioner and left.

Conclusion

The first half of the seventeenth century was probably the most complicated period for the Olomouc burghers' confessional profile. Following the development of the whole country Olomouc went through periods of different confessionalisation attempts, changing dominant confession several times during the half-century. Even though the Swedish army's capture of the city meant a serious blow to the development of Catholicism there, the end of the Thirty Years' War brought a clear decision that led the city to the one confession that prevailed in post-war Moravia.

The epilogue to this long period, in which various confessions lived side by side in Olomouc, was the initiation of a ritual cleansing of churches and the whole city. It was managed by perhaps the only cleric who stayed in the city throughout the Swedish occupation, Paulinus Zaczkowicz. Zaczkowicz was appointed by the papal nuncio as the titular bishop of Sarepta and equipped with special privileges from the papal curia. On 17 July the cemetery, cathedral and chapel of St Anne were reconstituted. On 23 July the church of St Maurice was ritually purified and on 24 July a procession was led through the city from St Maurice to the cathedral for a celebration of a *Te Deum*.[75] The city was cleansed from the defilement of heresy, and even though it was destroyed and depopulated it could begin to rally and develop under a single religion, as a Catholic city.

74. *Ibid.*, p. 605.
75. *Ibid.*, p. 611; Dudík, *Olmützer Sammel-Chronik*, p. 61.

5. The Evolution of Catholic Identity, 1650-1700

Radmila Prchal Pavlíčková

Pilgrimage and Baroque Spirituality

At the end of the 1660s Jan Andrýsek, a merchant and burgher of Olomouc, composed an account of events that occurred forty years earlier and led to the foundation of one of the most significant pilgrimage sites in baroque Moravia near Olomouc. According to this record Andrýsek vowed to construct a chapel dedicated to the Virgin Mary, although for some time he was unable to find a suitable location near the city. Spurred on by a vision of the Virgin Mary and the growth of his property, he finally began to search intensively around the area. On one of his journeys, at the end of February 1629, he was lost in a snowstorm and reached an unfamiliar, brightly lit hilltop similar to the place that appeared in one of his dreams. He exulted in finding a place suitable for the realisation of his pledge. He was even more pleased when he learned that it was located on a plot of church property, belonging to the Premonstratensian monastery of Hradisko, resting in close proximity to the Olomouc city walls. The rest of the text then focuses on the practical matters of the chapel's foundation.

Andrýsek's commemorative record symbolically unites three crucial periods in the history of the city. The event it describes took place at the turn of the twenties and thirties of the seventeenth century, when the mainly Lutheran population of the city had to reckon with governmental pressure to unify citizens of the state under the faith of the Catholic sovereign. A sequence of regulations and controls proposed by Ferdinand II was published as the Renewed Land Ordinance (in Moravia 1628), which established the Catholic confession as the only faith allowed in the state. The story was drawn up only forty years later in the time when after the generational shift, the departure of the Swedish army and the consolidation of the post-war conditions, expressions of Catholic spirituality could already be seen in the city. Its writing was probably encouraged by negotiations over the construction of a new church (1669-79) instead of Andrýsek's original chapel, which was consumed by fire in 1645 during the Thirty Years' War. At that time the first publications of the story were circulated in an extensive guide for pilgrims dedicated to Svatý Kopeček (the Holy Hill) pilgrimage site in 1680.[1] Finally, An-

1. [Bernard Wancke], *Mons praemonstratus, Das ist: Außführliche Beschreibung...*, Olmütz, Johann Joseph Kylian, 1679.

Figure 24: Svatý Kopeček, Basilica of the Virgin Mary, St Pauline chapel. *Founding the place for the chapel.*

drýsek's commemorative work was printed again in the 1730s, when two of the local festivals (the centennial anniversary of the pilgrimage church's foundation and the coronation of the stone relief of the Virgin, both in 1732) ranked among the great manifestations of baroque Catholic spirituality.[2]

A wealth of literature about pilgrimage sites, written in the seventeenth century in connection with the conversion of Bohemia and Moravia to Catholicism, closely relied on the attempts of church intellectuals to reconstruct a sacred history of the land. With the aid of antique venerability and holiness, it offered to the inhabitants an alternative to forbidden religions. Most of these works contained a section dedicated to the history of the pilgrimage site and a description of the miracles associated with it. Examples include the numerous works of Bohuslav Balbín about pilgrimage sites (for instance Tuřany in Southern Moravia); a treatise of the Jesuit Jan Tanner called *Via sancta* describing the road between Prague and Stará Boleslav (1679); and the book of his brother Matěj Tanner about the pilgrimage site near Štramberk in Moravia (1660-61).[3]

2. Miloš Sládek, *Malý svět jest člověk aneb výbor z české barokní prózy*, Jinočany, H&H, 1995, pp. 89-104.

3. Jan Kučera and Jiří Rak, *Bohuslav Balbín a jeho místo v české kultuře*, Prague, Vyšehrad, 1983; Matěj Tanner, *Hora Olivetská*, ed. by Jan Malura and Pavel Kosek, Brno, Host, 2001;

Andrýsek's commemorative work notably differs from the standard canon of pilgrimage literature. It lacks a historical justification for its holiness. It contains no tradition or medieval pre-Hussite esteem, no ancient source of faith to which a pious, post-White Mountain Catholic would turn. The story centres on the confident action of a rich burgher who decided to invest a portion of his property to celebrate God. This burgher had some characteristic attributes: ardent spirituality, devotion, a "courageous heart" and absolute trust in and reliance on the will of God. The construction of a pilgrimage site on Svatý Kopeček is interpreted as an act of the individual, in close cooperation with the traditional institution of the Catholic Church – the monastery of the old monastic order. Andrýsek is presented as a model of piety for the burghers of Olomouc and others: an economically successful merchant uses his fortune to build a new Catholic sanctuary. Thus he represents a new type of a Catholic pious burgher as created in the Olomouc environment during the second and third quarters of the seventeenth century.

The timeline of this process undoubtedly coincides with the departure of the last Swedish soldiers in July 1650. After eight years the city was freed from the non-Catholic military garrison. Immediately after that St Maurice church and St Wenceslas cathedral were re-consecrated. As mentioned in the previous chapter these church celebrations may be considered as demonstrative, renewing acts, expressing the definitive end of a two-hundred-year period in which city residents were able to profess different religious movements and confessions, and symbolising the beginning of the victory of Catholicism.[4]

A range of conditions influenced the adoption and deepening of Catholic baroque spirituality. At the legislative level a decisive step was taken by the monarch when he allowed Catholicism as the only faith of the subjects in the aforementioned Renewed Land Ordinance. The provisions in the Peace of Westphalia (1648), according to which the organisational arrangements of religion in the Empire should return to 1624, enabled him to take advantage of the rule of *cuius regio, eius religio* in this effort. It is certain, however, that the mere regulation of the sovereign was insufficient to boost and finalise the return of citizens to Catholicism. In this way, only the legislative framework for the privileged position of a single confession was constructed. In recent discussion on confessionalisation key questions concern the role of the state, the representatives of the church (bishop, chapter, male and female monastic communities, the Jesuit university, religious confraternities, the nearby pilgrimage site and so on) and the individual seeking his or her own salvation. The original conception of confessionalisation as formulated by Reinhard and Schilling in the early 1980s was grounded in the targeted actions of the state and church on the religious-moral disciplination of the population. But subsequent critical reflections on this approach further emphasised the role of participation and initiatives of communities and individual believers in confessional formation.

Howard Louthan, *Converting Bohemia. Force and Persuasion in the Catholic Reformation*, Cambridge, Cambridge University Press, 2009, pp. 244-276.

4. Martin Elbel, "Utváření katolické konfesijní identity v Olomouci", in *Olomoucké baroko*, vol. I, pp. 189-196.

Bishop Charles

It has been said many times that Olomouc occupied a privileged position within the land and the diocese. It was the traditional seat of the bishopric with its cathedral, chapter and consistory, the religious-judicial and administrative office of the diocese. It is therefore necessary to consider the role the bishops played in consolidating the Catholic identity of Olomouc's burghers. The latter, especially the German-speaking ones, were ardent supporters of Martin Luther's teachings. This was a thorn in the side of the bishops' endeavours at the turn of the sixteenth and seventeenth centuries. Bishops Stanislaus Pavlovský and Francis of Dietrichstein, on the contrary, were active supporters of Trent. These facts were mentioned in the previous chapters in detail. However, after the death of Cardinal Dietrichstein (1636) the situation at the bishop's seat radically changed.

Until 1664 for almost thirty years the episcopal seat was controlled by the Habsburg archdukes, first by Leopold Wilhelm (bishop 1637-62),[5] the youngest son of Ferdinand II. He was followed for a short time by Charles Joseph (1663-64), son of Ferdinand III. Olomouc was one of their many benefices. Leopold Wilhelm was recognised primarily in the military arena and in international diplomacy and became an important individual in the Habsburg power struggle. Little can be said about the active support of re-Catholicisation from the bishop at this time; the Olomouc diocese rested completely outside the interests of its top officials.

The situation changed radically with the arrival of the new bishop in 1664. The chapter elected Charles of Liechtenstein-Castelkorn, dean of the chapter of Salzburg and canon of Olomouc. Roughly the next thirty years (Bishop Charles died in the autumn of 1695) were marked by signs of the diocese's extensive renewal on many levels: Bishop Charles was able to restore and strengthen the political prestige of the bishop in the estate institutions, to stabilise the economic situation of the bishop's estate, to restore the bishop's seat as a significant cultural and artistic centre and to contribute to the religious unification of the diocese.[6] Not accidentally, all contemporary panegyric literary and visual production built on the contrast between the destruction of the diocese during the Thirty Years' War and its generous renewal during the reign of Bishop Charles.

A telling example is an Olomouc university thesis from 1678[7] that likens Bishop Charles to the sun whose rays warm the land, thawing "a variety of nights" (i.e. the heresies and heretics), as is emphasised in a sign carried by angels be-

5. Renate Schreiber, *"ein galeria nach meiner Humor", Erzherzog Leopold Wilhelm*, Wien, Kunsthistorisches Museum, 2004.

6. Radmila Pavlíčková, *Sídla olomouckých biskupů. Mecenáš a stavebník Karel z Liechtensteinu-Castelkorna 1664-1695*, Olomouc, Univerzita Palackého, 2001; *Archbishop's chateau & gardens in Kroměříž*, ed. by Ladislav Daniel, Marek Perůtka and Milan Togner, Kroměříž, National Institute for Preservation of Historical Monuments, district branch Kroměříž, 2009.

7. Pavel Zatloukal, "Univerzitní teze Františka Ernesta ze Schertzu, 1678, Biskup Karel z Liechtensteinu-Castelkorna jako slunce ozařující Moravu", in *Olomoucké baroko*, vol. II, pp. 402-403.

Figure 25: Bachelor thesis of Mathias Schmidt, *Předhradí and the fire of the New gate*, copperplate engraving, 1676.

Figure 26: Olomouc university thesis of Franz Ernest of Schertz, *Bishop Charles of Liechtenstein-Castelkorn as sun over Moravia*, 1678.

neath a portrait of the bishop. In the centre of the image a sitting female personification of Moravia holds in her hands a map of Moravia and Silesia. The map casts a shadow, the only dark place among the ray-drenched garden scenery. It hides the last remnants of heresy, represented by the devil, a snake and a bat. A putto kneels in front of the personification of Moravia, reading a book in which it is written that "because of the most noble Prince Bishop Charles many thousands of souls were returned to the faith". Another putto standing beside him ostentatiously gestures with his right hand toward the book and with his left hand gestures upward toward the portrait of Bishop Charles in an oval medallion flanked on both sides by eagles. While the central vertical axis of the image is reserved for the celebration of the bishop as restorer of the diocese's religious unity, all of the surrounding area is reminiscent of the cultural, artistic and patronage activities. The scene is set in a garden, clearly referring to the architecture of the floral garden that Bishop Charles built at his residence in Kroměříž, the principal town of his estates. The standing figures on the sides personify various Moravian towns or refer back to the bishop's foundational activities in inscriptions on fountains in the middle of both of the rows. The figure of Minerva sitting by the fountain on the left also refers to architecture and other arts, while symmetrically to the right a sitting woman represents prudent government blossoming in prosperity. Finally, in the lower left corner appears an allegory of science and wisdom, represented by the then-popular *camera obscura*, whereby the medallion of the bishop is projected from heaven to earth.

The depiction of the late 1670s celebrates the bishop on two levels: as a successful agent of re-Catholicisation and as a great founder and patron of the arts and sciences. Historiography of the twentieth and twenty-first centuries has focused primarily on the second area and is completely in line with contemporary panegyrics that celebrated Charles of Liechtenstein-Castelkorn as a patron who turned his episcopal residences into an artistic centre. His foundational activity also affected the city of Olomouc, location of the bishop's residence. At the beginning of his episcopate Bishop Charles rebuilt it into a mighty city palace that housed a portrait gallery of Olomouc bishops. The picture cycle pointed to the historicity of the diocese and its holy founders, Sts Cyril and Methodius, and to the secular and ecclesiastical power of the Olomouc prelates and their singular political position in the country. The municipal bishop's palace inside the walls of Olomouc played an important part in the two-day festive entrances of newly elected bishops,[8] and represented their power in the city during their frequent absences.

The vigour with which the new bishop began to manage his diocese in 1664 was also reflected in the care of souls. Immediately after his ascension Charles of Liechtenstein-Castelkorn began to implement steps to create a better spiritual administration for the diocese and to improve the quality of parish clergy. He followed key resolutions of the Council of Trent, which promoted the idea that the basis of religious revival is a new type of priest, a spiritual shepherd who through his own example and piety leads the flock to Christian perfection.

One of Bishop Charles' first steps was to issue a normative regulation (*Monitorium*, 1666) that contained instructions for the deans and parish priests of the church on administration and spiritual lifestyle.[9] The *Monitorium* stressed the residential duty of parish priests and formulated clear guidelines for the everyday life of the secular clergy, particularly concerning their appearance and the creation of their image before the lay community of believers. Unacceptable forms of behaviour were also described, such as concubinage, appearing in public with service women, dancing and drunkenness. It also regulated clothes and trimming of the beard and hair, etc. Moreover, it instructed on correct spiritual ministery, including in matters of preaching, explaining catechism to the youth, educating parishioners about the sacrament of marriage in the sense of Trent decretals, and compelling them to maintain fasts and participate in pilgrimages. The *Monitorium*, which became the norm for priestly life deep into the eighteenth century, was followed in the seventies and eighties by a series of episcopal regulations on various issues. They served to promote among the population true piety, the acceptance of Catholic discipline through pastors and essential issues like the observance of Sunday rest.

At the same time, the *Monitorium* laid the foundations for regular visitations as a basic instrument to control pastoral activities and to enforce the clergy's discipline. According to the regulation, deans were obliged to annually visit parishes

8. Martin Elbel, "Bishop's Secular Entry. Power and Representation in Inauguration Ceremonies of the Eighteenth-Century Bishops of Olomouc", in *Religious Ceremonials and Images. Power and Social Meaning (1400-1750)*, ed. by José Pedro Paiva, Coimbra, Palimage, 2002, pp. 47-60.

9. Rudolf Zuber, *Osudy moravské církve v 18. století: 1695-1777*, Prague, Ústřední církevní nakladatelství, 1987, pp. 97-110.

and send reports back to the consistory. Establishing an effective tool for monitoring the diocese depended on the redistribution of deaneries so that the size would be convenient for the administration and supervision of deans. It took place at the very beginning of his episcopate and was completed by the 1670s.

Another area the bishop considered problematic in the early years of his tenure was the liturgical purity of worship, such as in the conducting of marriage ceremonies and singing denominationally correct songs. Already in 1666 he directed the dissemination of Catholic songs to replace the old, often Lutheran, songs. These activities culminated in the mid-nineties with the publication of the diocesan agenda, *Novae agendae Olomucensis directorium chori*, as one of the primary liturgical manuals and the guide for church musicians. The selection of Latin choral songs and German and Czech songs sung before the sermon played a role in the confessionally orthodox hymnal.[10]

Equally important was the bishop's support of pilgrimage and the major pilgrimage sites in Moravia, many of which were within reach of Olomouc burghers. The bishop supported the development of the aforementioned pilgrimage site of Svatý Kopeček, close to Olomouc (where the new pilgrimage church had already replaced the poor chapel), and the pilgrimage sites of Tuřany, near Brno, less than eighty kilometres away from Olomouc to the south; Stará Voda, about forty kilometres from Olomouc to the north; and the Mount of Olives in the Jesuit estate near Štramberk, about eighty kilometres east. The landscape around Olomouc was gradually filled with holy sites thanks to the support of church authorities. The popularity of pilgrimage to nearby locations was an important religious, public and social experience for the parish and other communities who made the pilgrimage.

Although the bishop took several steps to reform church administration it is impossible to give him sole credit for the re-Catholicisation of the country and the city of Olomouc, as contemporary panegyrics did. Moreover, at the core of his clever self-stylisation was the imperial princely title combined with the preferred political status of the country, rather than the office of bishop as the good shepherd of the Borromean kind. This is metaphorically revealed in the bishop's correspondence with his Viennese agent, with whom he discussed the purchase of a collection of paintings. He commented that the collection contained many paintings with religious themes, which was perhaps suitable for a church but not for the residence of a prince.[11]

Bishop Charles had matured politically in the imperial court of the Salzburg Archbishops, who independently participated in imperial politics. This experience was probably crucial for his political ambitions and his ideas about the Olomouc bishop as a carrier of the imperial princely title. It influenced also his relationship to art, music, architecture, books and minting coins. In the court of the archbishops of Salzburg he got to know generous cultural investment and the significance of well-chosen, thoughtful patronage in fashioning one's own representation. It is

10. Jiří Sehnal and Jiří Vysloužil, *Dějiny hudby na Moravě*, Brno, Muzejní a vlastivědná společnost, 2001, s. 66.

11. Antonín Breitenbacher, *Dějiny arcibiskupské obrazárny v Kroměříži*, 2 vols., Kroměříž, 1925-1927.

thus clear that Bishop Charles dedicated much more of his attention to artistic and architectural patronage than to the spiritual administration of his diocese.

Revival of Catholic Piety

The authorities and bodies associated with the administration of the diocese were not the only ecclesiastical institutions within the city walls. In addition to the cathedral, the chapter and the consistory, there were four parish churches (St Peter, St Maurice, the Virgin Mary in Předhradí and St Blaise). Moreover, the city had a Jesuit college, in which the university functioned since the sixteenth century, six male monasteries or friaries of traditional medieval orders (Dominicans, Conventual Franciscans and Augustinian canons, Carthusians, Observant Franciscans and Capuchins) and three nunneries (Dominicans, Poor Clares, and Ursulines). Olomouc burghers shared their living space within the city walls with a large community of secular clergy and hundreds of monks and nuns who, in their colourful competition, offered diverse, often attractive ways to participate in spiritual life (i.e. to work for one's own salvation and help others to salvation, especially the deceased).

One of the decisions of the Council of Trent was crucial in forming a new concept of post-Reformation Catholic piety. It suggested that for the salvation of souls human free will was necessary to cooperate with the grace of God. Unlike the Reformation conception that denied any possibility of humans actively participating in their salvation (when salvation depended on justification by faith, the grace of God and Scripture alone), the resurgent Catholic religion was founded on the importance of human deeds. This brought into play traditional medieval ideas and practices and justified their usefulness and necessity. They included the monastic life, respect for the Virgin Mary and the saints, indulgence practice and requiems, pilgrimages, processions and so on. Through priests' sermons and catechesis and through spiritual and educational literary works believers were convinced that salvation could be achieved by faith, accompanied however by a denominationally correct way of life. Good deeds with their salvific power and active participation in Catholic public life played an essential role.

The reformed version of Catholic piety offered the faithful attractive, visually compelling, emotionally interesting components which they began to consider important, even necessary, for preservation of their earthly life and their salvation, and that of their loved ones. Many other factors played a role in the adoption of the new Catholic identity. These included a wide range of religious educational literature, prayer books, home catechisms, guides for a good death, hymnbooks, pilgrims' guides and other genres that dominated the Czech and German language book markets in the second half of the seventeenth century and introduced the faithful to a denominationally correct life and death in the context of Catholic piety.[12] This literature represented an ideal Catholic life, explained the usefulness of its implementation and provided specific instructions on how to achieve it. The

12. Louthan, *Converting Bohemia;* Marie Sobotková, "Literatura v barokní Olomouci", in *Olomoucké baroko*, 3 vols., *Výtvarná kultura let 1620-1780*, vol. III, *Historie a kultura*, ed.

Figure 27: Kryštof Šimšický, St Pauline's reliquary, 1639-40.

authors took into account the theological and intellectual capacity of the readers. They presented religious and moral standards in an accessible way and expressed complex theological issues in a simple and concise manner.

Catholic forms of piety had many attractive aspects. One was the conviction that a believer was not alone in his or her distress and poor conscience, but had a wide range of possibilities to handle every-day problems. Their daily prayers could reach directly to God and Christ and to the Virgin Mary and the plethora of saints. The latter were believed to have power in heaven to intercede for poor sinners on earth and to beg for God's mercy or miracles. The baroque heaven was not only broad and large, but also very specialised. The faithful could direct their plea to a personal patron saint, to the local or provincial patron saint, to patron saints of specific professions, or saintly protectors against diseases and misfortune. There was also a varied and codified hierarchy for gaining the help of the residents of Heaven. Believers could rely on prayers and pleas, as well as a more demanding and sophisticated resources that reflected the strength of the supplicant's ties to that saint. These included pious donations and even the dedication of the believer's life.

The Olomouc heaven offered the residents of the city a wide range of saints through consecrated churches and chapels that housed their relics. In the seventeenth century respect for the traditional city patron saints was enriched with completely new elements, or at least a new momentum. The first phenomenon is illustrated by the addition of a new patron saint – St Pauline – in the 1620s. The saint's relics (skull, bones and oil lamp) were won by Olomouc Jesuits in 1623. Her presence in the sacred procession on 8 October 1623 was believed to have ended the plague, and she became the prime patron of the city and its inhabitants. Her reliquary, stored in the Jesuit church of the Virgin Mary, complemented a considerable number of relics displayed in dozens of local churches.[13]

Due to the beginnings of her worship and the thoughtful and purposeful promotion of her cult by the Jesuits, Saint Pauline was promptly classified as the patron saint of the city. The development of the cult in the second half of the seventeenth century is evidenced by the construction of the chapel (completed in 1685 and co-financed by the city council) that permanently exhibited her relics in a magnificent reliquary on the altar. The uniqueness of the cult of St Pauline, in full bloom dur-

by Ondřej Jakubec and Marek Perůtka, Olomouc, Muzeum umění Olomouc, 2010, vol. III, pp. 199-210.

13. Elbel, "Utváření katolické konfesní identity v Olomouci", pp. 189-196.

Figure 28a: Antonín Martin Lublinský, *View of Olomouc from south-west with St Pauline*, 1674.
Figure 28b: detail.

ing the seventeenth century, is associated with protection against the plague. Its popularity among the city inhabitants in the second half of the seventeenth century is witnessed in preserved votive paintings and prints sponsored by individuals and ecclesiastical and municipal institutions.[14] The greatest attention to St Pauline's cult was naturally displayed by the Olomouc Jesuits. They owed to her the transformation of their complicated position in the eyes of non-Catholic burghers into one of a good neighbour capable of providing a new protector for the city. The timing of the relics' first use, when the epidemic was probably already subsiding, brought both the immediate success of the new saint and local recognition of the Jesuits, enhancing their prestige in the city. Using the saint's relics in processions against the plague was the easiest and most practical method of introducing Catholic devotion to the non-Catholic city. It was a well thought out move and an absolute triumph.[15] The Jesuits of Olomouc, thanks to their ability to distribute miracles, offered the city specialised "spiritual service" and continued to promote the cult of St Pauline through the spiritual administration of the chapel and the maintenance of her relics.

Apparently, they ordered a veduta of the city in 1674. It is the first work by Anton Martin Lublinský and captures the city from the southwest.[16] The Jesuits' design and sponsorship is evidenced in the print by the presence of St Pauline and a complex of Jesuit buildings in Předhradí with the newly built college accentuated in the city's skyline. The scene in the lower left corner of the frame puts the city in territorial, political and ethereal coordinates: the personification of the Margravate of Moravia is accompanied by a river god, representing the Morava River flowing through Olomouc, and Minerva, the symbol of wisdom and protection from war. Minerva hands a wreath of flowers to St Pauline, shown in a white robe with a floral wreath on her head and a lamp in her hand.[17] The saint is displayed in an exclusive position. She is the only representative of the celestial sphere in the city's skyline. Understandably so, since important corporate devotional acts were addressed to her to obtain protection for the city. In addition to the annual votive procession, her relics were featured in processions imploring protection from epidemics. Additionally, special days-long church services were held in her chapel when the city was threatened by plague, as in 1715. Many houses in Olomouc reportedly bore inscriptions and paintings venerating the patron. The belief in the protective power of St Pauline and the habit of organising a collective appeal for the protection of the urban community was documented as recently as the 1830s.[18]

14. Petra Zelenková, "Contra pestem nobis fave. Příspěvek k ikonografii sv. Pavlíny, patronky proti moru v barokní Olomouci", *Sborník prací Filozofické fakulty brněnské univerzity. Opuscula historiae artium* 55, no. 49 (2005), pp. 27-45: 27-35.

15. Louthan, *Converting Bohemia*, pp. 16-46; Ondřej Jakubec, "Olomoucký jezuitský kostel a protimorový kult P. Marie Sněžné", in *Olomoucké baroko*, vol. I, pp. 150-156.

16. Milan Togner, "Pohled na Olomouc od jihozápadu, Antonín Martin Lublinský 1674", in *Olomoucké baroko*, vol. II, pp. 301-302, fig. 145.

17. Milan Togner, *Barokní malířství v Olomouci*, Olomouc, Univerzita Palackého, 2008, p. 22.

18. Helena Zápalková, "Relikviář sv. Pavlíny z pokladu olomoucké katedrály", in *Olomoucké baroko*, vol. I, pp. 211-218; Jakubec, "Olomoucký jezuitský kostel", p. 154.

The renewed reverence for the diocesan patrons St Cyril and St Methodius had a quite different background and promotion. The saints were considered missionaries who brought Christianity to Moravia and consequently to Bohemia, and who founded the bishopric and became its first representatives. They were revered as the most important diocesan patrons and in that sense became fixed figures among Olomouc's protectors.[19] Antiquity and continuity of the country's religious foundation gained special value in the second half of the seventeenth century, especially in religious self-presentation. The desire to prove a strong link to the pre-Hussite and pre-Reformation period, understood as the golden age of true piety, and to provide evidence of traditional orthodoxy in a country that had recently earned the label of a heretical and rebellious place, was manifested also in the works of Catholic intellectuals, especially in historical treatises.[20] Strong expression of this tendency is also documented in art patronage. Artistic commisions using medieval Gothic forms aspired to prove the antiquity of the true faith and the essential contribution of individual religious institutions to the growth and defence of that faith.[21] The Olomouc chapter and bishops, most importantly in the case of Cardinal Dietrichstein, strongly supported the cult of Sts Cyril and Methodius, renewed by Charles of Liechtenstein-Castelkorn in the second half of the seventeenth century. For the representation of the bishopric it played a crucial role as a symbol of the country's ancient piety and the emergence of the institutional church, seated in Olomouc. Respect for the missionaries was manifested in contracts for the construction, decoration and furnishings of the cathedral, as well as in depictions of the founding legend in the graphic arts and book commissions of the bishop and chapter.[22]

In addition to these examples it is necessary for this period to mention the worship of the local priest Jan (John) Sarkander (1576-1620). Sarkander died in the city prison in Olomouc during the revolt of the estates from the consequences of torture and interrogation. After his death he was almost immediately revered as a martyr. Though his beatification and canonisation occurred quite late (1859

19. Land patron saints: St Wenceslas, St Cyril, St Methodius, St Adalbert, St Vitus, St Procopius, St Cristinus, St Ludmila and St Cordula. Cf. their presence on the Olomouc Holy Trinity Column on the main square, which is regarded as a presentation of the Olomouc heaven.

20. Louthan, *Converting Bohemia*, pp. 115-145.

21. Zdeněk Kalista, *Česká barokní gotika a její žďárské ohnisko*, Brno, Blok, 1970; Viktor Kotrba, *Česká barokní gotika: Dílo J. Santiniho-Aichla*, Prague, Academia, 1976; Mojmír Horyna, *Jan Blažej Santini-Aichel*, Prague, Karolinum, 1998.

22. Silver busts of Sts Cyril, Methodius and Ludmila were donated by Charles of Liechtenstein-Castelkorn to the high altar of the cathedral. See Helena Zápalková, "Olomoučtí zlatníci doby baroka", in *Olomoucké baroko*, vol. II, pp. 475-483: 476; Gabriela Elbelová, "Portrétní tablo olomouckých biskupů", in *Olomoucké baroko*, vol. II, p. 335, fig. 199; Pavel Suchánek, *Triumf obnovujícího se dne. Umění a duchovní aristokracie na Moravě v 18. století*, Brno, Barrister & Principal, 2013, s. 122-133; Tomáš Parma, "The Legacy of Sts Cyril and Methodius in the Plans of Recatholization of Moravia", in *The Cyril and Methodius Mission and Europe – 1150 Years since the Arrival of the Thessaloniki Brothers in Great Moravia. Proceedings from the International Scientific Conference 13th-17th May 2013*, ed. by Pavel Kouřil, Velehrad, Brno, The Institute of Archaeology of the Academy of Sciences of the Czech Republic, 2014, pp. 334-341 (in print).

and 1995), throughout the seventeenth and eighteenth centuries he enjoyed saintly reverence in Olomouc.[23] In the second half of the seventeenth century key motifs of the legendary narrative crystallised, along with the principal places and modes of his worship in Olomouc. As part of the first official attempts to initiate the beatification process his legend was published in the 1660s, foreshadowing the publishing boom of the early eighteenth century.

Thanks to this literature we are well informed both about the baroque literary and iconographic shaping of Sarkander's legend and the specific devotional and ritual practices that Olomouc burghers and visitors associated with the places of his torture and death. Their characteristics are a good indication of the magical power saints held in the eyes of believers, the abilities people attributed to them and the manner in which the laity complemented Catholic dogma with unofficial superstitions in an urban environment.[24]

The worship of Sarkander figured in the sacred topography of the city through two novelties. One was the grave established for him in the chapel of St Lawrence in the church of the Virgin Mary in Předhradí. The second was the city prison. In the years 1672-73 a part of the prison was adapted as a chapel, in accordance with conditions of religious worship of Jan Sarkander's martyrdom. It was decorated in the years 1703-04. The faithful attributed to both sites magical healing powers. This is documented by the hanging of anatomical and other small *ex voto* offerings at the grave and in the chapel close to the instruments of torture. It is manifested in the use of dust from the grave and water from the prison well as remedies for diseases. Protective power was also attributed to the wood from the rack and the wheel on which Sarkander was tortured. In their account of the saint contemporary legend writers described people flaking away chips and gathering them in their homes. Reportedly, Olomouc burgher Josef Weisbach had as many as forty small crosses made of these chips, which he reportedly dropped into the cellar of his house during a great fire in 1709 in hopes of avoiding the disaster. The local popularity of Olomouc's Counter-Reformation martyr and the supposed benefits of physical contact with his holy sites bear strong witness that for the city's faithful the attractive elements of Catholic piety included the opportunity to acquire earthly and posthumous benefits, to participate in spiritual life, to become a part of various religious organisations and to accumulate these benefits for heaven.

The topography of the other world played a key role in constructing post-Tridentine Catholic confessional identity. Belief in purgatory – the place where the soul of the deceased went if burdened with only minor sins and could be in unspeakable agony cleansed to stand before God without blemish – was harshly rejected by the Reformation theologians who could not find support for it in Scripture. The Catholic Church, by contrast, confirmed at the Council of Trent the effectiveness of purgatorial dogma and acts of mercy (especially masses, prayers,

23. Ondřej Jakubec, "Ikonografie barokního kultu Jana Sarkandera v Olomouci", in *Olomoucké baroko*, vol. I, pp 182-186; cf. also the previous chapter.

24. Kaspar von Greyerz, "Grenzen zwischen Religion, Magie und Konfession aus der Sicht der frühneuzeitlichen Mentalitätsgeschichte", in *Grenzen und Raumvorstellungen*, ed. by Guy P. Marchal, Zürich, Chronos, 1996, pp. 329-343.

Figure 29: Antonín Freindt, *View into the chapel of Jan Sarkander*, former city prison, engraving, 1712.

Figure 30: Antonín Freindt, *View into the chapel of St Laurence at the Virgin Mary church in Předhradí, Jan Sarkander's tomb*, engraving, 1712.

alms) to pass the suffering souls of the dead through purgatory. In 1577, only a few years after the end of the Council of Trent, the first privileged indulgence altar was created. Such altars were endowed with special liturgical privileges that under the fulfilment of certain conditions guaranteed spiritual grace for souls of the dead. Commemorative religious practice moved from the elite level, dependent on the financial resources of the individual and family, to the collective level where it became commonly available.

Post-Tridentine Catholicism emphasised an intense connection between communities of the living and the dead. The possibility of constant communication with the deceased through acts of mercy was very attractive to lay believers. It ensured close contact with the dead and filled the need for intensive preparation for one's own departure from earthly life and a creation of "safeguards against purgatory". Recent research in nearby Brno (in size and significance a comparable royal city) shows that the originally Lutheran majority population established these new forms of baroque piety precisely in the period at hand (post mid-seventeenth century). The Brno burghers accepted them completely as their own. This is externally reflected, for example, by abundant memberships in religious confraternities and the steep increase in pious legacies.[25]

Active Religious Life

The Council of Trent and the subsequent promotions of purgatory and caring for the souls of the deceased became one of the central points of baroque Catholic piety, fundamentally determining the religious practice of believers. Such habits were reflected most in the daily life of the laity. Due to their importance for human salvation, these habits significantly influenced the thinking and behaviour of the believers and shaped their new Catholic identity. Institutions and communities that were able to offer adequate pastoral assistance gained considerable popularity.

In post-Tridentine society volunteer communities gained a completely new role, mostly as religious confraternities, which were a phenomenon of post-Tridentine Catholic regions. They were free and open associations of the faithful with close links to a parish or convent and had the purpose of supporting a cult. They emphasized the securing of posthumous salvation, funeral services, intercessory requiem masses and obtaining indulgences. Confraternities offered attractive forms of participation in religious activities due to their blending of religious and social life. They provided insurance against purgatory, guaranteeing salvation and assurance that the deceased would be remembered by the confraternity in the form of prayers for the dead. At the same time, they had a strong ambition to shape the daily lives of their members through membership regulations and obligations and regular execution of individual devotional acts. Membership in the confraternity thus required the adoption of a confessionally aligned form of piety. This had a strong impact on the everyday religious and personal religiosity of Olomouc burghers. To instruct members in the correct spiritual life, the confraternities distributed publications – especially their own manuals containing statutes, lists of indulgences and detailed instructions for spiritual life that included prayers and songs. The confraternities were crucial to the social life of the urban community and provided their members with the chance to organize public events like religious festivals.

Some early modern confraternities were founded in the late Middle Ages while others were newly formed. From the last third of the sixteenth century confraternities emphasised a return to Catholicism and the public manifestation of that faith. This is demonstrated by several phenomena: the increasing aggressiveness of the Confraternity of the Rosary in promoting the cult of Mary; the Corpus Christi Confraternity's confronation of the Reformation denial of transubstantiation; and the Marian Brotherhood's combining of both of these efforts.[26] In late sixteenth-century Olomouc, like in other cities, the Jesuit Order dominated the restoring of traditional confraternities and the establishment of new ones. After the mid-seventeenth century other orders and priests became involved in these efforts.

25. Tomáš Malý, *Smrt a spása mezi Tridentem a sekularizací*, Brno, Matice moravská, 2010.

26. Vladimír Maňas and Zdeněk Orlita, "Olomouc v období jediného oficiálního vyznání a jeho náboženská bratrstva", in *Olomoucké baroko*, vol. III, pp. 90-99.

All confraternities were until the mid-seventeenth century managed by the Jesuits, with the exceptions of the Confraternity of the Rosary, founded in the late fifteenth century at the Dominican church of St Michael, and the Scapular Brotherhood, run by the Augustinian friary since 1641. In the 1570s and 1580s the order founded two Latin Marian sodalities dedicated to the Visitation of the Virgin Mary for students of university, and to the Assumption of the Virgin Mary, which was intended mainly for academics and alumni. Its character surpassed the city because it often brought together an exclusive, socially significant range of members from more distant regions. In the first decade of the seventeenth century there were two other smaller Latin sodalities for grammar school students.

These Latin sodalities differed considerably from the non-Jesuit brotherhoods. They were characterised by relatively stringent requirements for their members' religious discipline. Strict standards were maintained and compliance was severely controlled. Acts of devotion were based on the principles of Ignatian spirituality. They had a variety of meditative elements and encouraged private prayers and religious exercises, which reached to the level of the mysteries. Despite the relative intensity and closeness of the Latin sodalities, Jesuits accepted as members even those from external and non-university environments. These were mainly from the higher social strata and were often exempt from the strict rules. The members of Marian sodalities were Moravian nobles, the diocese's ecclesiastical elite and the richest and most powerful Olomouc burghers. The latter, especially the wealthiest families and members of the city council, thus became part of an elite "club" of major political, economic and religious figures centred around Jesuit confraternities.

Furthermore, Marian sodalities influenced city life with regular public religious and dramatic productions on its streets, like funeral and other processions at Marian feasts, carnival and Holy Week. They impressed residents with their solemn and spectacular character. Among the most typical and also most expressive was the flagellation procession of students during the carnival period before Ash Wednesday and Good Friday. In the pre-White Mountain era these processions were denominationally militant. They demonstrated allegiance to the Catholic faith in an ostentatious manner in the mainly non-Catholic city. In the second half of the seventeenth century, however, parades of self-flagellating young men in hoods with bare backs presented for onlookers exacting forms of physical self-denial.

A considerably more direct influence on the population was made by St Anne's Confraternity at the church of the Virgin Mary in Předhradí. It was founded in 1501 and since the late sixteenth century was managed by the Jesuits. It was a confraternity for Olomouc burghers of both sexes. The confraternity connected Marian devotion with Anne's traditional piety, especially pilgrimages to St Anne at Stará Voda near Libavá, some thirty kilometres away from Olomouc. The activities of the confraternity offered to its members a combination of common, popularly practised collective experiences, and participation in certain internal events like the Latin Marian sodality procession or liturgy associated with the order. The members thus shared in the devotion based on monastic spirituality. By combining elements of popular and the more demanding Marian devotion, the St Anne's Jesuit Confraternity became very popular, as evidenced by the number of members and pious donations. In 1630 the

Jesuits founded yet another confraternity, this one dedicated to the Immaculate Conception of the Virgin Mary. It was an organisation purely for artisans and focused on married, established burghers and free journeymen from Olomouc. Six years later the Confraternity of Our Lady at the Crib and St Isidore was founded for the rural population around the city. Thus, the Jesuits managed to offer to individuals of practically all social strata both in the city and immediate area a possibility of membership in a pious confraternity established under their influence.

The biggest factor in the confraternity boom and the massive increase in their numbers occurred under Bishop Charles of Liechtenstein-Castelkorn in the second half of the seventeenth century. Confraternities originated in parishes (for example, at the parish church of St Maurice the Confraternity of the Mortal Agony of Christ was founded in 1655 and a confraternity dedicated to the cult of Corpus Christi in 1677), but also in monastic churches. Their expansion in this period suggests, among other things, that Olomouc burghers already largely identified with the Catholic faith and maintained abundant, sometimes multiple, memberships in lay pious associations based on the principles of post-Tridentine Catholicism. For them it was a welcome opportunity to acquire merits towards heaven.

Monasteries too were major centres offering Olomouc burghers attractive participation in religious life. Already in the early eighteenth century the confraternities of St Ursula at the Ursuline Convent (1702) and of the Heart of the Virgin Mary at the Monastery of the Poor Clares were founded. Another specific form of association for secular parties arose in 1700 with the Third Order at the Franciscan convent in Olomouc, the first in the Bohemian lands.[27] Compared to the confraternities this offered greater association with an order. This was manifested, for example, in their monastic attire while attending meetings and a larger share of monastic indulgences. The Third Order of St Francis at the Olomouc convent experienced its greatest expansion in the first decade after its founding, which confirms the attractiveness of this deeper and more demanding form of religious life. It also confirms that Olomouc burghers were fully primed for it.

The city was densely populated with opportunities to participate in spiritual life through individual institutions. These institutions competed with each other for the favour of the burghers. They sought to maintain a positive image in the eyes of the townsfolk and to pursue extra activities such as organising pilgrimages, processions or stations of the cross, or making more unusual offers or exclusive forms of piety. The city became the scene of religious festivals in which city dwellers could participate and in which could be observed little resentments among the ecclesiastical institutions whose disputes often escalated from spectacular religious celebrations to skirmishes and bickering over precedence.

Competition for the symbolic dominance of space and the favour of the people during religious festivals was not just demonstrated by the activities of the Jesuits in establishing confraternities. Another example of such a strategy was the long and ultimately successful effort to build the Franciscan Chapel of the Holy Stairs in Olomouc. The townspeople conducted a ceremonial ground-breaking for

27. Martin Elbel, *Bohemia Franciscana. Františkánský řád a jeho působení v českých zemch v 17. a 18. století*, Olomouc, Univerzita Palackého, 2001, p. 75.

the foundations on 3 June 1702. According to the monastic chronicle they experienced exalted rapture during the sermon of a Franciscan superior, and over the next three days excavated the foundations for the construction of the chapel.[28] The interest that was aroused by the chapel, which was granted numerous indulgences in the year 1726, suggests that Olomouc burghers entered the new century as solid Catholics with a sense of the specific and demanding forms of Catholic piety.

Conclusion

The events of 1650 – the Swedish troops' withdrawal from the city and the ceremonial cleansing of the city churches – mark a turning point in the confessional development of Olomouc. After more than a century of confessional struggle and confessionalisation strategies and policy by outside authorities, the city entered on a path to a single confession: Catholicism. The Catholic revival was enabled by the re-Catholicisation policy of Bishop Charles and the active participation of the burghers in parishes and religious orders. Within the second half of the seventeenth century the citizens acquired a clear Catholic identity manifested by various religious festivities, and Catholicism again defined the city.

28. *Ibid.*, pp. 90-92; Martin Elbel, "Tanquam Peregrini. Pilgrimage Practice in the Bohemian Franciscan Province", in *Communities of Devotion: Religious Orders and Society in East Central Europe, 1450-1800*, ed. by Maria Craciun and Elaine Fulton, Farnham, Ashgate, 2011, pp. 227-243: 239-240.

6. Consolidation, 1700-1750

Martin Elbel

On 18 July 1700 Olomouc began celebrating the great jubilee promulgated by the pope earlier that year. Although the solemnity of the occasion was clouded by the menace of war – a local chronicler noted that the pope had declared the jubilee in an attempt to prevent a war over the Spanish succession – the jubilee was a joyful and promising event.[1] After all, the old traditional threats seemed to have been overcome: the last plague had struck twenty years earlier, the Ottomans were retreating after the defeat at Vienna and the witch-trials in the nearby region were waning. There was less fear of witches and less fear that the witch-finder Boblig of Edelstadt would extend his competence over the citizens of Olomouc.[2] The city was prosperous and so were its religious institutions. The jubilee lasted for two months. In order to obtain indulgences, believers were supposed to visit within a fifteen-day period four major places of worship in the city: the cathedral of St Wenceslas and the three parish churches of St Peter (a former cathedral), the Virgin Mary and St Maurice. Alternatively, they could say the required prayers in three of those churches, provided they visited them in a procession. This was the choice of many – not because it represented a concession to duty, but rather because processions provided additional solemnity and splendour. The first procession was held by the local Franciscans on the afternoon of the first day. It was a massive success, attracing much attention from onlookers who joined the friars. Soon the procession swelled so that it stretched through "the longest street in the town". Other processions followed in the next few days.

It was only fifty years earlier when a similar procession strode through the streets and squares of the impoverished and devastated city to reclaim its public space for the Catholic religion and the emperor.[3] At that time the procession consisted of only a handful of priests. Now there was a large and fairly complex body of clergy, both secular and religious. Moreover, the population of Olomouc consisted, at least nominally, of loyal Catholic believers who were bound by

1. MZA, E 21, Franciscans of Dačice, book no. 9, *Archivum Conventus Olomucensis*, pp. 125-6.

2. See Martin Elbel, "Strach z ďábelských sil v raném novověku", in *Olomoucké baroko*, vol. I, pp. 159-165.

3. *Chronik des Minoriten-Guardians des St. Jacobs-Klosters in Olmütz*, ed. by Beda Dudík, Wien, 1881, pp. 160-161.

formal or informal ties to individual churches, monasteries and religious confraternities.[4] Many of these institutions, including local guilds, sought to organise their own processions that linked their respective shrines with the four major churches. The processions covered the city with a web of routes that marked its sacred topography and manifested complex patterns of communal religious life. The whole jubilee thus became a celebration of the Catholic identity of the town, its institutions and citizens.[5]

Less than two years later the image of harmonious Catholic polity would be shattered by a conflict between the bishop's consistory and the city council. It would involve other important religious and secular institutions in the town and reveal serious ruptures under the seemingly unified confessional culture. As in the previous period, numerous groups and individuals shared allegiance to the Catholic faith yet continued to hold competing views and ambitions. The first half of the eighteenth century indeed represented a heyday of Catholic confessional culture that saw spectacular festivities and the construction of lavish religious buildings. Yet under that surface there was a struggle to maintain the balance of power, a constant negotiation of the contours of religious life and on-going adaptation of universal cults to local experience. These processes enabled the development of a yet more profound confessional culture, which survived even the transformation of the city into a huge fortress (commencing in 1742) and continued to influence city life into modern times.[6]

Balance of Power

The jubilee of 1700 was an important public event that attracted many institutions and individuals. One notable exception was the bishop of Olomouc. During the jubilee year Bishop Charles III of Lorraine failed to visit his diocese at all. He was a sharp contrast to his predecessor, Charles II of Liechtenstein-Castelkorn, who had dedicated much effort to the spiritual and material development of his bishopric. Charles of Lorraine was a nephew of Emperor Leopold I, who imposed thirteen-year-old Charles as a coadjutor to the ageing Liechtenstein in 1692. And when the old bishop died the emperor saw to it that the cathedral chapter elected Charles as his successor. Although the pope imposed some restrictions on Charles's right to use the bishopric's property until Charles reached prescribed age, the new bishop soon gained control over the estates and revenues. He visited his see for the first time seven years after the election, and his stay was rather short. Meanwhile he had been elected also as bishop of Osnabrück, which

4. Martin Elbel, "Utváření katolické konfesijní identity v Olomouci", in *Olomoucké baroko*, vol. I, pp. 189-196.

5. Cf. Will Coster and Andrew Spicer, "Introduction: The Dimensions of Sacred Space in Reformation Europe", in *Sacred Space in Early Modern Europe*, ed. by Will Coster and Andrew Spicer, Cambridge, Cambridge University Press, 2005, pp. 1-16.

6. See *Dějiny Olomouce*, vol. 2, ed. by Jana Burešová, Olomouc, Univerzita Palackého, 2009.

he chose as his permanent residence. The Olomouc see was thus reduced to a source of income to finance the bishop's own activities and the emperor's treasury, depleted by the war. It is no wonder that Charles's episcopate had a far from positive impact on the diocese, especially in financial terms.[7]

In spite of the absentee bishop the local church, at least within the city itself, proved to be remarkably self-sufficient. It was run efficiently by the bishop's consistory, presided over by the agile and severe dean Orlick, who diligently supervised the affairs of the local church. This period contributed to the professionalisation of church bureaucracy and the consolidation of religious life. Yet the profound differences between urban and rural areas survived. In Olomouc itself the Catholic confession flourished (the only non-Catholics were temporary visitors, especially journeymen and soldiers of the garrison), but the situation in countryside was more complicated and required constant attention. Unlike in the towns the parish network was inefficient and occasional visitations encountered serious gaps in pastoral care. For example, in one mountain village the priest had been neglecting preaching for thirty years and his parishioners allegedly did not know how to make the sign of the cross and could not answer the question of how many gods there were.[8] Although this was an extreme case the situation in the countryside was far from satisfactory and in many ways contrasted the situation in Olomouc.

The city and the countryside, however, were not separate entities; the affairs of Olomouc and the diocese were interconnected. This became apparent in one extraordinary case. When the witch trials in the diocese had stopped (the last witch was executed in 1703), the consistory started receiving petitions from rural parish priests asking for instructions. Their parishioners were complaining that the cadavers of some deceased people had been leaving their graves and tormenting their living neighbours. There had been several instances of vampirism already in the seventeenth century, mostly in northern mountainous parts of the diocese.[9] At the beginning of the eighteenth century the superstition re-emerged with increased intensity. People demanded destruction of the afflicted corpses. Although sceptical voices appeared, in most cases the consistory approved of exhumation. Its decisions were motivated mostly by petitions from uneasy parish priests directly exposed to pressure from anxious parishioners and partly by the fear that the people themselves would take matters into their own hands with less legal and orthodox means.[10] The situation was particularly delicate since some of the villages that reported cases of vampirism were part of the bishop's domains. This led the director of the bishop's estates, Karl Ferdinand Schertz, to publish a

7. Rudolf Zuber, *Osudy moravské církve v 18. století*, Prague, Ústřední církevní nakladatelství, 1987, pp. 91-104.

8. *Ibid.*, p. 207.

9. Giuseppe Maiello, *Vampyrismus v kulturních dějinách Evropy*, Prague, Nakladatelství Lidové noviny, 2005.

10. On fear and anxiety in pre-modern society see William J. Bouwsma, "Anxiety and the Formation of Early Modern Culture", in *After the Reformation: Essays in Honor of J.H. Hexter*, ed. by Barbara C. Malament, Manchester, Manchester University Press, 1980, pp. 215-246. Cf. Michel de Certeau, *The Possesion at Loudun*, transl. by M.B. Smith, Chicago and London, University of Chicago Press, 1999, p. 2.

book entitled *Magia Posthuma* in 1704.[11] Although Schertz did not deny the existence of vampires, he called for caution and dealt predominantly with the legal aspects of exhumations. Upon his advice the consistory insisted that exhumation only take place in the presence of its deputy and several physicians and surgeons from Olomouc. They found most of the bodies in a natural state of decomposition, but a few cases of cadavers showing "unusual signs" were enough to keep the panic alive. Its outbursts continued to re-appear in the following decades. During the culmination of the panic in the small town of Libavá, around eighty corpses, including sixty children, were exhumed and destroyed in a single year (1727).[12] The panic was, at least officially, suppressed only in 1755 when Empress Maria Theresa, encouraged by her physician and adviser Gerhard van Swieten, issued a decree condemning vampirism as ignorant superstition. She admonished the consistory and forbade further exhumations.[13]

Although the cases of vampirism remained limited to several villages and smaller towns in the region some twenty miles northwest of the city, Olomouc and its inhabitants were not immune to the panic. Schertz claimed that in the city there was a ghost that had unpleasant habit of throwing stones at people.[14] Rumours circulated in the city and the countryside and soon spread beyond the confines of the diocese. The consistory, uncertain how to proceed, sent an enquiry to Rome. They never got an answer however. Later some of the afflicted towns wrote similar petitions to universities. Even more important for the spread of the fame of Moravian vampires were the bishop's officials from Lorraine who were sending regular reports back home. One of them sent his remarks with a copy of Schertz's book to Dom Augustin Calmet, Abbot of Senones. Calmet found in the issue of bodies returning from their graves an interesting theological problem and decided to research the topic. In 1746 he published his *Dissertations sur les apparitions des anges, des démons et des esprits, et sur les revenants et vampires de Hongrie, de Bohême, de Moravie et de Silésie*, a book which – thanks to its sensational contents – later overshadowed even his monumental commentaries on the Bible.[15] It was soon translated into German, Italian and English and later became a major inspiration for Victorian vampire novels, including Stoker's *Dracula*.[16]

11. Carolus Ferdinandus de Schertz, *Magia Posthuma Per Juridicum Illud Pro et Contra Suspenso Nonnullibi Judicio Investigata*, Olomucii, 1704.

12. Jan Bombera, "O posmrtné magii na libavském panství v 18. století", in *Okresní archív v Olomouci* 1984, Olomouc, Státní okresní archiv, 1985, pp. 79-93.

13. Van Swieten was also an author of another treatise about the vampire superstition: *Remarques sur le Vampyrisme de Sylésie de l'an 1755*. See Gerhard van Swieten *Vampyrismus*, ed. by Piero Violante, Palermo, Flaccovio, 1988.

14. de Schertz, *Magia Posthuma*, s.p.

15. Augustin Calmet, *Dissertations sur les apparitions des anges, des démons et des esprits, et sur les revenants et vampires de Hongrie, de Bohême, de Moravie et de Silésie*, Paris, de Bure l'aîné, 1746.

16. The other contemporary works are a book by Giuseppe Davanzati, Bishop of Trani, published in 1739. Davanzati was informed about the vampires by Charles's successor to the Olomouc see, Cardinal Schrattenbach, during his sojourn in Italy. See Giuseppe Davanzati, *Dissertazione sopra i vampiri*, ed. by Giacomo Annibaldis, Bari, BESA, 1998.

While the vampire panic was mainly an issue of the countryside, within the city the consistory was involved in another problem. In spite, or perhaps because, of the progress and consolidation of Catholic confessional culture, the relationship between ecclesiastical and secular authorities was becoming increasingly complicated. A particularly tense situation occurred at the beginning of 1702. At that time the consistory was dealing with some marital litigation and decided to summon a local citizen, a merchant of Italian origin, as a witness. The city council – claiming that the merchant was under its jurisdiction and that the consistory had no right to interrogate him – forbade the merchant to attend the hearing. The councillors also suggested that they would interrogate the merchant themselves and send the protocol to the consistory. However, marriage disputes were closely related to sacraments, and as such were seen as the domain of the church. Dean Orlick took the magistrates' obstructions as an attack on ecclesiastical prerogatives and acted promptly. On 29 January the consistory's clerk nailed on the doors of local churches a decree that announced to the astonished citizens that members of the municipal council responsible for the obstruction had been excommunicated.[17] The council immediately fought back, complaining at the land government. Soon other institutions were involved in the case. Eventually the emperor declared that the church had no right to excommunicate public officials without a prior consultation with state authorities and ordered Orlick to cancel the excommunication. The dean first refused to give in to the pressure, but without a strong bishop's backing he could not resist for long. When the emperor threatened to confiscate the dean's estates, the dismayed and humiliated Orlick gave in and withdrew the excommunication.[18]

The whole affair is more than just an illustration of the growing influence of the state over church affairs. It reveals a complicated network of loyalties of individual institutions. While the Jesuits and most of the clergy seemed to support the consistory's decision (albeit with limited enthusiasm), others were more reluctant. Just a few days after the publication of the excommunication a rumour spread that the local Observant Franciscans had boycotted it. Not only had they allowed the councillors to attend their church, they also permitted them to receive the sacraments. Hieronymus Veit, the superior of the convent, was even accused of fraternising with the excommunicated councillors and attending feasts in their houses. The open disobedience and sheer lack of solidarity angered Orlick and scandalised most of the clergy. Even fellow friars from other convents were writing alarmed letters to their Olomouc brethren asking if those terrible calumnies were true.[19] The superior of the Olomouc convent sought to defend himself, claiming that the text of the excommunication decree was ambiguous; but apparently others did not share his view. The cancellation of the excommunication brought relief but it could hardly justify Veit's behaviour in the eyes of other clergy.

17. The whole affair documented in SOkA Olomouc, AMO, Zlomky registratur, inv. no. 190, cart. no. 8.

18. Rudolf Zuber, "Poslední exkomunikace laiků v olomoucké diecézi", *Ročenka Státního Okresního Archívu v Olomouci*, 20 (1993), pp. 162-169.

19. SOkA Olomouc, AMO, Zlomky registratur, inv. no. 401, cart. no. 13, fol. 201-202.

Although the reputation of the Olomouc Franciscans suffered among other clergy it seems the superior carefully weighed the risks, which eventually paid off. In his chronicle he openly admitted that his (almost exclusive) support in the times of crisis won the gratitude of the city council and eventually the whole town. Veit was shortly after appointed an extraordinary notary of the city and the convent was amply remunerated for its potential losses.[20] This is just one of the hints that the superior's haphazard behaviour was not a mere consequence of his disrespect to the delicate network of local ties. On the contrary, it seems to have been a logical step that followed traditional co-operation between the municipal council and mendicants. The councillors of the town had been major institutional and personal supporters of the convent. It was from their ranks that the Franciscans usually chose their "Spiritual Fathers" or apostolic syndics. In the eighteenth century many of them would join the newly established Third Order at the Franciscan convent (and thus virtually became members of the Franciscan family). In return, they found in the Franciscan church various spiritual benefits and a burial place. Their interest was not limited to the Franciscan convent but extended to other religious institutions in the town. Among these it was the mendicants' convents that proved to be the most efficient partners and allies. The economic and social vulnerability of the mendicants made them more sensitive toward the interests of the town, and its representatives in particular. Their co-operation helped both parties pursue their goals and to shape the town's religious life.

The superior had another agenda that inspired his bold attempt to win favours from the city council – perhaps even at the expense of the other mendicants. Before his appointment to Olomouc in 1700 he had spent several years as a missionary in Palestine and Egypt. Immediately after his arrival to Olomouc he started several projects intended to increase the popularity of his convent. Among other actions he introduced the Third Order and wrote a handbook for its members.[21] It seems his efforts were not without success; after his first year in office the number of communicants in the Franciscan church increased by half. Yet all these activities were just a prelude to an even more ambitious project. As the superior stated in the convent chronicle, already during his sojourn in the Middle East, Italy and Spain he had conceived an idea to build a new attractive shrine back home in his province. Eventually he decided on an imitation of the Lateran *Scala Sancta*, which would become the first such shrine in the region. He soon acquired papal indulgences for the place, a copy of *Volto Santo* and even succeeded in getting appropriate space next to the convent gate. The sudden excommunication of the city council was an unpleasant complication. However, his loyalty in the times of crisis definitely paid off. In summer 1702 he was able to proceed with construction. The beginning of the works was marked by festivities during which the superior delivered a particularly animated sermon. He announced his intentions to build the chapel and described the spiritual benefits of the shrine. The response of the people was

20. MZA Brno, E 21, Franciscans of Dačice, book no. 9, *Archivum Conventus Olomucensis*, p. 132.

21. Hieronymus Veit, *Regule, Aneb Spůsob Žiwota, Bratrůw a Sester, Třetjho Řžádu S. Otce Frantisska*, W Nowém M. Pražském, v Anny Worssyli Hamplowý, 1708.

highly enthusiastic. The gathered believers allegedly began spontaneously digging the foundations using their bare hands and handkerchiefs to carry the soil away. This lasted continuously for three days and nights, during which the people reportedly did the work that ten skilled workers were supposed to do for four weeks. The other clergy in the town were outraged however. They accused the Franciscan superior of simony and seducing the crowd with false promises. The Capuchins bitterly complained that the new shrine would attract all the alms at the expense of other mendicant convents, while the neighbouring Ursuline nuns accused the Franciscans of seizing ground that was supposed to become a part of their monastery. The abbot of a nearby Premonstratensian monastery was so disgusted by the superior's behaviour that he decided to withhold annual alms the monastery gave to the Franciscans and instead distributed them to other religious houses in the town.[22]

The quarrels triggered by a plan to build an attractive shrine reflect the complicated ties between church institutions in the city. The dynamic religious development in the previous century created a complex religious landscape, densely populated with churches, monasteries and chapels. In addition to the cathedral and four parish churches, in the first half of the eighteenth century Olomouc hosted several smaller chapels and seven male and three female monasteries. These included a Jesuit college with a university and newly rebuilt church of the Virgin Mary of the Snow, the Augustinian Canons, the Carthusians, the Dominicans, all three main branches of the Friars Minor (the Conventuals, Observants and Capuchins), the Dominican nuns, the Poor Clares and the Ursulines. Outside the town walls there were three hospital churches and a large Premonstratensian monastery (Hradisko) with a major pilgrimage church at Svatý Kopeček, four miles from the city.[23] Most of the churches offered privileged altars, miraculous statues, ancient relics, regular devotions and skilled preachers. Out of the city's estimated eight thousand inhabitants there were approximately five hundred priests, monks, friars and nuns.[24] This provided settings for rich religious life but also provoked tensions and competition. By the beginning of the eighteenth century local religious institutions reached a fragile equilibrium, a sort of religious balance of power. An attempt to introduce a new shrine for devotion threatened the balance, and other institutions immediately created an alliance to prevent it.[25] The religious institutions were not the only players in the city however. The city or its representatives and the state authorities wanted to have their say. They became increasingly influential in the negotiating process. It was only the support of the city council that helped the friars finally overcome the obstacles and complete, albeit with great delay in 1726, the construction of the chapel.

22. Martin Elbel, "Budování poutního místa. Svaté schody při františkánském klášteře v Olomouci", *Folia historica Bohemica*, 20 (2004), pp. 215-239.

23. Jana Oppeltová, "Premonstrátská kanonie Hradisko u Olomouce a její kulturní prostředí", in *Olomoucké baroko*, vol. III, pp. 53-65.

24. See the description by Florián Josef Loucký, *Popis královského hlavního města Olomouce sepsaný syndikem Floriánem Josefem Louckým roku 1746*, ed. by Vladimír Spáčil and Libuše Spáčilová, Olomouc, Vlastivědná společnost muzejní, 1991.

25. Similar situations were occurring in other royal cities, even in previous decades, when some religious orders wanted to get a hold in the town and found a monastery.

Figure 31: J.A. Schindler, *Scala santa at Observant Franciscans*, 1726.

It turned out that the fears of other monasteries were premature. Although the new shrine gained interest and popularity it never became a major pilgrimage shrine that attracted regular processions from outside Olomouc. The church of the Virgin Mary at Svatý Kopeček continued to be the principle local pilgrimage shrine. The main reason for that lay in the distinctively urban character of the new shrine and its focus on the Passion of Christ. As such, it encouraged regular individual devotions instead of the more spectacular collective festivities of rural pilgrimage churches (mostly dedicated to the Virgin Mary and other saints).[26] On the other hand, the Holy Stairs helped strengthen ties between the convent and its local sympathisers. It perhaps also helped to attract more believers (the number of citizens joining the Franciscan Third Order, at least, slightly increased in the years after the consecration of the chapel). The visitors to the Franciscan church nonetheless continued to distribute their interest and support among other local shrines.

Self-Assured Triumph

The wealth of cults and devotions became one of the assets of the urban sphere. Both burghers and visitors to the city had a great variety of choice and could shape their religious life according to their needs, social status, wealth, allegiance to professional corporations and family traditions. It could be structured on various levels with different patterns and intensity. In addition to attendance at their parish church people could visit services or sermons in the cathedral or churches of religious orders. They could participate in their specific devotions, make vows and foundations and sponsor altarpieces and devotional objects. The burghers could also join one or more religious confraternities and even enter a religious order.[27] Those seeking an even more profound and permanent relation with the shrines could secure a burial place in one of the crypts instead of the cemetery of their own parish church. This involvement and sponsorship was not limited to wealthier inhabitants of the town. People of all social layers could give donations or order a mass to be celebrated for a selected purpose. The fixed price of thirty *Kreutzer* (half a guilder) per mass made this option affordable, albeit on irregular basis, even to poorer inhabitants.

It was not just money, however, that shaped and influenced the position of individual church institutions in the town. Attendance and the number of penitents and communicants mattered too. So even the poor could "vote with their feet". This created a dynamic and stimulating environment in spite of the tension aroused by some of the more ambitious projects. Individual church institutions

26. Several years later the Franciscans incorporated the *Scala Sancta* (together with the older chapel of the Holy Sepulchre) into the newly erected Way of the Cross, another novel and arguably more successful devotion they introduced into the city.

27. Vladimír Maňas and Zdeněk Orlita, "Olomouc v období jediného oficiálního vyznání a jeho náboženská bratrstva", in *Olomoucké baroko*, vol. III, pp. 90-99. See also *Zbožných duší úl. Náboženská bratrstva v kultuře raněnovověké Moravy. Katalog výstavy*, ed. by Vladimír Maňas, Zdeněk Orlita and Martina Potůčková, Olomouc, Muzeum umění Olomouc – Arcidiecézní muzeum Olomouc, 2010.

supported by rich individuals or groups of burghers competed for attention and introduced new cults and devotions. Their endeavours were not only manifested by the patronage of new paintings, statues and liturgical objects, but also by conspicuous building activity, which culminated in the first three decades of the eighteenth century.[28] Some of the new buildings altered the skyline of the town, especially the new Dominican church of St Michael with its three domes on the hill (1676-1707). The most active builders were the Jesuits. They bought several houses in their neighbourhood to expand their premises. Gradually they rebuilt their college (1711-22), the church of the Virgin Mary of the Snow (1712-19), the Seminary of St Francis Xavier (1717-20) and finally the New College (*convictus*) with the Corpus Christi chapel (1721-24). They created a vast complex of buildings that stretched along the town walls and occupied a central position between the ecclesiastical suburb (Předhradí) and the town itself.

Even the two big catastrophes that afflicted the town in the first two decades of the eighteenth century proved to be stimuli rather than serious impediments to building activities. The first was the fire in 1709, which destroyed a large part of the town. It also hit the Dominican church of St Michael, but the damage was repaired within a few years. The real victims of the fire were mostly private houses.[29] The restoration was costly and tedious, but eventually major streets gained a new, more representative outlook. The fire led to the construction of new fountains in the town. The older fountains of St Florian, Neptune and Hercules were joined by fountains of Tritons (1709), Caesar (1725) and Mercury (1727). These were predominantly situated in the quarters most heavily afflicted by the fire. In 1735 the statue at the Florian fountain was replaced with a new statue of Jupiter. Thus the whole set of fountains was unified and based on Classical mythology and history. It emphasised the glory of the town while containing strong references to the emperors (Hercules, Caesar, Jupiter). Especially the fountain of Caesar utilised the myth of the city's foundation by Gaius Julius himself. The fountain with the equestrian statue is located in the corner of the main square. Caesar, however, is not looking toward the open space (and the town hall); instead, his gaze is fixed on the façade of houses, beyond which stands one of the town's three hills (with St Michael's church). This hill was claimed to be the hill of Julius, the location of the original Roman settlement. This gave Olomouc its origin story and name (*Juliomontium – Olomucium*). At the same time, Caesar is coincidentally looking into the windows of the house that belonged to one of the city councillors, who promoted the construction of the fountain. Here as in other cases, the combination of public interests and private ambitions of prominent citizens became an important factor in the rebuilding of early modern cities.[30]

Five years after the fire the citizens faced another disaster: a plague outbreak. Although the first cases appeared at the end of 1714 the epidemic fully erupted in the spring of the following year. In June a quarantine was imposed on the town.[31]

28. Milan Togner, "Triumf baroka", in *Olomoucké baroko*, vol. III, pp. 17-20.

29. Stanislava Kovářová, "Požár Olomouce v roce 1709", in *Olomoucké baroko*, vol. I, pp. 136-141.

30. Simona Jemelková, "Caesarova kašna", in *Olomoucké baroko*, vol. I, pp. 119-122.

31. Eduard Wondrák, *Historie moru v Českých zemích: O moru, morových ranách a boji proti nim, o zoufalství, strachu a nadějích i o nezodpovězených otázkách*, Prague, Triton, 1999.

Figure 32: Olomouc, New College, Corpus Christi chapel, J.K. Handke, the vault fresco, 1728.

The gates were locked and the town was surrounded with military guards. The epidemic lasted until February 1716. Although the reports that two-thirds of the population were killed are exaggerations, the plague left a strong impact on the city's religious life. The cult of the city's patron St Pauline, especially, whose relics were kept in the Jesuit church, received a new impetus. Immediately after the quarantine was cancelled the town and the Jesuits organised an eight-day thanksgiving ceremony with processions and prayers to the saint. St Pauline's feast (6 June) was annually observed with renewed vigour and a new altar dedicated to her was erected in the parish church of St Maurice. Yet the centre of the cult remained in the Jesuit church where the relics were kept in a new chapel. The church was being rebuilt at that time and the plague experience permeated the whole shrine. This motif appears several times in the main fresco in the nave, but even more significantly in the new dedication of the church; in 1716 it was changed to that of the Virgin Mary of the Snow, which bore strong anti-plague connotations.[32]

In the town's public space the plague epidemic gave rise to two commemorative columns. The first was commissioned by count Leopold Anton Sack of Bohunowitz. It was to be erected on the Lower Square and decorated at the top with a statue of the Virgin Mary and two groups of major plague saints: Sebastian, Rochus, Francis Xaverius and Charles Borromeo on the lower level, and Pauline, Barbara, Catherine and Rosalia on the upper level. The commission was given to Wenceslas Render, the most prolific architect in the town.[33] Render, having some substantial means but no heirs, made his own proposal. He suggested to the municipal council that he would build at his own expense another taller, more ornate column on the Upper Square. Since the construction of Sack's column was already in progress Render gave up his idea to build a "plague column" and instead designed his column as a celebration of the Roman Catholic Church. The column would be decorated with eighteen statues of saints divided into three storeys (six holy knights and rulers on the first level, holy bishops and popes on the second, and the Holy Kinship on the third), while the summit of the tall column would carry a huge statue of the Holy Trinity.[34]

All this building activity contrasted with the little attention given to the cathedral. The permanent absence of the bishop was a decisive factor in this, even though the cathedral chapter took over some of the bishop's roles. At that time the chapter was a rather closed and elite community.[35] It was relatively wealthy, yet in the first half of the eighteenth century it still consisted of only fourteen residential and sev-

See also Leoš Mlčák, "Mor, hlad, války a živelné pohromy v Olomouci", in *Olomoucké baroko*, vol. I, pp. 125-135.

32. Ondřej Jakubec, "Olomoucký jezuitský kostel a protimorový kult P. Marie Sněžné", in *Olomoucké baroko*, vol. I, pp. 150-156.

33. Gabriela Elbelová, "Václav Render – zbožnost za časů moru", in *Olomoucké baroko*, vol. I, pp. 142-149.

34. Martin Elbel, "Čestný sloup Nejsvětější Trojice v Olomouci", in *Ročenka Státního okresního archivu v Olomouci VI (XXV) 1997*, ed. by Vladimír Spáčil, Olomouc, Okresní archiv, 1998, pp. 87-97.

35. Pavel Suchánek, "Metropolitní kapitula v Olomouci a umění v 18. století", in *Olomoucké baroko*, vol. III, pp. 43-52.

enteen non-residential canons, in spite of the bishop's previous efforts to increase the number. This was a significantly smaller number than at similar chapters in the Empire or other countries. It made membership in the Olomouc chapter a prestigious and lucrative post. It was, of course, strictly limited to sons of aristocratic origin. On the other hand, the chapter insisted on the proper education of its members. Three years of study at one of the colleges in Rome or at a university approved by the emperor was a condition *sine qua non.* These two conditions enhanced the importance of the individual canons and the whole body of the chapter. Because of their aristocratic origin the canons could use family ties and contacts at important state offices, even at the imperial court. Their studies in Rome allowed them to meet and cultivate relationships with influential people and to keep abreast of recent news and trends in the church. Membership in the Olomouc chapter was indeed an important step in an ecclesiastical career. Many of the canons held simultaneous canonicates in Salzburg, Wrocław, Passau, Prague, and other places. One fifth of them would eventually acquire a bishopric – in Olomouc or another see in the Empire.[36]

The canons played an invaluable role as patrons of the arts and ecclesiastical activities. Their importance during the first decade of the eighteenth century increased, and so did the tension between the chapter and the absentee bishop. In 1711, however, a sudden hope emerged when it became known that Charles III of Lorraine was likely to gain the archbishopric of Trier. Although there was still the danger that Charles could get a papal concession to keep the Olomouc bishopric as well, the canons welcomed his ambitions. When the news of his successful election reached Olomouc the canons acted immediately; in spite of Charles's protests they hastily proceeded with the election of the new bishop. This time they resisted the pressure of the imperial court (Charles's brother Francis Anthony of Lorraine was the next favourite). Ultimately, they reached a compromise with the emperor and elected Wolfgang Hannibal of Schrattenbach. The new bishop was aware of his precarious situation and decided to reconcile with the Viennese court in matters of the Olomouc bishopric and offer the emperor his services. Charles VI, who ascended to the throne just a few months earlier and was overwhelmed by the conflict over the Spanish succession, accepted the offer. As a sign of goodwill he asked the pope to award Schrattenbach a cardinal's hat. The new cardinal solemnly entered his diocese in October 1712, but already early the next year he left for Vienna again. The cardinal and bishop would not dwell in his diocese for long. In 1714 Schrattenbach left for Rome where he was appointed emperor's ambassador to the Holy See. Although the emperor promised to pay the cardinal an annual rent, Schrattenbach had to pay most of his expenses from his own income. The steady flow of revenues depended on his brother Otto, a canon of the Olomouc chapter who stayed in the diocese to ensure that all the resources of the bishop's estates were mobilised. Schrattenbach thus followed the legacy of his predecessor who used the bishopric as a source of income to sponsor his personal ambitions. He did not return to his diocese until 1722 (meanwhile moving to Naples as an ambassador in 1719). After his return he preferred to stay in his palace in Brno or his residence in Vyškov. He visited Olomouc only occasionally.

36. Zuber, *Osudy moravské církve v 18. století*, p. 68.

The bishop's conspicuous absence from the city was not just due to his other duties or deteriorating health; it was also a consequence the ambiguous role of the prince-bishop and of the complicated relations with the city of Olomouc and Moravian society in general (see Chapter 5). But even Schrattenbach's successor Jacob Ernst, who was personally more involved in the affairs of the diocese and pastoral care, paid more attention to other towns. Frontier areas close to Silesia or Hungary were exposed to real or imagined Protestant influence, while in lesser towns it was necessary to negotiate church affairs with their aristocratic lords. Under such circumstances a personal visit of a bishop could provide decisive help and support. Olomouc on the other hand was by that time a confessionally stable and developed city with a plethora of religious institutions. Ceremonial and liturgical duties could be performed either by an auxiliary bishop or members of the cathedral chapter. In 1726 Schrattenbach successfully petitioned the pope to give the right to wear the mitre to the dean of the chapter and three other prelates. This was the same right that the abbots of local Augustinian and Premonstratensian monasteries had had.[37]

Schrattenbach even, in spite of his promises, would not attend some of the most spectacular celebrations in the diocese. Toward the end of 1726 Pope Benedict XIII canonised eight new saints. On 10 December he canonised a Dominican nun Agnes of Montepulciano, a Franciscan friar James of the Marches and an archbishop Turibius of Mogrovejo. On 27 December these were followed by a Servite friar Pellegrino Laziosi, a Carmelite John of the Cross and another Franciscan Francis Solanus. Finally, on the last day of the year, two Jesuits concluded the line: Aloysius Gonzaga and Stanislaus Kostka. Five of the new saints – the Jesuits, the Franciscans and the Dominican nun – belonged to religious orders with monasteries in the town. The joint canonisation inspired spectacular celebrations in which all the mentioned religious orders closely co-operated. The Franciscan celebrations commenced on 10 August 1727 and lasted the usual eight days (*octiduum*). When it finished the Jesuits took over and began their celebrations on 18 August. On each day of those celebrations there was a solemn mass celebrated by one of the canons or prelates of local monasteries and a sermon delivered by a secular or religious preacher. Although we have no information about the Dominican celebrations, we might expect they were held in the same period, perhaps preceding the celebrations of the Observant Franciscans. In any case, the Dominicans took an active part in the other celebrations, both as invited preachers and members of the procession.[38]

All these celebrations were an ouverture to another, more spectacular festivity. On 19 March 1729 Benedict XIII canonised the last of his numerous saints – a Bohemian priest John of Nepomuk (d. 1393). In Bohemia the canonisation was celebrated with great splendour in 1730. In Moravia it was postponed and begun only on 10 June 1731. On the eve of the festivity the bells of all the churches rang for one hour. The festivity itself was opened at seven in the morning by the procession, led by the auxiliary bishop Egkh. It consisted of the chapter, local religious orders, confraternities and congregations, the city council and all the guilds. It departed from the cathedral and took a complicated route through major streets and squares

37. *Ibid.*, p. 56.
38. *Ibid.*, p. 124.

of the city. Then it returned to the cathedral where Egkh celebrated Mass on behalf of Cardinal Schrattenbach. While this general procession covered most of the city and involved all religious institutions in the town, the following days were dedicated to special processions that linked individual churches with the cathedral. This involved the negotiation of several compromises. The procession on the second day belonged to the secular clergy. The most important role was given to the prior of St Maurice, who led the procession from his church. He was accompanied by the clergy of the two other parish churches (Assumption of the Virgin Mary and St Peter) and by several confraternities (Corpus Christi, St Joseph, St Anne and St Isidore). Then it was the turn of the religious orders. On the third day it was the Augustinian Canons accompanied by the student sodality *Latina Major Beatae Virginis in Coelos Assumptae*. On the fourth day it was the Dominicans. The fifth day belonged to the university with all its students. The sixth day was dedicated to the Friars Minor. This probably needed some careful negotiation since all three rival branches (Conventuals, Observants and Capuchins) had to cooperate and walk together. They were followed on the seventh day by the Jesuits with all the scholars and students. On the eighth and final day was repeated the same general procession as on the first day. Then, Cardinal Schrattenbach made one of his rare appearances and celebrated Mass in the cathedral. During the ceremony the cardinal granted three prelates of the chapter the right to wear a mitre – the privilege he had negotiated with the pope. In addition to this there were numerous processions from the countryside led by their respective priests. Each day there were also sermons in German (in the cathedral) and Czech (outside the cathedral).[39]

The celebrations of John of Nepomuk, however splendid and spectacular they were, were only a prelude to another festivity. In 1732 the pilgrimage church of the Visitation of the Virgin Mary on Svatý Kopeček was about to celebrate its centenary, and the anniversary was eagerly anticipated. At that time the shrine had already been firmly established as a popular pilgrimage site. With tens of thousands of pilgrims frequenting it every year it occupied a prominent position among the country's shrines. The magnificent church, which had replaced the original chapel in the 1670s, was extended several times and redecorated during the first decades of the eighteenth century. After the two wings adjacent to the frontal façade of the church were built (1720-21) the church looked – together with an alley of trees running down the hill – like a large cross lying on the slope of the hill. The church stood outside the city walls and belonged to the Premonstratensian Order (or to its Hradisko monastery). But as mentioned in the previous chapter its origin was associated with one of the local citizens, and its proximity to the city made it an integral part of the sacred topography of Olomouc.

Olomouc and its ecclesiastical and secular institutions indeed played an important role in the upcoming festivity. The celebrations at Svatý Kopeček began on 8 September after the arrival of a huge procession from the city with members of the city council and hundreds of townsmen. The celebrations lasted the usual

39. *Brevis Synopsis Devotionis Octiduanae Olomucii in Cathedrali Ecclesia Sancti Wenceslai in Venerationem Sancti Martyris Joannis Nepomuceni Institutae*, s.l., 1731. Cf. MZA Brno, E 21, Franciscans of Dačice, book no. 9, *Archivum Conventus Olomucensis*, pp. 214-6.

eight days and followed the pattern used during the Nepomuk festivities, including regular devotions, processions coming from all corners of the country and regular sermons (again, in German inside and Czech outside the church). Unlike the previous year Cardinal Schrattenbach did not take any public role in the ceremonies. The highest church official to perform the rites was Jacob Ernst of Liechtenstein-Castelkorn, bishop of Seckau and canon of the Olomouc chapter (and future bishop of Olomouc), accompanied by the four prelates of the chapter with the privilege of wearing the mitre. Schrattenbach still contributed to the festivity though. He used his connections in Rome to negotiate the canonical coronation of the miraculous image – the privilege that the Vatican chapter awarded to the most notable Marian churches. In summer the measures and a draft of the miraculous relief were sent to Rome. The crowns, however, arrived only on the day after the end of the celebrations. So another three-day festivity was held a few days after. This culminated on 21 September when the auxiliary bishop Otto Honorius of Egkh and Hungersbach crowned the image.[40]

New Challenges

The Svatý Kopeček festivities were another result of successful co-operation among local institutions. While the homage paid to John of Nepomuk linked Olomouc with Bohemia, and eventually also with other lands of the Habsburg monarchy, the anniversary of the pilgrimage shrine signified the city's own contribution to the sacred landscape of the monarchy. As such, it had much stronger local accents. In retrospect the 1730s marked the triumph and heyday of Catholic confessional culture in Olomouc. The lavish ceremonies and building activities, however, masked tensions within the town and discrepancy between the urban and rural areas. The church was triumphant and civic culture flourishing. But the year 1740 brought a sudden end to this. On 20 October Charles VI died and in December the king of Prussia Frederick II invaded Silesia in spite of the Pragmatic Sanction. The city suffered from shortages and high taxation, but the situation was about to become even worse. In December 1741 the Prussian army appeared at the outskirts of the city. Undermanned and underequipped, the garrison stood no chances against the invader's troops. On 28 December the commander signed a capitulation and the Prussians entered the town. Marshal Schwerin found accommodation in the bishop's palace, while common soldiers were lodged in private houses and monasteries. A high military contribution was levied on the city and its citizens.[41]

40. *Enthronisticum Parthenium: Sive Gloria Et Honor Neo-Inauguratæ ... Reginæ Mariæ ... ; Prope Metropolim Olomucensem in Marchionatu Moraviæ ... Et Prima In Orbe Marcomanno Corona Regali Aurea De Urbe Missa Ritu Vaticano, Solemnissimóque applausu Coronata*, Olomucii, typis Francisci Antonii Hirnle, 1733. Cf. Howard Louthan, *Converting Bohemia: Force and Persuasion in the Catholic Reformation*, Cambridge, Cambridge University Press, 2009, p. 271.

41. Vítězslav Prchal, "Války s Pruskem a přeměna Olomouce v pevnost", in *Olomoucké baroko*, vol. I, pp. 285-292.

Figure 33: K. J. Haringer, A. and J. Schmutzer, *View of the interior of the church of the Visitation of the Virgin Mary at Svatý Kopeček*, 1733.

Figure 34: Olomouc, Teresian armoury, northern façade, 1769-71.

The occupation ended up being much shorter than the Swedish one a century earlier; the Prussian army left after four months. There were immediate economic consequences but the real impact of the event was far-reaching. The quick collapse of Olomouc contrasted with its growing strategic influence. It was situated on an important route to Vienna and after the Prussian conquest of Silesia Olomouc became an important buffer zone. Maria Theresa and her military advisors were aware of its importance. Thus, immediately in 1742 Olomouc was promoted to *Königliche Haupt- und Grenzfestung*, the royal main and border fortress, and construction of the new fortification system was commenced.[42] Olomouc had a status of a fortress since 1655, and as such had constant military garrison. Its commanders were, after all, important guests at religious festivities and sponsors of some altars and devotions. Now, however, the situation started changing.

The whole city was gradually surrounded with a complicated network of bastions, ravelins and other fortifications. No buildings were allowed within a certain distance from the perimeter (the Premonstratensian Monastery Hradisko was one notable exception). Everyday life in the town, including religious customs, had to be subdued to the regime of the fortress. The influence and visibility of the military in public spaces increased – in many ways at the expense of the church. There were two such symbolic gestures that framed the shift in favour of the army. First, in 1745 the empress forbade the garrison commander to assume his traditional place in the

42. Vladimír Kupka, "Olomoucké fortifikace na plánech a ve skutečnosti", in *Olomoucké baroko*, vol. I, pp. 293-300.

inauguration parade of new bishops and limited the number of gun salvos to be fired on this occasion. In 1768 she approved the construction of huge artillery armoury right in front of the bishop's palace (completed in 1778) as a visible marker of the state's priorities. This presaged more radical changes in the 1780s when the military would be given the former Jesuit buildings and some other dissolved monasteries.

These visible and immediate changes were accompanied by broader transformations on the state level that were triggered by the war and that afflicted religious life. The local church, however, was not entirely unprepared. The chapter's emphasis on the proper education of its canons and their studies abroad started paying off. The canons were relatively well-read, well-travelled and had broad international connections. Many of them were interested in the new trends in the church that sought reform in ecclesiastical organisation and religious life. One of these, count Francis Giannini, kept regular contacts with Ludovico Antonio Muratori, whose books *Della Carità Cristiana* (Modena, 1723) and *Della Regolata Divozione de' Cristiani* (Venice, 1747) played a principal role in the Catholic Enlightenment.[43] When Schrattenbach died in 1738 most of the canons, albeit with hesitation, gave their votes to Jacob Ernst of Liechtenstein-Castelkorn, a nephew of the esteemed bishop Charles II. With him they were not only electing a new bishop but introducing a new generation of bishops. By the time of his election in Olomouc Liechtenstein-Castelkorn was already known for his pious life, his dedication in office and his ecclesiastical policy. In 1731, as a bishop of Seckau (Styria), he refused to join the strict religious policy of his Salzburg superior, Archbishop Leopold Anton von Firmian, who expelled more than 20,000 non-Catholic believers from the territory of his archbishopric. Instead, Jacob Ernst pleaded for a more moderate approach, better religious education and intensive pastoral care. His episcopate in Olomouc, however, was rather short. In 1745 he was elected the Archbishop of Salzburg. He accepted the position and resigned from Olomouc. In the same year the chapter promptly and unanimously elected another reform-minded candidate Ferdinand Julius Troyer.[44]

With this election the canons were also making a choice and an open statement about their policy toward Maria Theresa, the state and the on-going changes. Already Liechtenstein was an ardent supporter of Maria Theresa. He openly criticised the betrayal of the Bohemian estates and their election of the rival candidate Charles Albert (and it was Liechtenstein who later crowned Maria Theresa as the Queen of Bohemia, instead of the discredited Archbishop of Prague). With Troyer – who had been known as *"totus caesareus"* – they confirmed their stance and their will for unambiguous co-operation. In return, Maria Theresa asked the pope to give Troyer the dignity of a Cardinal. This was granted to him just before his formal inauguration in Olomouc.[45]

43. Eleonore Zlabinger, *Lodovico Antonio Muratori und Österreich*, Innsbruck, Kommissionsverlag der Österreichischen Buchhandlung, 1970, pp. 58-60.

44. Zuber, *Osudy moravské církve v 18. století*, p. 144.

45. Martin Elbel, "Bishop's Secular Entry: Power and Representation in Inauguration Ceremonies of the Eighteenth-Century Bishops of Olomouc", in *Religious Ceremonials and Images: Power and Social Meaning*, ed. by José Pedro Paiva, Coimbra, Palimage, 2002, pp. 47-60.

Figure 35: F. V. Korompay (follower), *Entry of Bishop Troyer*, 1783.

During his episcopacy Troyer continued his close co-operation with the empress (sometimes even against the pope) and dedicated much time to the affairs of the diocese. He also made first attempts to limit pomp and eccentricity of some devotions. For example, in 1747 he prohibited flagellant processions and drastic representations of Christ's suffering on Good Fridays – a decision which might have been inspired by the new and simpler Way of the Cross devotion introduced by the Franciscans in 1743. What was, however, of crucial significance was the fact that Troyer was the first bishop who made again – after many decades – a proper and thorough visitation to the diocese between 1754 and 1756.[46]

In the meantime, construction of the fortress advanced at a rapid pace. It was finished just in time to withstand another Prussian siege in 1758. The successful defence justified the construction of the fortress and all the expense and sacrifice it required, and revived the military pride of the city that had been shattered by the inglorious events of 1642 and 1741. Already before the successful defence, however, there had been other two public events that encouraged local patriotism. In 1748 Maria Theresa, the first Habsburg ruler since King Matthias in 1616, and her husband arrived to the city. They even repeated their visit again in 1754. Both the bishop and the city did their best to prove they were excellent hosts and prepared a rich programme to entertain the royal couple. Although both visits were motivated mainly by the practical reason of inspecting the new fortress, they had some strong religious aspects too.

In 1754, for example, Maria Theresa and her husband witnessed the consecration of the Holy Trinity column, finally completed after almost four decades. After the death of Wenceslas Render, the founder of the column, the construction was supervised by the city council which imposed its own ideas about the role and meaning of the column. The councillors ensured that only local artists and craftsmen would work on the monument and they introduced some changes in the decoration. The overall structure and iconographic programme remained but the councillors replaced some of the saints so that each statue would represent

46. Zuber, *Osudy moravské církve v 18. století*, p. 152.

one of the local churches, chapels or monasteries. The emphasis thus shifted from celebrating the Roman Church (as suggested by its founder Wenceslas Render) to glorifying the local church. This idea, among others, fitted in with Maria Theresa's ecclesiastical policy.[47]

The importance of local traditions and their role in the state's needs was emphasized by the visits of Maria Theresa and Francis of Lorraine to the grave of local martyr John Sarkander in 1748 and 1754. At that time Sarkander's cult was firmly rooted in Olomouc but still lacked official approval. The first lukewarm steps towards the beatification process were already made by Cardinal Schrattenbach with the approaching centenary of Sarkander's death. Now the cult received several new impulses. The first was the successful canonisation of John of Nepomuk, a Bohemian saint and a patron of the Secret of Confession. Sarkander, who had been similarly tortured in order to reveal the contents of confessions, was seen as his (Moravian) counterpart. The second and more imminent reason was the war with Prussia, and its religious aspects. Under these circumstances Sarkander could be seen as an obvious "state protector against the Protestant intruder".[48] Indeed, already in 1747 Cardinal Troyer with the support of Maria Theresa initiated the beatification process in Rome. On 5 March 1748 Troyer announced in his Olomouc palace the opening of the process and invited people to provide documents and testimony about Sarkander's martyrdom and miracles. The first files handed personally by Troyer to Benedict XIV, however, failed to convince the Congregation of the Sacred Rites. The gathering of evidence continued into the 1750s but Troyer's death in 1758 and the outbreak of the Seven Year's War hampered the efforts. As mentioned earlier, the beatification of Sarkander had to wait until 1859 (and canonisation until 1995).

Royal visits and preparations for Sarkander's process attracted the attention of all strata of society. Yet in the background of these events were other processes, more socially restricted but with substantial cultural impact. In 1746 Canon Francis Giannini and Slovenian noblemen Baron Joseph von Petrasch founded

47. Elbel, "Čestný sloup Nejsvětější Trojice v Olomouci", pp. 87-97.

48. Stefan Samerski, *"Wie im Himmel, so auf Erden"? Selig- und Heiligsprechung in der katholischen Kirche 1740 bis 1870*, Stuttgart, Kohlhammer, 2002, pp. 171-197.

Figure 36: Josef Freindt, *Holy Trinity column*, engraving.

Societas eruditorum incognitorum in terris Austriacis, the first learned society in the Habsburg lands.[49] The society was soon joined by Ludovico Antonio Muratori and other influential scholars, both from Moravia and abroad. The core group held regular meetings in Baron Petrasch's palace on the main square, and kept in touch with other members by letters and the periodical *Olmützer Monathlichen Auszüge Alt- und Neuer Gelehrter Sachen.* The society promoted German language and culture (instead of Latin and French) and mediated some Enlightenment ideas. It earned some limited support from the state, but fierce opposition from the local Jesuits and their university. In addition to Giannini there were other society members from the ranks of the clergy, including influential prelates like Andrzej Stanisław Załuski, Archbishop of Cracow, and Cardinal Domenico Silvio Passionei. Although Cardinal Troyer seemed to be more cautious, his support of Maria Theresa and the needs of her state opened the way to further reforms and gave career opportunity to several reform-minded clergymen.

Conclusion

Under Troyer and his followers Olomouc and its bishopric became one of the centres of Reform Catholicism in the Habsburg monarchy. This might seem a sharp contrast with the situation in 1700. But it was a consequence rather than a negation of previous developments. Under the surface of festivities and building activities there was a successful process of consolidation. The tension and constant necessity to negotiate the local religious situation contributed to the adaptability and flexibility of the local church. Moreover, the successful synthesis of general patterns and local traditions helped develop a vital confessional culture, which – thanks to the wealth and variety of its institutions, cults and rituals – could flexibly react to new conditions and challenges. The local church entered the reform era of the eighteenth century – which culminated in Josephinism – not as a victim or enemy of reforms but as an active partner capable of negotiation.

49. Filip Hradil, "Olomouc ve druhé polovině 18. století", in *Olomoucké baroko*, vol. I, pp. 313-332; Antonín Kostlán, *Societas incognitorum. První učená společnost v českých zemích*, Prague, Archiv Akademie věd ČR, 1996.

Afterword

Graeme Murdock

The transformation of religious life in Olomouc between the fifteenth and eighteenth centuries offers extraordinarily vivid insight into the history of the lands of the Bohemian crown and also into the complex relationship between urban communities and religious change in late medieval and early modern Europe. Our focus here will be on the latter issue, and this afterword will reflect on some of the key features identified in this volume about the changing character of religious life in Olomouc set in the context of historiography on other cities and towns across the Continent.

During the late medieval and early modern periods many European cities and towns witnessed challenges to traditional religious authorities, and demonstrations of both elite and popular support for reform movements.[1] Cities and towns were sites of discussion and debate about rival religious ideas, and arenas for both official action and popular violence against heresy (most notably in the French monarchy).[2] Some cities acted as places of refuge for religious exiles and also as hubs for mission efforts.[3] Historians have devoted attention to the varied ways in which urban

1. By way of example, see analysis of the spread of incidents of iconoclasm in Carlos Eire, *War Against the Idols: The Reformation of Worship from Erasmus to Calvin*, New York, Cambridge University Press, 1986, and in Lee Palmer Wandel, *Voracious idols and violent hands. Iconoclasm in Reformation Zurich, Strasbourg and Basel*, Cambridge, Cambridge University Press, 1994.

2. On popular religious violence in French cities and towns see Natalie Zemon Davis, *Society and culture in early modern France*, Stanford, Stanford University Press, 1975; Barbara Diefendorf, *Beneath the Cross: Catholics and Huguenots in sixteenth-century Paris*, New York, Oxford University Press, 1991; Philip Benedict, *Rouen during the wars of religion*, Cambridge, Cambridge University Press, 1981; Penny Roberts, *A City in Conflict: Troyes during the French wars of religion*, Manchester, Manchester University Press, 1996; Philip Connor, *Montauban and southern French Calvinism during the wars of religion*, Aldershot, Ashgate, 2002; Judith P. Meyer, *Reformation in La Rochelle: Tradition and change in early modern Europe, 1500-1568*, Geneva, Droz, 1998; Graeme Murdock, Penny Roberts and Andrew Spicer, eds., *Ritual and Violence: Natalie Zemon Davis and Early Modern France*, Oxford, Past and Present Supplement Series, 2012; Allan Tulchin, *That Men Would Praise the Lord: The Triumph of Protestantism in Nîmes, 1530-1570*, Oxford, Oxford University Press, 2010.

3. Andrew Pettegree, *Emden and the Dutch Revolt: Exile and the development of Reformed Protestantism*, Oxford, Clarendon, 1992; E. William Monter, *Calvin's Geneva*, New York, John Wiley, 1967; William Naphy, *Calvin and the consolidation of the Genevan Reformation*, Manchester, Manchester University Press, 1994.

communities responded to ideas about reform and acted as engines for religious change in the Netherlands, Scotland and in England.[4] There has also been considerable debate over why ideas about religious reform seem to have had a particular resonance in the cities and towns of the German lands during the sixteenth century. Some authors have focused attention on the social groups in towns who embraced ideas about reform. Others have emphasised the significance of the ways in which cities in the Empire were governed, or considered the space provided within towns for social and intellectual communication and exchange, or assessed the importance of ideas about the sacral character of urban communities. Historians have also examined why many towns rejected reform movements, and explored deep internal divisions within cities over matters of faith. Other historians have suggested that the degree of difference between towns and the countryside has been exaggerated, and argued that rural and urban societies shared ideals about how the relationship between church and community should be re-configured.[5]

The history of religious life in Olomouc as set out in this volume reveals points of comparison and contrast with research on other cities and towns across the Continent. In Olomouc we find a complex picture of evolving relations between state authorities, church institutions, the city council and the urban community. This predominantly German-speaking royal and episcopal city was impacted by successive waves of religious reform in Hussite, Lutheran and Catholic guises between the fifteenth and eighteenth centuries. War, fire and plague afflicted the city, destroying lives and disrupting commerce. As a result the population of Olomouc fluctuated wildly from around 5,000 people during the fifteenth century, to 10,000 by the late sixteenth century, only to collapse to 2,000 by the mid-seventeenth century, then rising again to 8,000 by the early eighteenth century. Olomouc had some particular features of long-term significance in the development of its religious life. For exam-

4. Guido Marnef, *Antwerp in the age of Reformation: Underground Protestantism in a commercial metropolis, 1550-1577*, Leiden, Brill, 1996; Christine Kooi, *Liberty and Religion: Church and State in Leiden's Reformation, 1572-1620*, Leiden, Brill, 2000; Benjamin J. Kaplan, *Calvinists and Libertines: Confession and community in Utrecht, 1578-1620,* Oxford, Clarendon, 1995; Michael Lynch, *Edinburgh and the Reformation*, Edinburgh, Edinburgh University Press, 1981; Susan Brigden, *London and the Reformation*, Oxford, Oxford University Press, 1989; John Craig, *Reformation, Politics, and Polemics: The Growth of Protestantism in East Anglian Market Towns, 1500-1610*, Aldershot, Ashgate, 2001; David Underdown, *Fire from Heaven: Life in an English town in the seventeenth century*, New Haven, Yale University Press, 1992.

5. Bernd Moeller, *Reichsstadt und Reformation*, Gütersloh, Gerd Mohn, 1962; Heide Stratenwerth, *Die Reformation in der Stadt Osnabrück*, Wiesbaden, F. Steiner, 1971; Steven E. Ozment, *The Reformation in the Cities: The Appeal of Protestantism to Sixteenth-Century Germany and Switzerland*, New Haven, Yale University Press, 1975; Thomas A. Brady, *Class, Regime and Reformation at Strasbourg, 1520-1555*, Leiden, Brill, 1978; Lorna Jane Abray, *Magistrates, Clergy and Commons in Strasbourg, 1500-1598*, Ithaca, Cornell University Press, 1985; Heinrich Richard Schmidt, *Reichsstädte, Reich und Reformation. Korporative Religionspolitik 1521-1529/30*, Stuttgart, F. Steiner, 1986; Lyndal Roper, *The Holy Household: Women and Morals in Reformation Augsburg*, Oxford, Clarendon, 1991; Peter Blickle, *Communal Reformation: The Quest for Salvation in Sixteenth-Century Germany*, London, Humanities Press, 1992; Berndt Hamm, *Bürgertum und Glaube. Konturen der städtischen Reformation*, Göttingen, Vandenhoeck und Ruprecht, 1996.

ple, the city was internally divided with a wall separating the main part of the city from the former castle district which became the town's ecclesiastical centre around the cathedral of St Wecenslas. However, Catholic buildings, signs and symbols dominated the urban landscape across the city with a number of impressive parish churches and monasteries, and a Jesuit academy that was founded in 1566.

The example of Olomouc highlights that divisions between Utraquists and Catholics in the fifteenth century were far more than a mere precursor to the later challenges posed to Rome by Lutheran and Calvinist movements. Hussitism failed to gain a foothold in Olomouc. How should we understand the city's rejection of Hus and the reform movements of the fifteenth century? Loyalty to Rome was certainly bolstered by the presence of the bishop and cathedral chapter (with notable leadership offered by Bishop John the Iron). Aside from Wrocław, Olomouc was the only place in the lands of the Bohemian crown to retain a consecrated bishop throughout the Hussite period. Catholics from other cities lost to the Hussites sought refuge in Olomouc which acted to strengthen Catholic loyalism in the city. The Czech vernacular played an important role in Hussite culture, perhaps another factor in limiting the appeal of Utraquism in mostly German-speaking Olomouc. The city resisted Hussite armies during the wars of the 1420s and 1430s at considerable cost with severe economic disruption. Some of the difficulties experienced by the city's residents were taken out on the small Jewish community of around 200 people. Olomouc welcomed John of Capestrano on a preaching tour against the Hussites in 1451 and 1454. With no Utraquist heretics available to persecute, resident Jewish families were thrown out of the city in 1454.

Olomouc's Catholic loyalism was noted in Rome. In 1462 Pius II encouraged the people of the city "to persevere in the faith of their fathers".[6] The bishop and city authorities abandoned the Hussite king George of Poděbrady in favour of Matthias Corvinus. Matthias was duly grateful and described the church in Olomouc as "a sole rose among the thorns and a lantern tightly confined by the darkness".[7] Olomouc's identity as a bastion of Catholicism and royalism was tested during the 1470s by rivalry between two Catholic monarchs. Olomouc was the site for the 1479 confirmation of peace between Matthias and Wladislas Jagiellon, with Matthias retaining control over Moravia. We should also note that there were significant internal tensions in the city during this period. In particular, the council sought to develop their own school to rival the school run by the cathedral chapter. The city authorities gained papal consent in 1466 and then royal confirmation in 1473 for the right to establish their new school. The character of religion in Olomouc also reflected wider developments in Catholic culture during the latter decades of the fifteenth century with both humanist influences and a rise in popularity of Franciscan piety. A new Observant Franciscan friary was founded during the 1450s while the Dominicans also retained their prominent place in the city, notably through public disputations against the Unity of Brethren.

When King Louis visited Olomouc in 1523 he witnessed a public burning of heretical books from Saxony. This occasion was intended to provide public

6. See above, p. 42.
7. See above, p. 48.

affirmation of the city's ongoing loyalty to Rome. There were few reasons at this stage to predict that Olomouc's established brand of Catholic royalism would be threatened any more by Luther than it had been by Hus. It is difficult to be certain about the pace, extent and depth of growing support for the Lutheran cause. There were no obvious divisions in the social reception of Lutheranism between rich and poor, or between different districts within the city, or between different occupation groups, or between different generations. The city school that the council had battled to establish in the late fifteenth century provided an important early focus of Lutheran activity. By the middle decades of the sixteenth century there were public challenges to Lenten regulations, the vernacular was used in some church services, and Communion was distributed in both kinds.

It seems more straightforward to explain how Lutheran ideas reached Olomouc than to understand why they were so readily accepted by a very substantial proportion of the urban community. Analysis of the spread of ideas about religious reform across Europe has often focussed on the role of urban centres. Cities and towns were key spaces within which Bibles and books were printed and discussed (and burned), public debates and synods were held, clergy were trained, academies and schools were established, and church institutions were developed. Books and people quickly spread ideas between towns along river systems and through well-established trade and communication networks. In the case of Olomouc, long-standing social and economic links provided channels of communication between the city and other towns impacted by Lutheranism in Silesia and beyond. Ease of communication with other German-speaking cities as well as shared access to printed texts in German help to explain how Lutheran ideas spread to Olomouc. Indeed German-speakers in towns across the Czech lands, as well as in towns in Hungary and the Transylvanian principality, and around the Baltic coast in Poland, Estonia, Sweden and Denmark, were often the first to engage with Lutheran ideas and provided conduits for Lutheranism to then spread to other vernacular communities.[8]

How might we explain the readiness of the people of Olomouc to embrace reform in the sixteenth century when they had rejected reform in the previous century? The language in which ideas about reform were communicated is of obvious importance. The significance of vernacular culture was certainly bolstered in this period through the greater role played by printed texts in the transmission of ideas. However, understanding the appeal of Lutheranism in Olomouc cannot be reduced to a mere function of linguistic affinity with Saxon reformers. We should also consider the irony that Olomouc's rejection of Hussitism was vital in maintaining the city's integration into the mainstream of Catholicism that in turn proved crucial in the reception of later ideas about reform. The political context

8. Howard Louthan and Graeme Murdock, eds., *A Companion to the Reformation in Central Europe*, Leiden, Brill, 2015; Márta Fata, *Ungarn, das Reich, der Stephanskrone, im Zeitalter der Reformation und Konfessionalisierung. Multiethnizität, Land und Konfession 1500 bis 1700*, Münster, Aschendorff, 2000; Michael G. Müller, *Zweite Reformation und städtische Autonomie im königlichen Preussen. Danzig, Elbing und Thorn in der Epoche der Konfessionalisierung*, Berlin, Akademie Verlag, 1997; Ole Peter Grell, ed., *The Scandinavian Reformation: From Evangelical Movement to Institutionalisation of Reform*, Cambridge, Cambridge University Press, 1995.

was also important. The council attempted to shape the pace and character of the process of reform, at times coming under some degree of popular pressure. The council attempted throughout to maintain good order in the town although there were particular tensions during the 1550s and some incidents of popular disruption of Catholic services with lusty Lutheran hymn-singing during the 1560s.

During a visit to Olomouc by Maximilian II in 1563 the council put forward a request that Lutherans in Olomouc should have the legal right to practise their religion. While this plea was rejected, private Lutheran services continued to take place in the city while other Lutherans travelled on Sundays to worship in neighbouring villages on the lands of sympathetic nobles. This practice of *Auslauf* was an enduring feature of religious life in different political and legal contexts across the Continent. During the latter decades of the sixteenth century thousands of Lutherans packed the roads out of Vienna on Sunday mornings to be able to attend public services. Likewise thousands of Parisian Calvinists travelled to attend the nearest legal church at Charenton under rights gained by the Edict of Nantes. Religious minorities in the Empire also gained rights after 1648 to travel to attend services including Calvinists in Aachen who left their city to worship in an enclave of the Dutch Republic.[9]

Lutherans in Olomouc lacked any legal clarity on their rights and pressed for greater religious liberties. For example, Lutherans wanted to be buried in their own parish churches in the city with the prominence that their social status deserved. In 1570 a dispute erupted over the burial in a city church of a Lutheran merchant, Georg Thaller.[10] The bishop ordered that Thaller should be exhumed. This order was ignored and the bishop claimed that "they [the Lutherans] wanted to chop me to pieces".[11] On the whole the Lutheran-dominated council preferred to seek compromise or adopted tactics of delay and obfuscation rather than enter into open conflict with Catholic institutions and the court. A 1577 order of Rudolf II that non-Catholics should not serve on the councils of royal cities was simply ignored in Olomouc. This defiance was based on Lutheran dominance of the city, and in 1580 Bishop Pavlovský does not seem to have been greatly exaggerating when he complained that there were "few Catholics in Olomouc".[12]

While Lutherans were strong in numbers, the lack of formal legal rights delayed the emergence of autonomous Lutheran church institutions. The advance of Protes-

9. For a micro-history on religious life around the city of Aachen during the eighteenth century see Benjamin J. Kaplan, *Cunegonde's Kidnapping: A Story of religious conflict in the age of Enlightenment*, New Haven, Yale University Press, 2014.

10. Issues around burial caused problems in other contested religious environments. See for example, Jérémie Foa, "An unequal apportionment: The conflict over space between Protestants and Catholics at the beginning of the war of religion", *French History*, 20 (2006), pp. 369-386; Penny Roberts, "Contesting sacred space: burial disputes in sixteenth-century France", in *The Place of the Dead: Death and Remembrance in late medieval and early modern Europe*, ed. by Bruce Gordon and Peter Marshall, Cambridge, Cambridge University Press, 2000, pp. 131-148; Peter Marshall, "Confessionalization and community in the burial of English Catholics, c. 1570-1700", in *Getting Along? Religious Identities and Confessional Relations in Early Modern England*, ed. by Nadine Lewycky and Adam Morton, Farnham, Ashgate, 2012, pp. 57-76.

11. See above, p. 84.

12. See above, p. 68.

tantism in Olomouc during the latter decades of the sixteenth century seems to have been bloodless but rather anaemic.[13] A certain social understanding seems to have developed in the city about how to live in an uncertain but mixed religious environment. Whether best labelled as multi-confessionalism or supra-confessional Christianity or pluralism or everyday ecumenism, this capacity to "get along" with people of different or unclear beliefs was a feature of religious life in Olomouc as in many parts of Europe.[14] However, this period of informal Lutheran dominance of Olomouc was also inherently unstable. It remained a function of a particular set of political circumstances in the Czech lands during the latter decades of the sixteenth century which meant that neither the Lutheran council nor the court and Catholic authorities held sufficient political resources to resolve matters decisively in their favour.

From where did the sources of Catholic recovery come? The Habsburg court and resident bishops proved in the end to be vital agents in reviving the Catholic cause. The Jesuits were also prominent in attempts to mobilise remaining Catholics in the city. A 1590s inscription on the cathedral door expressed optimism about the potential recovery of Catholic fortunes in Olomouc; "as a kind mother opens her arms to converts, let the lost souls return to the church of Christ".[15] In 1602 Rudolf ordered the expulsion of non-Catholic clergy from royal cities, and insisted that councils must be exclusively Catholic. When pressure was later placed on Matthias in the Moravian estates to concede rights of worship to non-Catholics, he temporised and set up a commission to investigate matters. Some grew tired of waiting for concessions and in 1610 an illegal initiative was undertaken to build a place of Lutheran worship in Olomouc. After the Moravian diet of 1619 an anti-Habsburg coup in Olomouc installed a new council that supported the estates' party. Within months Catholic property was confiscated, the Jesuits were expelled, and cathedral canons were arrested. Abraham Scultetus subsequently lead a service in the Jesuit church in Olomouc during the visit to the city of Frederick of the Palatinate. One Catholic commentator found the sight of local Lutherans attending their new Reformed king hard to take and decried "Lutheran bootlickers dressed in Calvinist skin".[16]

13. On the application of this phrase see Robert Evans, "Calvinism in East-Central Europe: Hungary and her neighbours", in *International Calvinism, 1541-1715*, ed. by Menna Prestwich, Oxford, Clarendon, 1985, pp. 176-177.

14. Benjamin J. Kaplan, *Divided by Faith: Religious conflict and the practice of toleration in early modern Europe*, Cambridge, Harvard University Press, 2007; Keith Cameron, Mark Greengrass, and Penny Roberts, eds., *The adventure of religious pluralism in early modern France*, Bern, Peter Lang, 1999; Gregory Hanlon, *Confession and community in seventeenth-century France: Catholic and Protestant Coexistence in Aquitaine*, Philadelphia, University of Pennsylvania Press, 1993; Keith Luria, *Sacred Boundaries: Religious Coexistence and Conflict in Early Modern France*, Washington DC, The Catholic University of America Press, 2005; Thomas Max Safley, *A Companion to Multiconfessionalism in the Early Modern World*, Leiden, Brill, 2011; William Sheils, "'Getting on' and 'Getting along' in Parish and Town: Catholics and their neighbours in England", in *Catholic Communities in Protestant States: Britain and the Netherlands, c. 1570-1720*, ed. by Benjamin Kaplan, Bob Moore, Henk van Nierop and Judith Pollmann, Manchester, Manchester University Press, 2009, pp. 67-83.

15. See above, p. 88.

16. See above, p. 105.

Amid this apparent triumph for Lutheran Olomouc, the martyrdom of Jan Sarkander provided Catholics with a usable hero for the future. And, Lutheran joy quickly turned to disaster. In January 1621 the imperial army entered Olomouc. Before the end of that month the Jesuits were back in the city and all non-Catholic clergy were interned. Catholic church property was restored, while the property of leading rebels was confiscated. The revival of Catholicism in Olomouc was in the first place a direct result of the changing military and political fortunes of the Habsburg dynasty in the Bohemian lands. The results were apparently dramatic with Bishop Dietrichstein claiming before his death in 1636 that 110,000 of 150,000 Moravian non-Catholics had converted to Rome. What sort of converts were these?[17] Some in Olomouc were certainly inspired by the procession of the relics of St Pauline that saw the grip of plague weaken in 1624. Others were perhaps more affected by direct legal pressure to convert. A 1625 decree required that all who did not want to become Catholics must sell their property and leave within months. The 1628 Renewed Land Ordinance outlawed the practice of all non-Catholic religion in Moravia. Some suspicion between "old" and "new" Catholics lingered. The author of a chronicle called Valentin Ecker identified himself with "*wir evangelische*" in 1625 but by 1626 Ecker wrote of belonging to the ranks of "*unkatholische*" before lapsing into judicious silence on any religious matters.[18]

When the tide turned again with the Swedish occupation of the city in 1642, only 176 people in Olomouc registered as Catholics. In 1643 the Jesuits were expelled again, and Lutheran public services were restored. However, this final Lutheran episode proved no more than an interlude. Once the Swedes finally left in 1650, Catholics performed elaborate rituals to cleanse and re-consecrate churches in the city. From the second half of the seventeenth century, religious life in Olomouc was transformed once more with the development of new styles of Catholic piety. There is evidence of growing private ownership of prayer-books and catechisms, of popular commitment to participate in religious festivals, processions and pilgrimages, and of an increasing number of confraternities supported by the Jesuits. The popularity of confraternities in particular seems to speak to a Catholic answer to the challenge of providing for lay participation in religious life and the communalisation of the church. The cult of Jan Sarkander, the local martyr for Catholic Olomouc, was also deliberately fostered with the first printed text on Sarkander published in the 1660s.

The Catholic church once more dominated the city and its surrounding countryside. This was most notably the case in the church built on the Holy Hill to the north-east of Olomouc. This new building highlights the role of the laity in reviving and reshaping Catholicism in Olomouc. A wealthy citizen called Jan Andrýsek saw the Virgin in a dream indicate where he should build a shrine. Andrýsek paid for a small chapel to be constructed at the site by 1632. This building was burned

17. Compare with broader arguments about the role of the state and church in transforming religious cultures in Howard Louthan, *Converting Bohemia: Force and Persuasion in the Catholic Reformation*, Cambridge, Cambridge University Press, 2009, and in Trevor Johnson, *Magistrates, Madonnas and Miracles: The Counter Reformation in the Upper Palatinate*, Aldershot, Ashgate, 2009.

18. See above, p. 113.

down in 1645, but in 1679 the bishop consecrated a larger church and residence for Premonstratensians on the same site. Public spaces in the city also reflected new styles of piety with a substantial commemorative column following an outbreak of plague in the 1710s, and a later monumental column designed as a celebration of the Catholic church.[19] Work on this Holy Trinity column began in 1717 in the city's upper square and was only completed in 1754 with a consecration ceremony led by Bishop Troyer and attended by Maria Theresa. The initiative for this column had been taken by a mason called Wenceslas Render who designed the column and bequeathed his estate to finance its completion.

By the early eighteenth century Catholic culture flowered in Olomouc. This culture had some remarkable features as Catholic belief engaged with popular traditions. The last witch was executed in the diocese of Olomouc in 1703. However, rural parish priests in the area continued to report complaints that some of the dead (including children) had been leaving their graves. Popular celebrations also speak to the character of Catholicism in this period, not least the 1732 anniversary of the pilgrimage church on Holy Hill which had become an integral part of the sacred landscape of Olomouc. Olomouc was home to considerable numbers of clergy who made up a substantial proportion of the urban population. This concentration of priests and members of different orders inevitably led to competition and tension as well as creative energy. There were also ongoing divisions between the interests of bishops and the council. A brief occupation by the Prussian army in 1741 saw the development of Olomouc as a military fortress that was able to withstand a Prussian siege in 1758. This marked a new involvement of the state in shaping the character of Olomouc but these threats to the city also provided the context for a campaign for the beatification of Jan Sarkander led by Bishop Troyer and supported by Maria Theresa.

The military, political and legal power exerted by the Habsburg court was a vital component in the revival of Catholicism in Olomouc. The state provided exclusive rights of religious practice to the Catholic church but did not solely determine the contours of the city's confessional culture. Local clergy as well as ordinary lay people played an important role in shaping the vibrant forms of Catholic piety of the city. The impact of war and demographic shocks to the city's population during the early seventeenth century also broke chains of memory that might otherwise have sustained elements of the religious culture of earlier generations.[20] The new sacred landscape of Olomouc asserted the historicity and continuity of Catholicism with almost every trace of the presence of heretics entirely eradicated. As churches expanded and were decorated more richly, and columns were embellished and grew taller, there is perhaps just a lingering sense that the city was trying a little too hard to demonstrate its Catholic credentials and to forget its heretical past.

19. See case-studies on ideas about sacred space in Will Coster and Andrew Spicer, eds., *Sacred space in early modern Europe* , Cambridge, Cambridge University Press, 2005, and in Andrew Spicer and Sarah Hamilton, eds., *Defining the holy: Sacred Space in late medieval and early modern Europe*, Aldershot, Ashgate, 2005.

20. Danièle Hervieu-Léger, *Religion as a Chain of Memory*, New Brunswick, Rutgers University Press, 2000.

List of Olomouc Bishops, 1397-1776

The bishopric of Olomouc was re-founded in 1063 (an earlier tradition existed). In 1777 it was elevated to the status of archbishopric. Two periods were problematic: the disputes in 1416-20 and 1482-97. In the first case John the Iron won the bishopric, supported by the Council of Constance, Pope Martin V and King Sigismund. In the other case, Jan Filipec was elected by the chapter and supported by King Matthias. But he was never confirmed by the pope, who appointed another bishop, John Vitéz (with temporary royal support), and two cardinals. None of the three ever visited Olomouc.

John (Jan) Mráz	1397-1403
Lacek (Ladislas, Laczko) of Kravaře	1403-1408
Conrad of Vechta	1408/1410-1413 (elected/consecrated)
Wenceslas Králík of Buřenice	1413-1416
Aleš of Březí	1416-1420 (claiming the office)
John the Iron (Jan Železný)	1416/1418-1430 (elected/appointed)
Conrad of Zvole	1431-1434
Paul of Miličín	1434/1435-1450 (elected/consecrated)
John	1450-1454
Bohuslaus of Zvole	1454/1455-1457 (elected/consecrated)
Prothasius (Tas) of Boskovice	1459-1482
John Filipec	1483-1490 (*administrator*)
John Vitéz the Younger	1487-1489
Ardicino della Porta	1489-1493
Giovanni Borgia (Juan Borja)	1493-1497
Stanislaus Thurzo	1497-1540
Bernard Zoubek of Zdětín	1540-1541
John Dubravius	1541-1553
Mark Kuen	1553-1565
William Prusinovský	1565-1572
John Grodecký	1572-1574
Thomas Albín of Helfenburk	1574-1575
John	1576-1578
Stanislaus Pavlovský	1579-1598

Francis of Dietrichstein	1599-1636
John Ernest of Plattenstein	1636-1637
Leopold Wilhelm	1637-1662
Charles Joseph	1663-1664
Charles of Liechtenstein-Castelkorn	1664-1695
Charles Joseph of Lorraine	1695-1711
Wolfgang Hannibal Schrattenbach	1711-1738
Jacob Ernst of Liechtenstein-Castlekorn	1738-1745
Ferdinand Julius Troyer	1745-1758
Leopold Friedrich Egkh	1758-1760
Maximilian, earl of Hamilton	1761-1776

List of Figures

List of Abbreviations

ACO	Arcibiskupská konzistoř Olomouc (Archbishop's Consistory Olomouc)
AMO	Archiv města Olomouce (Olomouc City Archives)
AO	Arcibiskupství Olomouc (Archbishopric Olomouc)
ASV	Archivio segreto vaticano (Vatican Secret Archives)
BAV	Biblioteca apostolica vaticana (Vatican Apostolic Library)
DL	Diplomatikai levéltár (Collection of pre-1526 charters)
MCO	Metropolitní kapitula Olomouc (Metropolitan Chapter Olomouc)
MNL OL	Magyar Nemzeti Levéltár Országos Levéltára (Hungarian National Archives, State Archive, Budapest)
MZA	Moravský zemský archiv v Brně (Moravian Land Archives, Brno)
SOkA	Státní okresní archiv (State District Archives)
VKOL	Vědecká knihovna Olomouc (Research Library, Olomouc)
ZAO-O	Zemský archiv Opava, pobočka Olomouc (Land Archives Opava, branch Olomouc)

Archival Sources

Brno, Moravský zemský archiv (MZA)
E 21, Franciscans of Dačice, book no. 9, *Archivum Conventus Olomucensis*
G 83, Matice moravská, Kopiáře biskupské korespondence (Cartularies of bishops' correspondence)

Budapest, Magyar Nemzeti Levéltár (MNL)
Országos Levéltár, DL 36087, 66756

Città del Vaticano, Archivio Segreto Vaticano (ASV)
Reg. Lat. 629, 635
Reg. Suppl. 580, 589, 957
Reg. Vat. 420, 531

Città del Vaticano, Biblioteca Apostolica Vaticana (BAV)
Fondo Boncompagni–Ludovisi, E 12
Vat. lat. 3922

Olomouc, Státní okresní archiv (SOkA)
AMO, Knihy (Books), sign. 677, 1540, 1562
AMO, Listiny (Charters), inv. no. 206, 237, 240, 247, 252, 253, 255, 256, 258, 263, 264, 265, 267, 269, 273, 275, 277, 278, 284, 367, 528, 1203, 1209, 1378, 1380, 1381
AMO, Zlomky registratur (Fragments of registers), inv. no. 190, 401, 531, 1374, 1527, 1590, 1877/1, 4405, 4587, 4631

Olomouc, Vědecká knihovna (VKOL)
sign. II 32070, II 39012, M I 10, M I 302, M II 91

Olomouc, Zemský archiv Opava, pobočka Olomouc (ZAO-O)
ACO, ms. 109a, 109b
AO, Kopiáře biskupské korespondence (Cartularies of bishops' correspondence)
AO, Pergameny (Parchments), sign. C I b 10, C I b 11

MCO, Listiny (Charters), sign. A IV c 4, A IV d 3/6, A IV a 28, A IV a 29, A IV b 22, A IV b 23, E I 4

MCO, sign. C.O. 538, Magnoald Ziegelbauer, *Olomucium Sacrum quo Historici Ecclesiastica Moraviae et eius Episcopatus exponitur,* vol. II, 1798

Prague, Národní archiv (NA)

Stará manipulace (SM), sign. R 109/14

Rome, Biblioteca Angelica

Ms. 1077

Bibliography

Abray, Lorna Jane. *Magistrates, Clergy and Commons in Strasbourg, 1500-1598*. Ithaca, Cornell University Press, 1985.

Acta Tomiciana, 17 vols., ed. by Stanislaus Górski. Poznań, 1852-1999.

Archbishop's chateau & gardens in Kroměříž, ed. by Ladislav Daniel, Marek Perůtka and Milan Togner. Kroměříž, National Institute for Preservation of Historical Monuments, district branch Kroměříž, 2009.

Archiv Český, 39 vols., ed. by František Palacký et al. Prague, 1840-2004.

Babler, Otto F. "Ein englischer Reisender des 16. Jahrhunderts über Olmütz." *Mährisch-Schlesische Heimat,* 1 (1968), pp. 42-48.

Bachmann, Adolf, ed. *Urkundliche Nachträge zur österreichisch-deutschen Geschichte im Zeitalter Kaiser Friedrich III.* (Fontes rerum austriacarum II/46). Vienna, Tempsky, 1892.

Bailey, Michael D. *Battling Demons. Witchcraft, Heresy, and Reform in the Late Middle Ages*. University Park, Pennsylvania State University Press, 2004.

Balcárek, Pavel. *Brno versus Olomouc. O primát hlavního města Moravy. Pod Špilberkem proti Švédům*. Brno, Jota, 1993.

Baletka, Tomáš. "Olomoucké biskupství v době sedisvakance. Osoby a instituce ve víru vzájemných interakcí (1482-1497)." In *Sacri canones servandi sunt: ius canonicum et status ecclesiae saeculis XIII-XV,* ed. by Pavel Krafl. Prague, Historický ústav AV ČR, 2008, pp. 540-544.

Baletka, Tomáš. *Páni z Kravař: Z Moravy až na konec světa*. Prague, Nakladatelství Lidové noviny, 2003.

Benedict, Philip. *Rouen during the Wars of Religion*. Cambridge, Cambridge University Press, 1981.

Bílý, Jiří Libor and Zdeněk Kašpar. *Staromoravští rodové I. Olomoučtí protestanté ve zmocňovací listině z roku 1610 I*. Ostrava, Key Publishing, 2013.

Blaschke, Karlheinz and Siegfried Seifert. "Reformation und Konfessionalisierung in der Oberlausitz." In *Welt – Macht – Geist. Das Haus Habsburg und die Oberlausitz 1526-1635,* ed. by Joachim Bahlcke and Volker Dudeck. Zittau, Städtische Museen Zittau, 2002, pp. 121-128.

Blickle, Peter. *Communal Reformation: The Quest for Salvation in Sixteenth-Century Germany*. London, Humanities Press, 1992.

Bombera, Jan. "O posmrtné magii na libavském panství v 18. století." In *Okresní archív v Olomouci 1984*. Olomouc, Státní okresní archiv, 1985, pp. 79-93.
Boubín, Jaroslav. *Žaloby katolíků na mistra Jana z Rokycan*. Rokycany, Státní okresní archiv, 1997.
Bouwsma, William J. "Anxiety and the Formation of Early Modern Culture." In *After the Reformation: Essays in Honor of J.H. Hexter*, ed. by Barbara C. Malament. Manchester, Manchester University Press, 1980, pp. 215-246.
Brady, Thomas A. *Class, Regime and Reformation at Strasbourg, 1520-1555*. Leiden, Brill, 1978.
Brandl, Vincenc, ed. *Spisy Karla staršího ze Žerotína, Oddělení I, Žerotínovi zápisové o soudě panském*. Brno, 1866.
Breitenbacher, Antonín. *Dějiny arcibiskupské obrazárny v Kroměříži*, 2 vols. Kroměříž, 1925-1927.
Bretholz, Berthold. "Die Übergabe Mährens an Herzog Albrecht V. von Österreich im Jahre 1423. Beiträge zur Geschichte der Husitenkriege in Mähren." *Archiv für österreichische Geschichte,* 80 (1894), pp. 251-349.
Brevis Synopsis Devotionis Octiduanae Olomucii in Cathedrali Ecclesia Sancti Wenceslai in Venerationem Sancti Martyris Joannis Nepomuceni Institutae. S.l., 1731.
Brigden, Susan. *London and the Reformation*. Oxford, Oxford University Press, 1989.
Burian, Vladimír. *Vývoj náboženských poměrů v Brně*. Brno, ÚNV, 1948.

Calmet, Augustin. *Dissertations sur les apparitions des anges, des démons et des esprits, et sur les revenants et vampires de Hongrie, de Bohême, de Moravie et de Silésie*. Paris, de Bure l'aîné, 1746.
Cameron, Keith, Mark Greengrass and Penny Roberts, eds. *The Adventure of Religious Pluralism in Early Modern France*. Bern, Peter Lang, 1999.
Christensen, Carl C. *Art and Reformation in Germany*. Athens, OH, Ohio University Press, 1979.
Connor, Philip. *Montauban and Southern French Calvinism during the Wars of Religion*. Aldershot, Ashgate, 2002.
Čornej, Petr and Milena Bartlová. *Velké dějiny zemí Koruny české,* vol. VI, *1437-1526*. Prague and Litomyšl, Paseka, 2007.
Coster, Will and Andrew Spicer, eds. *Sacred Space in Early Modern Europe*. Cambridge, Cambridge University Press, 2005.
Craig, John. *Reformation, Politics, and Polemics: The Growth of Protestantism in East Anglian Market Towns, 1500-1610*. Aldershot, Ashgate, 2001.
Csepregi, Zoltán. "Court Priests in the Entourage of Queen Mary of Hungary." In *Mary of Hungary. The Queen and Her Court 1521-1531,* ed. by Orsolya Réthelyi, Beatrix F. Romhányi, Enikő Spekner and András Végh. Budapest, Budapest History Museum, 2005, pp. 49-61.

d'Elvert, Christian, ed. *Mährische und schlesische Chroniken,* vol. I. Brünn, 1861.
Davanzati, Giuseppe. *Dissertazione sopra i vampiri*, ed. by Giacomo Annibaldis. Bari, BESA, 1998.

Davis, Natalie Zemon. *Society and Culture in Early Modern France*. Stanford, Stanford University Press, 1975.

de Certeau, Michel. *The possesion at Loudun*, transl. M.B. Smith. Chicago and London, University of Chicago Press, 1999.

de Schertz, Carolus Ferdinandus. *Magia Posthuma Per Juridicum Illud Pro et Contra Suspenso Nonnullibi Judicio Investigata*. Olomucii, 1704.

Dedic, Paul. "Die Geschichte des Protestantismus in Olmütz IV." *Jahrbuch der Gesellschaft für die Geschichte des Protestantismus im ehemaligen und neuen Österreich,* 55 (1934), pp. 69-112.

Dějiny Olomouce, 2 vols., ed. by Jindřich Schulz and Jana Burešová. Olomouc, Univerzita Palackého, 2009.

Derwich, Marek. "Jean Capistran et les Juifs. Exemple de Silésie." In *Les Chrétiens et les Juifs dans les sociétés de rite grec et latin: approche comparative,* ed. by Michel Dmitriev, Christian Tollet and Élisabeth Teito. Paris, Honoré Champion, 2003, pp. 59-72.

Deventer, Jörg. "Grenzen überschreiten. Konversionen zum Katholizismus in Böhmen und Schlesien im späten 16. und im 17. Jahrhundert." In *Náboženský život a církevní poměry v zemích Koruny české ve 14.-17. století,* ed. by Lenka Bobková and Jana Konvičná. Prague, Filozofická fakulta Univerzity Karlovy v Praze, Casablanca, 2009, pp. 670-682.

Diefendorf, Barbara. *Beneath the Cross: Catholics and Huguenots in Sixteenth-Century Paris*. New York, Oxford University Press, 1991.

Dudík, Beda, ed. *Chronik der Stadt Olmütz über die Jahre 1619 und 1620.* Brünn, Rohrer, 1851.

Dudík, Beda, ed. *Chronik des Minoriten-Guardians des St. Jacobs-Klosters in Olmütz.* Wien, 1881.

Dudik, Beda, ed. "Chronik des Minoriten-Guardians des St. Jakobs-Kloster in Olmütz, P. Paulinus Zackowic über die Schwedenherrschaft in Olmütz vom 1642 bis 1650." *Archiv für österreichische Geschichte*, 62 (1881), pp. 451-611.

Dudík, Beda, ed. *Olmützer Sammel-Chronik vom Jahre 1432 bis 1656.* Brünn, Rohrer, 1858.

Dudík, Beda, ed. "Ex Diario r.mi Patris Schönberger, rectoris Collegii Societatis Iesu Olomucii." *Archiv für österreichische Geschichte*, 62 (1881), pp. 612-624.

Dudík, Beda, ed. "Tagebuch des feindlichen Einfalls der Schweden in das Markgrafthum Mähren während ihres Aufenthaltes in der Stadt Olmütz 1642-1650 geführt von dem Olmützer Stadtschreiber und Notar Magister Friedrich Flade." *Archiv für österreichische Geschichte,* 65 (1884), pp. 307-485.

Eire, Carlos. *War Against the Idols: The Reformation of Worship from Erasmus to Calvin*. New York, Cambridge University Press, 1986.

Elbel, Martin. "Bishop's Secular Entry: Power and Representation in Inauguration Ceremonies of the Eighteenth-Century Bishops of Olomouc." In *Religious Ceremonials and Images: Power and Social Meaning,* ed. by José Pedro Paiva. Coimbra, Palimage, 2002, pp. 47-60.

Elbel, Martin. *Bohemia Franciscana. Františkánský řád a jeho působení v českých zemch v 17. a 18. století.* Olomouc, Univerzita Palackého, 2001.

Elbel, Martin. "Budování poutního místa. Svaté schody při františkánském klášteře v Olomouci." *Folia historica Bohemica,* 20 (2004), pp. 215-239.

Elbel, Martin. "Čestný sloup Nejsvětější Trojice v Olomouci." *In Ročenka Státního okresního archivu v Olomouci 6 (25) 1997*, ed. by Vladimír Spáčil. Olomouc, Okresní archiv, 1998, pp. 87-97.

Elbel, Martin. "Dva světy? Konfesijní hranice za švédské okupace Olomouce 1642-1650." In *Historická Olomouc XIII, Konec švédské okupace a poválečná obnova ve 2. polovině 17. století,* ed. by Martin Elbel and Milan Togner. Olomouc, Univerzita Palackého, 2002, pp. 99-105.

Elbel, Martin. "Kult sv. Jana Kapistrána v českých zemích." *Acta Universitatis Palackianae Olomucensis. Philosophica – Aesthetica,* 16 (1998), pp. 81-99.

Elbel, Martin. "Tanquam Peregrini. Pilgrimage Practice in the Bohemian Franciscan Province." In *Communities of Devotion: Religious Orders and Society in East Central Europe, 1450-1800*, ed. by Maria Craciun and Elaine Fulton. Farnham, Ashgate, 2011, pp. 227-243.

Elm, Kaspar. "Johannes Kapistrans Predigtreise diesseits der Alpen (1451-1456)." In Kaspar Elm, *Vitasfratrum: Beiträge zur Geschichte der Eremiten- und Mendikantenorden des zwölften und dreizehnten Jahrhunderts,* ed. by Dieter Berg. Werl, Dietrich Coelde, 1994, pp. 321-337.

Enee Silvii Piccolominei postea Pii PP. II De Europa, ed. by Adrianus van Heck (Studi e Testi 398). Città del Vaticano, Biblioteca Apostolica vaticana, 2001.

Enthronisticum Parthenium: Sive Gloria Et Honor Neo-Inauguratæ ... Reginæ Mariæ ... ; Prope Metropolim Olomucensem in Marchionatu Moraviæ ... Et Prima In Orbe Marcomanno Corona Regali Aurea De Urbe Missa Ritu Vaticano, Solemnissimóque applausu Coronata. Olomucii, typis Francisci Antonii Hirnle, 1733.

Eschenloer, Peter. *Geschichte der Stadt Breslau,* 2 vols., ed. by Gunhild Roth. Münster, Waxmann, 2003.

Evans, Robert. "Calvinism in East-Central Europe: Hungary and Her Neighbours." In *International Calvinism, 1541-1715*, ed. by Menna Prestwich. Oxford, Clarendon, 1985, pp. 167-196.

Fata, Márta. *Ungarn, das Reich der Stephanskrone, im Zeitalter der Reformation und Konfessionalisierung. Multiethnizität, Land und Konfession 1500 bis 1700.* Münster, Aschendorff, 2000.

Fiala, Jiří. "Dějiny jezuitského konviktu v Olomouci." In Jiří Fiala, Leoš Mlčák and Karel Žurek, *Jezuitský konvikt – sídlo uměleckého centra Univerzity Palackého v Olomouci. Dějiny, stavební a umělecké dějiny.* Olomouc, Univerzita Palackého, 2002, pp. 33-158.

Fiala, Jiří. "Jezuitská akademie a univerzita v Olomouci (1573-1773)." In Jiří Fiala et al., *Univerzita v Olomouci (1573-2009).* Olomouc, Univerzita Palackého, 2009, pp. 25-58.

Foa, Jérémie. "An Unequal Apportionment: The Conflict over Space between Protestants and Catholics at the Beginning of the War of Religion." *French History*, 20 (2006), pp. 369-386.

Foltýn, Dušan et al. *Encyklopedie moravských a slezských klášterů.* Prague, Libri, 2005.

Forster, Marc. *The Counter-Reformation in the Villages. Religion and Reform in the Bishopric of Speyer, 1560-1720*. Ithaca and London, Cornell University Press, 1992.

Fraknói, Vilmos, ed. *Mátyás király levelei, külügyi osztály,* 2 vols. Budapest, Magyar tudományos akadémia, 1893-1895.

Gál, Gedeon, Jason M. Miskuly, and Ottokar Bonmann. "A Provisional Calendar of St. John Capistran's Correspondence II." *Franciscan Studies,* 49 (1989), pp. 255-345.

Gecser, Ottó. "Itinerant Preaching in Late Medieval Central Europe. St. John Capistran in Wrocław." *Medieval Sermon Studies,* 47 (2003), pp. 5-20.

Gecser, Ottó. "Preaching and Publicness. St John of Capestrano and the Making of His Charisma North of the Alps." In *Charisma and Religious Authority. Jewish, Christian and Muslim Preaching 1200-1500,* ed. by Katherine L. Jansen and Miri Rubin. Turnhout, Brepols, 2010, pp. 145-159.

Göllner, Charles. "La Milice Chrétienne, un instrument de croisade au XVIIe siècle." *Mélanges de l'École Roumaine en France,* 12 (1936), pp. 59-118.

Gotwald, William Kurtz. *Ecclesiastical Censure at the End of the Fifteenth Century.* Baltimore, Johns Hopkins University Press, 1927.

Grell, Ole Peter, ed. *The Scandinavian Reformation: From Evangelical Movement to Institutionalisation of Reform.* Cambridge, Cambridge University Press, 1995.

Hamm, Berndt. *Bürgertum und Glaube. Konturen der städtischen Reformation.* Göttingen, Vandenhoeck und Ruprecht, 1996.

Hanlon, Gregory. *Confession and Community in Seventeenth-Century France: Catholic and Protestant Coexistence in Aquitaine.* Philadelphia, University of Pennsylvania Press, 1993.

Hermann, Amandus. *Capistranus Triumphans. Seu Historia Fundamentalis de Sancto Joanne Capistrans.* Coloniae, B. J. Endterum, 1700 (repr. Nabu Press, 2011).

Hervieu-Léger, Danièle. *Religion as a Chain of Memory.* New Brunswick, Rutgers University Press, 2000.

Heymann, Frederick G. *George of Bohemia: King of Heretics.* Princeton, NJ, Princeton University Press, 1965.

Hlobil, Ivo. "Bernardinské symboly Jména Ježíš v českých zemích šířené Janem Kapistránem." *Umění,* 44 (1996), pp. 223-234.

Hlobil, Ivo. "Heraldické svorníky mořického kostela v Olomouci z r. 1483 a případná zpodobnění jejich autora." *Vlastivědný věstník moravský,* 33 (1981), pp. 214-218.

Hlobil, Ivo. "Pochází Madona svatokopecká z Itálie?" In *Město v baroku, baroko ve městě*, ed. by Ladislav Daniel and Filip Hradil. Olomouc, Vlastivědné muzeum v Olomouci and Univerzita Palackého, 2012, pp. 130-135.

Hofer, Johannes. "Die wiener Predigten des hl. Johannes Kapistran im Jahre 1451." *Jahrbuch der Österreichischen Leo-Gesellschaft,* 1 (1927), pp. 122-146.

Hofer, Johannes. "Zur Predigttätigkeit des hl. Johannes Kapistran in den deutschen Städten." *Franziskanische Studien,* 13 (1926), pp. 120-158.

Holinková, Jiřina. *Dvě studie z dějin městské školy na Moravě v předbělohorském období.* Olomouc, Univerzita Palackého, 2005.

Horyna, Mojmír. *Jan Blažej Santini-Aichel.* Prague, Karolinum, 1998.

Housley, Norman. *Crusading and the Ottoman Threat 1453-1505.* Oxford, Oxford University Press, 2012.

Housley, Norman. "Giovanni da Capistrano and the Crusade of 1456." In *Crusading in the Fifteenth Century: Message and Impact,* ed. by Norman Housley. Basingstoke, Palgrave Macmillan, 2004, pp. 94-115.

Hradil, Miroslav. "Adam Schäffer – poslední olomoucký mincmistr." In *Ročenka Státního okresního archivu v Olomouci 1990.* Olomouc, Státní okresní archiv, 1991, pp. 80-84.

Hrubý, František. "Luterství a kalvinismus na Moravě před Bílou horou." *Český časopis historický,* 40 (1934), pp. 265-299.

Hrubý, František. "Moravská šlechta r. 1619, její jmění a náboženské vyznání." *Časopis Matice moravské,* 46 (1922), pp. 107-169.

Hrubý, František. "Pád českého povstání na Moravě 1620." *Český časopis historický*, 29 (1923), pp. 71-120, 358-388.

Iohannes Rabensteinensis. *Disputacio,* ed. by Bohumil Ryba. Budapest, Egyetemi nyomda, 1942.

Jacob, Eugen. *Johannes von Capistrano,* vol. II, *Die auf der Königlichen und Universitäts-bibliothek zu Breslau befindlichen handschriften Aufzeichnungen von Reden und Tractaten Capistrans, XLIV sermones Vratislaviae habiti a. D. MCCCCLIII.* Breslau, Max Woywod, 1911.

Jakubec, Ondřej. "Confessional Aspects of the Art Patronage of the Bishops of Olomouc in the Period before the White Mountain Battle." *Acta Historiae Artium,* 47 (2006), pp. 121-127.

Jakubec, Ondřej. "Kaple sv. Anny na Olomouckém hradě a svatoanenský kult na Moravě kolem roku 1600." In *Arcidiecézní muzeum na Olomouckém hradě / The Archdiocesan Museum at Olomouc Castle. Articles from the International Conference,* ed. by Ondřej Jakubec. Olomouc, Muzeum umění Olomouc, 2010, pp. 197-209.

Jakubec, Ondřej. "Konfesionalizace a rituály potridentského katolicismu na předbělohorské Moravě." In *Per saecula ad tempora nostra. Sborník prací k 60. narozeninám prof. Jaroslava Pánka,* ed. by Jiří Mikulec and Miloslav Polívka. Prague, Historický ústav AV ČR, 2007, pp. 360-366.

Jakubec, Ondřej. *Kulturní prostředí a mecenát olomouckých biskupů potridentské doby: Umělecké objednávky biskupů v letech 1553-1598, jejich význam a funkce.* Olomouc, Univerzita Palackého, 2003.

Jakubec, Ondřej. "Poutní místa, poutě a milostné obrazy v mecenátu a politice olomouckých biskupů raného novověku. Několik poznámek k poznání konfesionalizačních praktik na předbělohorské Moravě." In *Pielgrzymowanie i sztuka. Góra Świętej Anny i inne miejsca pielgrzymkowe na Śląsku,* ed. by Joanna Lubos-Kozieł. Wrocław, Uniwersytet Wrocławski, 2005, pp. 307-321.

Jakubec, Ondřej. "'Sebekonfesionalizace' a manifestace katolicismu jako projev utváření konfesní uniformity na předbělohorské Moravě." *Acta Universitatis Palackianae Olomucensis. Historica,* 31 (2003), pp. 101-119.

Jan z Rabštejna. *Dialogus,* ed. by Bohumil Ryba. Prague, Matice česká, 1946.

Jezuitský konvikt. Sídlo uměleckého centra Univerzity Palackého v Olomouci. Dějiny – Stavební a umělecké dějiny – Obnova a využití, ed. by Jiří Fiala, Leoš Mlčák and Karel Žurek. Olomouc, Univerzita Palackého, 2002.

Johnson, Trevor. *Magistrates, Madonnas and Miracles: The Counter Reformation in the Upper Palatinate*. Aldershot, Ashgate, 2009.

Kadlec, Jaroslav. *Katoličtí exulanti čeští doby husitské.* Prague, Zvon, 1990.

Kalista, Zdeněk. *Česká barokní gotika a její žďárské ohnisko.* Brno, Blok, 1970.

Kalous, Antonín. "Boskovice urai Mátyás király diplomáciai és politikai szolgálatában." *Századok,* 141 (2007), pp. 375-389.

Kalous, Antonín. "Declaratio brevis Corone immaculate virginis: A source for the late medieval popular piety." *Umění/Art,* 55 (2007), pp. 40-44.

Kalous, Antonín. "Spor o biskupství olomoucké v letech 1482-1497." *Český časopis historický,* 105 (2007), pp. 1-39.

Kameníček, František, ed. "Jednání sněmovní a veřejná v markrabství moravském." In *Archiv český,* vol. X, ed. by Josef Kalousek. Prague, 1890.

Kaminsky, Howard. *A History of the Hussite Revolution.* Berkeley and Los Angeles, University of California Press, 1967.

Kaplan, Benjamin J. *Calvinists and Libertines: Confession and Community in Utrecht, 1578-1620.* Oxford, Clarendon, 1995.

Kaplan, Benjamin J. *Cunegonde's Kidnapping: A Story of Religious Conflict in the Age of Enlightenment*. New Haven, Yale University Press, 2014.

Kaplan, Benjamin J. *Divided by Faith. Religious Conflict and the Practice of Toleration in Early Modern Europe.* Cambridge, MA and London, Belknap, 2007.

Kašpar, Zdeněk. "Prameny k dějinám Olomouce 16. století v kopiářích olomouckých biskupů I." *Ročenka Státního okresního archivu v Olomouci,* 8 (1999), pp. 179-196.

Kašpar, Zdeněk. "Prameny k dějinám Olomouce 16. století v kopiářích olomouckých biskupů IV." *Olomoucký archivní sborník,* 2 (2004), pp. 190-203.

Kašpar, Zdeněk. "Prameny k dějinám Olomouce 16. století v kopiářích olomouckých biskupů V." *Olomoucký archivní sborník,* 3 (2005), pp. 176-186.

Kašpar, Zdeněk. "V době předbělohorské." In Jindřich Schulz, ed., *Olomouc. Malé dějiny města.* Olomouc, Univerzita Palackého, 2002, pp. 93-110.

Kaufmann, Thomas. *Dreißigjähriger Krieg und Westfälischer Friede. Kirchengeschichtliche Studien zur lutherischen Konfessionskultur.* Tübingen, Mohr Siebeck, 1998.

Knoz, Tomáš. *Karel starší ze Žerotína. Don Quijote v labyrintu světa.* Prague, Vyšehrad, 2008.

Kobliha, Anton, ed. *Urkunden-Sammlung betreffend die Privilegien und Rechte des Hochwürdigst-getreuen Metropolitankapitels zu Olmütz.* Olmütz, Verlag des Metropolitankapitels, 1890.

Kohout, Štěpán. "Pobyt Jana Kapistrána v Olomouci." *Ročenka Státního okresního archivu v Olomouci,* 3 (1994), pp. 117-140.
Kooi, Christine. *Liberty and Religion: Church and State in Leiden's Reformation, 1572-1620.* Leiden, Brill, 2000.
Koslofsky, Craig. "Honour and violence in German Lutheran funerals in the confessional age." *Social History,* 20 (1995), pp. 315-337.
Kostlán, Antonín. *Societas incognitorum. První učená společnost v českých zemích.* Prague, Archiv Akademie věd ČR, 1996.
Kotrba, Viktor. *Česká barokní gotika. Dílo J. Santiniho-Aichla.* Prague, Academia, 1976.
Kráčmer, Mořic. *Dějiny metropolitního chrámu sv. Václava v Olomouci.* Olomouc, R. Prombergr, 1887.
Králík, Oldřich. "Dvě zprávy o olomouckých humanistech." *Časopis Matice moravské,* 68 (1948), pp. 283-327.
Krása, Josef. *České iluminované rukopisy 13.-16. století.* Prague, Odeon, 1990.
Kučera, Jan and Jiří Rak. *Bohuslav Balbín a jeho místo v české kultuře.* Prague, Vyšehrad, 1983.
Kux, Hans. *Geschichte von Olmütz.* Olmütz, 1937.
Kux, Hans. "Von der Reformation bis zur Gegenreformation." In *Aus der Geschichte des Protestantismus in Olmütz*, ed. by Friedrich Müller. Olmütz, 1927.
Kux, Johann. "Das Olmützer Judenregister vom Jahre 1413-1420." *Zeitschrift des Deutschen Vereines für die Geschichte Mährens und Schlesiens,* 9 (1905), pp. 385-423.

Loucký, Josef. *Popis královského hlavního města Olomouce sepsaný syndikem Floriánem Josefem Louckým roku 1746*, ed. by Vladimír Spáčil and Libuše Spáčilová. Olomouc, Vlastivědná společnost muzejní, 1991.
Louthan, Howard. *Converting Bohemia. Force and Persuasion in the Catholic Reformation.* Cambridge, Cambridge University Press, 2009.
Louthan, Howard and Graeme Murdock, eds. *A Companion to the Reformation in Central Europe*. Leiden, Brill, 2015.
Luria, Keith. *Sacred Boundaries: Religious Coexistence and Conflict in Early Modern France.* Washington DC, The Catholic University of America Press, 2005.
Lynch, Michael. *Edinburgh and the Reformation*. Edinburgh, Edinburgh University Press, 1981.

Macek, Josef. *Víra a zbožnost jagellonského věku.* Prague, Argo, 2001.
Macourek, Vladimír A. "Počátky katolické restaurace na Moravě za biskupa Prusinovského (1565-1572)." *Sborník historického kroužku,* 28 (1927), pp. 42-48, 96-102; 29 (1928) pp. 69-73, 122-128; 30 (1929) pp. 59-61, 113-121; 31 (1930) pp. 27-33, 102-109, 175-183; 32 (1931) pp. 8-13, 79-86, 196-201, 264-268; 33 (1932) pp. 19-28, 83-87, 133-138, 199-202; 34 (1933) pp. 28-32, 73-83.
Maiello, Giuseppe. *Vampyrismus v kulturních dějinách Evropy.* Prague, Nakladatelství Lidové noviny, 2005.

Malý, Tomáš. "Confessional Identity in Moravian Royal Towns in the 16th and 17th Centuries?" In *Public Communication in European Reformation. Artistic and other Media in Central Europe 1380-1620*, ed. by Milena Bartlová and Michal Šroněk. Prague, Artefactum, 2007, pp. 323-334.

Malý, Tomáš. *Smrt a spása mezi Tridentem a sekularizací.* Brno, Matice moravská, 2010.

Maňas, Vladimír, Zdeněk Orlita, and Martina Potůčková, eds. *Zbožných duší úl. Náboženská bratrstva v kultuře raněnovověké Moravy. Katalog výstavy.* Olomouc, Muzeum umění Olomouc – Arcidiecézní muzeum Olomouc, 2010.

Marek, Jaroslav. *Sociální struktura moravských královských měst v 15. a 16. století.* Prague, Nakladatelství Československé akademie věd, 1967.

Marnef, Guido. *Antwerp in the Age of Reformation: Underground Protestantism in a Commercial Metropolis, 1550-1577.* Leiden, Brill, 1996.

Marshall, Peter. "Confessionalization and Community in the Burial of English Catholics, c. 1570-1700." In *Getting Along? Religious Identities and Confessional Relations in Early Modern England*, ed. by Nadine Lewycky and Adam Morton. Farnham, Ashgate, 2012, pp. 57-76.

Maur, Eduard. "Příspěvek k biografii biskupa Aleše z Březí." In *Táborský archiv. Sborník Státního okresního archivu v Táboře.* Tábor, Státní okresní archiv, 1998, pp. 11-35.

Meyer, Judith P. *Reformation in La Rochelle: Tradition and Change in Early Modern Europe, 1500-1568.* Geneva, Droz, 1998.

Mezník, Jaroslav. "Markrabě a páni (K mocenskému dualismu na Moravě v době předhusitské)." *Sborník prací filozofické fakulty brněnské univerzity. Studia minora facultatis philosophicae Universitatis Brunensis,* C 42 (1995), pp. 39-50.

Mezník, Jaroslav. *Lucemburská Morava 1310-1423.* Prague, Nakladatelství Lidové Noviny, 1999.

Miller, Jaroslav. *Urban Societies in East-Central Europe: 1500-1700.* Aldershot, Ashgate, 2008.

Miller, Jaroslav et al., eds. *Konfliktní soužití: Královské město – šlechta – duchovenstvo v raném novověku. Edice. Knihy půhonné a nálezové královského města Olomouce (1516-1616).* Olomouc, Danal, 1998.

Mlčák, Leoš. "Manýristická poutní kaple na sv. Kopečku u Olomouce." In *Ročenka Státního okresního archivu v Olomouci 2000.* Olomouc, Státní okresní archiv, 2001, pp. 88-109.

Moeller, Bernd. *Reichsstadt und Reformation.* Gütersloh, Gerd Mohn, 1962.

Molnár, Amedeo. "Protivaldenská politika na úsvitu 16. století." *Historická Olomouc*, 3 (1980), pp. 153-174.

Monter, E. William. *Calvin's Geneva.* New York, John Wiley, 1967.

Müller, Michael G. *Zweite Reformation und städtische Autonomie im königlichen Preussen. Danzig, Elbing und Thorn in der Epoche der Konfessionalisierung.* Berlin, Akademie Verlag, 1997.

Murdock, Graeme, Penny Roberts and Andrew Spicer, eds. *Ritual and Violence: Natalie Zemon Davis and Early Modern France.* Oxford, Past and Present Supplement Series, 2012.

Muzzarelli, Maria Giuseppina. *Pescatori di uomini. Predicatori alla fine del Medioevo.* Bologna, Il Mulino, 2005.

Myslivečková, Hana. "Epitafy v renesanční sepulkrální sochařské tvorbě Moravy a českého Slezska." In *Ku věčné památce. Malované renesanční epitafy v českých zemích,* ed. by Ondřej Jakubec. Olomouc, Muzeum umění Olomouc, 2007, pp. 73-81.

Naphy, William. *Calvin and the Consolidation of the Genevan Reformation.* Manchester, Manchester University Press, 1994.

Nather, Wilhelm and Friedrich Nather. *Die Olmützer Häuserchronik,* 2 vols., ed. by Vladimír Spáčil. Olomouc, Univerzita Palackého, 2005-2006.

Nemeth Papo, Gizella. *Pippo Spano. Un eroe antiturco antesignano del Rinascimento.* Gorizia, Edizioni della Laguna, 2006.

Nešpor, Václav. *Dějiny Olomouce.* Brno, Muzejní spolek v Brně, 1936 (repr. Olomouc, Votobia, 1998).

Nešpor, Václav. "Kdy a jak byla provedena protireformace v Olomouci." *Časopis Vlastivědného spolku muzejního v Olomouci*, 57 (1948), pp. 45-47.

Odložilík, Otakar. *The Hussite King: Bohemia in European Affairs, 1440-1471.* New Brunswick, NJ, Rutgers University Press, 1965.

Ohlidal, Anna. "Kirchenbau in der multikonfessionellen Stadt. Zur konfessionellen Prägung und Besetzung des städtischen Raums in den Prager Städten um 1600." In *Stadt und Religion in der Frühen Neuzeit. Soziale Ordnungen und ihre Repräsentationen*, ed. by Vera Isaiasz. Frankfurt am Main, Campus, 2007, pp. 79-80.

Olomoucké baroko: Výtvarná kultura z let 1620-1780, 3 vols. Vol. I, *Úvodní svazek: Proměny ambicí jednoho města,* ed. by Martin Elbel and Ondřej Jakubec. Vol. II, *Katalog,* ed. by Ondřej Jakubec and Marek Perůtka. Vol. III, *Historie a kultura,* ed. by Ondřej Jakubec and Marek Perůtka. Olomouc, Muzeum umění Olomouc, 2010-2011.

Orlita, Zdeněk. "Olomoučtí jezuité a náboženská bratrstva v 16.-18. století." *Střední Morava*, no. 20 (2005), pp. 43-54.

Ozment, Steven E. *The Reformation in the Cities: The Appeal of Protestantism to Sixteenth-Century Germany and Switzerland.* New Haven, Yale University Press, 1975.

Pacelli, Vincenzo. "Il 'Monogramma' bernardiano: origine, diffusione e sviluppo." In *San Bernardino da Siena predicatore e pellegrino. Atti del convegno nazionale di studi bernardiniani* (Maiori, 20-22 giugno 1980), ed. by F. D'Episcopo. Galatina (Lecce), Congedo, 1985, pp. 253-259.

Palacký, František, ed. *Documenta Magistri Ioannis Hus vitam, doctrinam, causam in Constantiensi concilio actam et controversias de religione in Bohemia, annis 1403-1418 motas illustrantia.* Pragae, F. Tempsky, 1869 (repr. Osnabrück, Biblio-Verlag, 1966).

Palacky, Franz, ed. *Urkundliche Beiträge zur Geschichte Böhmens und seine Nachbarländer im Zeitalter Georg's von Podiebrad (1450-1471)* (Fontes rerum austriacarum II/20). Vienna, 1860.

Paprocký z Hlohol, Bartoloměj. *Zrcadlo Slavného Markrabství Moravského.* Olomouc, 1593.

Parma, Tomáš. "The legacy of Sts Cyril and Methodius in the plans of Recatholization of Moravia." In *The Cyril and Methodius Mission and Europe – 1150 Years since the Arrival of the Thessaloniki Brothers in Great Moravia. Proceedings from the international scientific conference 13th-17th May 2013, Velehrad,* ed. by Pavel Kouřil. Brno, The Institute of Archeology of the Academy of Sciences of the Czech Republic, 2014, pp. 334-341 (in print).

Parma, Tomáš. "Modernus Olomucensis dioecesis meae status. Le visite ad limina del Francesco cardinale Dietrichstein, vescovo di Olomouc (1570-1636) e le sue relazioni sullo stato della diocesi." *Römische Historische Mitteilungen,* 50 (2008), pp. 335-382.

Parma, Tomáš. "Neznámý jezuitský pramen o švédské okupaci Olomouce." In *Město v baroku, baroko ve městě,* ed. by Ladislav Daniel and Filip Hradil. Olomouc, Vlastivědné muzeum v Olomouci and Univerzita Palackého, 2012, pp. 13-22.

Parma, Tomáš. "Řád Křesťanského rytířstva: mezi řeholní společností a konfraternitou." *Folia historica Bohemica,* 26, no. 1 (2011), pp. 247-265.

Pavlíčková, Radmila. *Sídla olomouckých biskupů. Mecenáš a stavebník Karel z Liechtensteinu-Castelkorna 1664-1695.* Olomouc, Univerzita Palackého, 2001.

Petrů, Eduard and Ivo Hlobil. *Humanism and the Early Renaissance in Moravia.* Olomouc, Votobia, 1999.

Petrů, Eduard. *Humanisté o Olomouci.* Prague, Památník národního písemnictví, 1977.

Pettegree, Andrew. *Emden and the Dutch Revolt: Exile and the Development of Reformed Protestantism.* Oxford, Clarendon, 1992.

Pii II Commentarii rerum memorabilium que temporibus suis contigerunt, 2 vols., ed. by Adrian van Heck. Città del Vaticano, Biblioteca Apostolica Vaticana, 1984.

Pii Secundi Pontificis Maximi Commentarii, 2 vols., ed. by Ibolya Bellus and Iván Boronkai. Budapest, Balassi Kiadó, 1993.

Po-Chia Hsia, Ronnie. *Social Discipline in the Reformation: Central Europe 1550-1750.* London and New York, Routledge, 1989.

Pötzl-Malikova, Maria. "Die Feiern anlässlich der Heiligsprechung des Ignatius von Loyola und Franz Xaver im Jahre 1622 in Rom, Prag und Olmütz." In *Bohemia Jesuitica 1556-2006,* 2 vols., ed. by Petronilla Čemus. Prague, Karolinum, 2010, vol. II, pp. 1239-1254.

Pumprla, Václav. "Odvoz knih z Olomouce do Švédska na konci třicetileté války." In *Ročenka Státního okresního archivu v Olomouci 1997.* Olomouc, Státní okresní archiv, 1998, pp. 63-76.

Reinhard, Wolfgang. "Was ist katholische Konfessionalisierung?" In *Die katholische Konfessionalisierung,* ed. by Wolfgang Reinhard and Heinz Schilling. Gütersloh, Verein für Reformationsgeschichte, 1995, pp. 419-452.

Réthelyi, Orsolya. *Mary of Hungary in Court Context (1521-1531).* PhD dissertation, Central European University, Budapest, 2010.

Říčan, Rudolf, ed. *The History of the Unity of Brethren: A Protestant Hussite Church in Bohemia and Moravia,* transl. C. D. Crews. Betlehem, PA, Moravian Church, 1992.

Roberts, Penny. *A City in Conflict: Troyes during the French Wars of Religion.* Manchester, Manchester University Press, 1996.

Roberts, Penny. "Contesting sacred space: burial disputes in sixteenth-century France." In *The place of dead: death and remembrance in late medieval and Early Modern Europe*, ed. by Bruce Gordon and Peter Marshall. Cambridge, Cambridge University Press, 2000, pp. 131-148.

Roper, Lyndal. *The Holy Household: Women and Morals in Reformation Augsburg.* Oxford, Clarendon, 1991.

Safley, Thomas Max. *A Companion to Multiconfessionalism in the Early Modern World.* Leiden, Brill, 2011.

Samerski, Stefan. *"Wie im Himmel, so auf Erden"? Selig- und Heiligsprechung in der katholischen Kirche 1740 bis 1870.* Stuttgart, Kohlhammer, 2002.

Schieche, Emil. "Umfang und Schicksal der von den Schweden 1645 in Nikolsburg und 1648 in Prag erbeuteten Archivalien." *Bohemia,* 8 (1967), pp. 111-133.

Schilling, Heinz. "Die konfessionelle Stadt – eine Problemskizze." In *Historische Anstöße. Festschrift für Wolfgang Reinhard zum 65. Geburtstag am 10. April 2002,* ed. by Peter Burschel. Berlin, Akademie Verlag, 2002, pp. 60-83.

Schmidl, Joannes. *Historiae Societatis Iesu Provincie Bohemiae Pars II.* Pragae, Typis universitatis Carolo Ferdinandeae in Collegio S. J. Ad S. Clementem, per Jacobum Schweiger Factorem, 1749.

Schmidt, Heinrich Richard. *Reichsstädte, Reich und Reformation. Korporative Religionspolitik 1521-1529/30*. Stuttgart, F. Steiner, 1986.

Schreiber, Renate. *"ein galeria nach meiner Humor". Erzherzog Leopold Wilhelm.* Vienna and Milan, Kunsthistorisches Museum and Skira, 2004.

Sedlák, Jan. "K činnosti Jana Železného." *Studie a texty k náboženským dějinám českým,* 3 (1919), pp. 92-104.

Sehnal, Jiří and Jiří Vysloužil. *Dějiny hudby na Moravě.* Brno, Muzejní a vlastivědná společnost, 2001.

Šembera, Alois Vojtěch. *Paměti a znamenitosti města Olomouce.* Vienna, 1861.

Setton, Kenneth M. *The Papacy and the Levant (1204-1571),* vol. II, *The Fifteenth Century.* Philadelphia, The American Philosophical Society, 1978.

Sheils, William. "'Getting on' and 'Getting along' in Parish and Town: Catholics and Their Neighbours in England." In *Catholic Communities in Protestant States: Britain and the Netherlands, c. 1570-1720*, ed. by Benjamin Kaplan, Bob Moore, Henk van Nierop and Judith Pollmann. Manchester, Manchester University Press, 2009, pp. 67-83.

Sibutus, Georgius. *Adpotentissimum atque invictissimum Ferdinandum Hungariae & Bohemię, Dalmatię et Croatiae &c. regem ... Georgii Sibuti medici poetae & oratoris Panegyricus ... Eiusem illustratio in Olomuncz.* Vienna, 1528.

Sládek, Miloš. *Malý svět jest člověk aneb výbor z české barokní prózy.* Jinočany, H&H, 1995.

Šmahel, František. *Die Hussitische Revolution,* 3 vols. Hannover, Hahnsche Buchhandlung, 2002 (MGH Schriften 43).

Šmahel, František. "Spectaculum fidei českomoravské mise Jana Kapistrána." *Z kralické tvrze,* 14 (1987), pp. 15-19.

Šmahel, František. "Svoboda slova, svatá válka a tolerance z nutnosti v husitských Čechách." *Český časopis historický,* 93 (1994), pp. 644-679.

Smejkal, Bohumír. *Svatý Kopeček. Poutní chrám Navštívení Panny Marie.* Velehrad, 1994.

Snopek, František. "Akta kardinála Ditrichštejna z let 1619-1635." *Časopis Matice moravské,* 39 (1915), pp. 98-194.

Soukup, Daniel. "The Alleged Conversion of the Olomouc Rabbi Moses in 1425. Contribution to the Host Desecration Legends in Mediaeval Literature." *Judaica Bohemiae,* 48, no. 1 (2013), pp. 5-38.

Spáčilová, Libuše and Vladimír Spáčil, eds. *Památná kniha olomoucká (kodex Václava z Jihlavy) z let 1430-1492, 1528.* Olomouc, Univerzita Palackého, 2004.

Spicer, Andrew and Sarah Hamilton, eds. *Defining the Holy: Sacred Space in Late Medieval and Early Modern Europe.* Aldershot, Ashgate, 2005.

Staré letopisy české z rukopisu křižovnického, ed. by František Šimek and Miloslav Kaňák. Prague, SNKLHU, 1959.

Steinerová, Alžběta. *Zbožné odkazy v testamentech olomouckých měšťanů v 16. století.* MA Thesis, Department of History, Masaryk Univerzity, Brno 2014.

Stratenwerth, SHeide. *Die Reformation in der Stadt Osnabrück.* Wiesbaden, F. Steiner, 1971.

Suchánek, Pavel. *Triumf obnovujícího se dne. Umění a duchovní aristokracie na Moravě v 18. století.* Brno, Barrister & Principal, 2013.

Swieten, Gerhard van. *Vampyrismus,* ed. by Piero Violante. Palermo, Flaccovio, 1988.

Szewczyk, Aleksandra. "The Bishop as Shepherd and as Duke: Some Aspects of the Patronage of Art by the Bishops of Wrocław in the Sixteenth Century." In *Public Communication in European Reformation. Artistic and other Media in Central Europe 1380-1620,* ed. by Milena Bartlová and Michal Šroněk. Prague, Artefactum, 2007, pp. 219-227.

Tadra, Ferdinand. *K pobytu Jana Kapistrana v zemích českých. Sedmnácte listův z rukopisu národní knihovny Římské.* Prague, Královská česká společnost nauk, 1889.

Tanner, Matěj. *Hora Olivetská,* ed. by Jan Malura and Pavel Kosek. Brno, Host, 2001.

Taurinus Olomucensis, Stephanus. *Stauromachia, id est Cruciatorum servile bellum,* ed. by Ladislaus Juhász. Budapest, Egyetemi Nyomda, 1944.

Tenora, Jan and Josef Foltynovský. *Bl. Jan Sarkander. Jeho doba, život a blahoslavení.* Olomouc, Matice cyrilometodějská, 1920.
Theiner, Augustin, ed. *Vetera Monumenta Poloniae et Lithuaniae gentiumque finitimarum historiam illustrantia,* vol. II. Roma, Typis Vaticanis, 1861.
Togner, Milan. *Barokní malířství v Olomouci.* Olomouc, Univerzita Palackého, 2008.
Trinkaus, Charles. *The Spiritual Power: Republican Florence under Interdict.* Leiden, Brill, 1974.
Tulchin, Allan. *That Men Would Praise the Lord: The Triumph of Protestantism in Nîmes, 1530-1570.* Oxford, Oxford University Press, 2010.

Uhrová-Vávrová, Olga, ed. *Listář olomoucké univerzity 1566-1946.* Olomouc, 1946.
Underdown, David. *Fire from Heaven: Life in an English Town in the Seventeenth Century.* New Haven, Yale University Press, 1992.
Urbánek, Rudolf. *České dějiny,* part III, *Věk poděbradský,* vol. 3. Prague, Jan Laichter, 1930.
Urbánek, Rudolf. *České dějiny,* part III, *Věk poděbradský,* vol. 4. Prague, Academia, 1962.
Urbánková-Hrubá, Libuše. *Povstání na Moravě v roce 1619. Z korespondence moravských direktorů.* Prague, Archivní správa, 1979.

Válka, Josef. *Dějiny Moravy,* 2 vols. Brno, Muzejní a vlastivědná společnost, 1991-1995.
Válka, Josef. *Husitství na Moravě. Náboženská snášenlivost. Jan Amos Komenský.* Brno, Matice moravská, 2005.
Válka, Josef. "Karel starší ze Žerotína a problém jeho zrady." In *Morava v době renesance a reformace,* ed. by Tomáš Knoz. Brno, Moravské zemské muzeum, 2001, pp. 8-16.
Veit, Hieronymus. *Regule, Aneb Spůsob Žiwota, Bratrůw a Sester, Třetjho Ržádu S. Otce Frantisska.* W Nowém M. Pražském, v Anny Worssyli Hamplowý, 1708.
Videman, Jan and Dan Suchomel. *Mincovnictví olomouckých biskupů a arcibiskupů (1608-1820).* Kroměříž, ČNS Kroměříž, 1997.
von Greyerz, Kaspar. "Grenzen zwischen Religion, Magie und Konfession aus der Sicht der frühneuzeitlichen Mentalitätsgeschichte." In *Grenzen und Raumvorstellungen,* ed. by Guy P. Marchal. Zürich, Chronos, 1996, pp. 329-343.
Vorel, Petr. "Nacionalita a konfese v politickém životě jagellonských Čech (Utváření nového modelu společenské normy prostřednictvím Viléma z Pernštejna)." *Theatrum historiae,* 2 (2007), pp. 71-79.
Vrána, Jakub. "Kartuziánský klášter v Dolanech u Olomouce." In *Archeologické památky střední Moravy,* vol. XIII. Olomouc, Archeologické centrum Olomouc, 2007, pp. 19-22.

[Wancke, Bernard.] *Mons praemonstratus, Das ist: Außführliche Beschreibung Des heilig- und mit Gnaden leuchtenden Mariae Bergs Welchen die*

Gebenedeyte Mutter Gottes Unweit der Königlichen Haubtstadt Ollmütz in Mähren Vnter dem Gebiet des Marggräfflichen Stiffts und Kloster Radisch Praemonstratenser Ordens jhr selbsten zu einer Wohnung zu Schutz und Nutz deß Vatter-Landes zu Trost Zuflucht und Heyl deß Volckes außerwöhlet, Vnd wunderlicher Weise hat vorgewiesen. Olmütz, Johann Joseph Kylian, 1679.

Wandel, Lee Palmer. *Voracious idols and violent hands. Iconoclasm in Reformation Zurich, Strasbourg and Basel.* Cambridge, Cambridge University Press, 1995.

Wenzel, Kai. "Abgrenzung durch Annäherung – Überlegungen zu Kirchenbau und Malerie in Prag im Zeitalter der Konfessionalisierung." *Bohemia,* 44 (2003), pp. 29-66.

Winkelbauer, Thomas. *Gundaker von Liechtenstein als Grundherr in Niederösterreich und Mähren. Normative Quellen zur Verwaltung und Bewirtschaftung eines Herrschaftskomplexes und zur Reglementierung des Lebens der Untertanen durch einen adeligen Grundherrn sowie zur Organisation des Hofstaats und der Kanzlei eines „Neufürsten" in der ersten Hälfte des 17. Jahrhunderts.* Vienna, Böhlau, 2008.

Wojtyska, Henricus Damianus, ed. *Acta nuntiaturae Poloniae,* vol. II, *Zacharias Ferreri (1519-1521) et nuntii minores (1522-1553).* Roma, Institutum historicum Polonicum Romae, 1992.

Wondrák, Eduard. *Historie moru v Českých zemích: O moru, morových ranách a boji proti nim, o zoufalství, strachu a nadějích i o nezodpovězených otázkách.* Prague, Triton, 1999.

Wondrák, Eduard. "Mor a některé moravské protimorové spisy v 17. století." In *Ročenka Státního okresního archivu v Olomouci 1982.* Olomouc, Státní okresní archiv, 1983, pp. 73-86.

Wörster, Peter. *Humanismus in Olmütz: Landesbeschreibung, Stadtlob und Geschichtsschreibung in der ersten Hälfte des 16. Jahrhunderts.* Marburg, Elwert, 1994.

Zela, Stanislav. *Náboženské poměry v Olomouci za biskupa Marka Kuena (1553-1565).* Olomouc, 1931.

Zelenková, Petra. "Contra pestem nobis fave. Příspěvek k ikonografii sv. Pavlíny, patronky proti moru v barokní Olomouci." *Sborník prací Filozofické fakulty brněnské univerzity. Opuscula historiae artium* 55, no. 49 (2005), pp. 27-45.

Zlabinger, Eleonore. *Lodovico Antonio Muratori und Österreich.* Innsbruck, Kommissionsverlag der Österreichischen Buchhandlung, 1970.

Zuber, Rudolf. *Osudy moravské církve v 18. století: 1695-1777.* Prague, Ústřední církevní nakladatelství, 1987.

Zuber, Rudolf. "Poslední exkomunikace laiků v olomoucké diecézi." In *Ročenka Státního okresního archivu v Olomouci 20, 1992.* Olomouc, Státní okresní archiv, 1993, pp. 162-169.

Index

Printed in Szczecin, Poland,
by Booksfactory
August 2015